Managing and Negotiating Disagreements

Managing and Negotiating Disagreements: A Contemporary Approach for Conflict Resolution

BY

BHAWANA BHARDWAJ
Central University of Himachal Pradesh, India

AND

DIPANKER SHARMA
Central University of Himachal Pradesh, India

United Kingdom – North America – Japan – India – Malaysia – China

Emerald Publishing Limited
Emerald Publishing, Floor 5, Northspring, 21-23 Wellington Street, Leeds LS1 4DL.

First edition 2024

Copyright © 2024 Bhawana Bhardwaj and Dipanker Sharma.
Published under exclusive licence by Emerald Publishing Limited.

Reprints and permissions service
Contact: www.copyright.com

British Library Cataloguing in Publication Data
A catalogue record for this book is available from the British Library

ISBN: 978-1-83797-972-1 (Print)
ISBN: 978-1-83797-971-4 (Online)
ISBN: 978-1-83797-973-8 (Epub)

INVESTOR IN PEOPLE

Contents

List of Abbreviations

ADR	Alternative dispute resolution
AI	Artificial intelligence
BATNA	Best alternative to a negotiated agreement
NLP	Natural language processing
NSS	Negotiation support systems
ODR	Online dispute resolution
PEP	Personal excellence program
RAT	Role analysis technique
RNT	Role negotiation technique

About the Authors

Bhawana Bhardwaj is Assistant Professor, HPKV Business School, Central University of Himachal Pradesh, Dharmshala, India. She has 19 years of teaching and research experience in organizational behavior and human resource management. Throughout her education, she has been recognized for her merit and has received merit scholarships. She has contributed to the academic field as a dedicated academician and prolific writer by raising numerous social and organizational issues.

She has published research papers and book chapters in prestigious national and international journals with international publishers such as Elsevier, Emerald, Taylor & Francis, etc. She has presented papers as well as acted as a resource person at national and international conferences. She has also attended and organized numerous faculty development programs and workshops. As a resource person, she has been immensely appreciated by the organizers for her pedagogy and content. She has been conferred with "The Young Researcher Award," "National Budding Researcher Award," and the "Education Excellence Award in Human Resource Management." She has published books on contemporary issues such as artificial intelligence (AI), emotional intelligence, women empowerment, and conflict management. Her research interests include conflict management, AI, Green Human Resource Management (GHRM), skilled migration, and organizational ambidexterity.

Dipanker Sharma is Professor and Head, HPKV Business School, Central University of Himachal Pradesh, Dharmshala, India. He has a total work experience of 19 years and his areas of interest are human resource management and organizational behavior. With an illustrious industrial experience of over a decade as a corporate trainer with many renowned MNCs, his contribution to academia is unparalleled.

His academic career has been extraordinary. He has many patents and SCOPUS indexed books in his name. He has published research articles in nationally and internationally acclaimed journals with high cite scores and impact factors. He has presented research papers at several national and international conferences in and outside India. He has received national and international awards for his work. He has done short assignments in Asian countries like Hong Kong, Dubai, Bhutan, and Singapore and has taken up many research projects on women empowerment and related issues. He was conferred with the National

Researcher Award by Trigarth, Department of Tourism, in collaboration with Himachal Tourism, Government of Himachal Pradesh. His area of research includes migration studies, brain circulation of human capital, leadership, work–life balance, workforce diversity and knowledge management.

Foreword

Conflicts are common. Our lives are filled with conflicts: within the individual, between two individuals, between groups, among the groups, between organizations, communities, societies, nations, and many more. In fact, our lives are filled with conflicts and sometimes one feels if there are no conflicts, there is no life. Conflicts can be on goals, methods, values, systems, processes, and many more points.

Recognizing and managing conflicts within ourselves from time to time makes us productively or less productively use our time and energy and succeed or fail. Succeed or fail in our relationships, professional endeavors, or societal interactions, we frequently find ourselves facing divergent perspectives and conflicting interests. How we navigate these disagreements often defines the quality of our relationships, the success of our endeavors, the harmony of our communities, and the success of the organizations.

This book by Dr Bhawana Bhardwaj and Prof Dipanker Sharma *Managing and Negotiating Disagreements: A Contemporary Approach for Conflict Resolution* is a comprehensive text book that offers practical insights and strategies for effectively addressing and resolving conflicts in various contexts. Written by integrating research and practical experiences with exercises and case studies, this book serves as a beacon of wisdom for anyone seeking to enhance their conflict management skills.

Drawing from extensive research and real-world experiences, the chapters illuminate the intricacies of disagreement dynamics and provide readers with a comprehensive toolkit for constructive engagement. From understanding the underlying causes of conflicts to mastering the art of active listening and empathetic communication, each chapter equips readers with valuable techniques for fostering mutual understanding, finding mutually beneficial solutions, and developing negotiation skills.

What sets this book apart is its holistic approach to conflict resolution, which transcends simplistic notions of winning or losing. Instead, the emphasis is placed on cultivating collaborative mindsets, fostering trust, and nurturing resilient relationships that can withstand the test of disagreement. Through illustrative case studies, practical exercises, and insightful anecdotes, readers are invited on a transformative journey toward becoming more adept conflict navigators.

The book certainly benefits management graduates, professionals, practitioners, and academic fraternity with its comprehensive approach to develop proficiency for creating win–win situations while negotiating or dealing with conflicts of a variety. Whether you are a seasoned negotiator, a budding leader, or simply someone navigating the complexities of everyday interactions, this book offers invaluable guidance that will empower you to turn conflicts into opportunities for growth, understanding, and mutual gain.

The purpose of this book is to delve into the intricacies of negotiation, mediation, and conflict resolution within organizational contexts and complexities. This book advocates proactive approaches to conflict resolution by reframing conflict as a normal and potentially beneficial phenomenon. Through the lens of active listening, empathy, creativity, and principled bargaining, these 17 chapters of this book aim to empower readers to approach conflicts constructively.

This book has 17 chapters. The first chapter itself introduces and discusses the contemporary notion of conflict including what is conflict, conflict life cycle, speculating nature of conflict, various schools of thought on conflict, and diagnosis of conflict and discusses if conflict is always harmful. The second chapter presents various types of conflict (intra-personal, inter-personal, inter-group, intra-group, intra-organizational, and inter-organizational conflicts). The third chapter discusses the stages and processes of conflict. The fourth chapter discusses the styles of conflict management. The fifth chapter deals with conflict management styles (avoiding, competing, accommodating, compromising, and collaborating). The next chapters discuss the dynamics of personality and conflict including transactional analysis and ego-states. There are chapters devoted to conflict resolution strategies, resolving intergroup and intra-organizational conflict through role analysis and role negotiation techniques. A full chapter is devoted to negotiating conflicts including the temperaments that people bring to the negotiation table (harmonizing, controlling, pragmatic, and action driven) and how they impact negotiations. There are four chapters devoted to negotiation, dynamics of negotiation, team negotiation, and negotiation skills. The book also presents the best alternatives to negotiated agreements popularly known as BATNAs. This is a very comprehensively written book on conflict management. The book has various case studies, self-assessments, review questions, glossary, and group activities. The authors deserve to be congratulated to bring out such a comprehensive book with examples, case studies, and self-assessment tools.

I am very sure the ideas expressed, solutions provided, and approaches described in this book serve as a compass, guiding the readers toward a future where conflicts and disagreements are not obstacles to be feared but rather invitations to deepen connections and forge a more harmonious world. In the era of digitalization, there has been a significant drift in the management practices and negotiations are now managed online and through several AI tools. The discourse on using contemporary tools like negotiation support system and online dispute resolution is per se a prodigious contribution of this book which will benefit and enable the readers to fine-tune with this changing paradigm.

The authors, Dr Bhawana Bhardwaj and Prof Dipanker Sharma, have done a remarkable job and as they embark on this journey of educating and training various groups of professionals, teachers, and students, I appreciate their undaunted efforts in developing this book and congratulate them.

Best Wishes!!
T. V. Rao
Chairman, T V Rao Learning Systems Pvt. Ltd
Former Professor IIM (A)

Preface

Welcome to *Managing and Negotiating Disagreements: A Contemporary Approach for Conflict Resolution*. Human interaction will always involve conflict, especially in contexts like organizations where people with different personalities, objectives, and points of view come together. Even though conflict is frequently associated with negativity, when handled skillfully, it may also offer chances for development, creativity, and stronger bonds between people. The capacity to resolve conflicts and negotiate agreements is a critical talent for both individuals and companies in today's linked and fast changing world.

The purpose of this book is to present a conflict management that delves into the intricacies of negotiation, mediation, and conflict resolution in the context of organizations. The book support proactive methods to conflict resolution by encouraging readers to recognize conflict as a normal and potentially beneficial phenomenon. It does this by highlighting active listening, empathy, creativity, and principled bargaining. It also emphasizes how crucial it is to create an environment where candid communication, helpful criticism, and cooperative problem solving are valued in order to resolve disputes before they become more serious.

This book examines different aspects of conflict, negotiation, and resolution via 17 chapters. It starts with an introduction to conflict as a modern concept and goes into its numerous levels, stages, and procedures. The complexities of conflict management techniques, the relationship between personality and conflict, and conflict resolution and preventive tactics will all be covered in detail for readers.

The negotiation chapters provide insightful information about the nature of negotiations, negotiation styles, temperaments, and successful negotiating techniques. In order to obtain a deeper knowledge of the dynamics at play during negotiations, readers will also learn about crucial concepts like best alternative to a negotiated agreement and the significance of perception in negotiation.

This book also looks at the function of teams in negotiations, the significance of post-negotiation assessment, and the possibility of third parties stepping in to mediate disputes. It also looks at how conflict management is evolving in the digital era and how artificial intelligence and technology are used to resolve disputes. To encourage active learning and reinforce important concepts, each chapter is enhanced with self-assessment tasks, review questions, case studies, group activities, and glossaries.

Conflict management techniques suggested in the books are useful tools for fostering harmony, innovation, and organizational resilience, as disputes continue to affect organizational dynamics and outcomes. This book is a great tool for developing competence and confidence in handling and resolving conflicts, whether you're a professional, a student, an academician, a researcher, or an individual looking to improve your conflict resolution abilities.

In order to help you become an expert negotiator and conflict resolution practitioner, we believe that *Managing and Negotiating Disagreements: A Contemporary Approach for Conflict Resolution* will be a useful manual and a source of motivation.

Happy reading and learning!
Dr Bhawana Bhardwaj
Prof Dipanker Sharma

Chapter 1

Introduction to Conflict: A Contemporary Notion

Learning Objectives:

- Understanding the Concept and Nature of Conflict.
- Conflict Life Cycle.
- Various Schools of Thought on Conflict.
- Is Conflict Always Harmful?
- How To Diagnose a Conflict?

The changing dynamics of the modern workplace have posed new challenges to sustaining harmony and teamwork. Managers are reported to spend 9 to 15 weeks of the year dealing with workplace conflict and disagreements.[1] According to a research, 65% of problems related to performance occur due to employee conflicts, causing a colossal expense for organizations.[2] Thus, managing the human resource has become even more challenging. There are numerous explanations for conflict in the workplace, but the most general and evident is that every person is unique. When people with individual differences work together, they may disagree over things owing to competitive goals, personality differences, or the accomplishment of plans. Furthermore, managing workplace disagreements is the most reducible expense in organizations today and is perhaps the least known domain of cost minimization.

The word "conflict" conjures up images of squabbles, battles, riots, and war. However, the nature and scope of conflict extend well beyond this. We can

---

[1]https://www.prnewswire.com/news-releases/new-research-time-spent-on-workplace-conflict-has-doubled-since-2008-301652771.html.
[2]Collins, S. D., & O'Rourke, J. S. (2009). *Managing conflict in the workplace*. Cengage Leaning.

Managing and Negotiating Disagreements:
A Contemporary Approach for Conflict Resolution, 1–14
Copyright © 2024 by Bhawana Bhardwaj and Dipanker Sharma
Published under exclusive licence by Emerald Publishing Limited
doi:10.1108/978-1-83797-971-420241001

choose not to have any conflicts at work. All we must do is to locate an employment that does not involve interacting with others. Since it is nearly impossible, we will witness the conflict in one form. Consequently, conflict is inevitable and cannot be avoided. Most of us are constantly confronted with conflicting situations, either directly or indirectly. Though the type of conflict varies depending on the circumstance, there is one universal truth that remains "Conflict is unavoidable." The best thing we can do is learn how to manage it effectively or recognize its benefits.

1.1. What is Conflict?

The term "conflict" derives its origin from the Latin word "Confligere" that means striking two things together.[3] The outcome of the conflict is often portrayed as a fight or war between two or more parties, but the fact is far more intricate. "Conflict is an expressed struggle between two or more parties who perceive incompatible goals, scarce resources, and interference from others in achieving their goals."[4] However, it does not necessarily involve a riot, war, or a fight. According to Coleman (2000), "Conflict is an anticipated frustration entailed in the choice of either alternative."[5] According to Bartos and Wehr (2002), conflict is "a situation in which actors use conflict behavior against each other to attain incompatible goals and/or to express their hostility."[6]

Conflict occurs when one party feels that another party has negatively impacted or is about to negatively impact something significant to the first party. It is also called friction or opposition resulting from actual or perceived differences or incompatibilities.[7] Fisher (2000) states that conflict is "an incompatibility of goals or values between two or more parties in a relationship, combined with attempts to control each other and antagonistic feelings towards each other."[8]

According to Roloff (2014), "Organizational conflict occurs when members engage in activities that are incompatible with those of colleagues within their network, members of other collectivizes, or unaffiliated individuals who utilize the services or products of the organization."[9] Fig. 1 describes the nature of the conflict. Conflict can be a mental struggle to decide or choose among alternatives; it can be a clash or disagreement between two or more parties or can be described as incompatibilities of goals or opposition of ideas.

---

[3]http://www.latin-dictionary.net
[4]Wilmot, W., & Hocker, J. L. (2017). *Interpersonal conflict* (p. 384). McGraw-Hill Education.
[5]Coleman, P. T. (2000). Intractable conflict. In M. Deutsch and P. T. Coleman (Eds.), *The handbook of conflict resolution: Theory and practice* (pp. 428–450). Jossey-Bass Publishers.
[6]Bartos, O. J., & Wehr, P. (2002). *Using conflict theory*. Cambridge University Press.
[7]http://www.businessdictionary.com/definition/conflict.html.
[8]Fisher, R. J. (2000). Intergroup conflict. In M. Deutsch & P. T. Coleman (Eds.), *The handbook of conflict resolution: Theory and practice* (pp. 166–184). Jossey-Bass.
[9]Roloff, M. R. (2014). Conflict and communication: A roadmap through the literature. In N. A. Burrell, M. Allen, B. M. Gayle, & R. W. Preiss (Eds.), *Managing interpersonal conflict: Advances through meta-analysis* (pp. 42–58). Routledge. https://doi.org/10.4324/9780203149041

Fig. 1.   Nature of Conflict. *Source*: Authors' creation.

When actions or aims are contradictory, conflict can arise. Alternatively, it is a situation in which interdependent people have (manifest or latent) disparities in meeting their respective needs and interests and are hampered by one another in doing so. It also involves a competition between parties who believe they have incompatible needs, aims, aspirations, or ideals. Burton (1990) states that unmet needs also contribute to conflict. In a struggle to satisfy these needs conflict may arise.[10] John Galtung[11] emphasized that dispute arises because of inequalities embedded in social structure. Violence is one of the possible responses to such conflicting situations. In such situations, conflict comprises three phases: before, after, and during the violence.

1.2. Conflict Life Cycle

Conflict is a dynamic process and comprises three stages described below and exhibited in Fig. 2.

1.2.1. Stage I: Contradiction

A contradiction occurs when individuals and groups have incompatible goals or competition. It can also prevail due to personality differences, background, age, education, perception, and attitude. In this stage, incompatibility may exist between two or more parties. Example – an employee may have to work with an arrogant boss.

1.2.2. Stage II: Attitude

At this stage, the contradiction and apparent differences in goals or resource competition may result in the creation of negative attitudes such as hostility, competition,

---

[10]Burton, J. (1990). *Conflict: Resolution and prevention*. St. Martins Press.
[11]http://www.transcend-netz.de/upload/dokument_1328270221.pdf

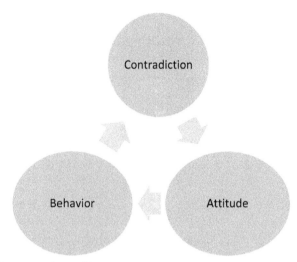

Fig. 2. Life Cycle of Conflict. *Source*: Authors' creation.

distrust, frustration, or other negative emotions between the parties involved. Example – the employee feels stressed due to the arrogant behavior of his boss.

1.2.3. Stage III: Behaviors

In this stage, the negative attitudes and emotions from the previous stage may manifest in observable behaviors. These behaviors may include open conflicts, debates, confrontations, violence, or other activities that indicate the partners' increased stress and hatred. Example – the employee argues with the boss.

1.3. Speculating Nature of Conflict: Various Schools of Thought

Conflict does not always bring adverse outcomes.[12] It may prevent the obsolescence of the system and promote creativity and innovation. Similarly, few thinkers advocate that conflict is always negative. Thus, various schools of thought have emerged to understand the nature of conflict. These three schools of thought offer distinct views on conflict and how it should be addressed in organizations and human interactions. The conventional school argues for conflict avoidance, the HR school recognizes conflict as a fundamental aspect of human connections but promotes resolution, and the interactionist school emphasizes the potential benefits of conflict if managed properly. Each viewpoint provides useful insights and can influence how disputes are treated and managed in different circumstances. Organizations can use components from each school to create comprehensive conflict resolution solutions.

---

[12]Coser, L. (1957). Social conflict and the theory of social change, *The British Journal of Sociology*, *8*(3), 197–207.

a. *Traditional school of thought*: This school emphasizes that conflict is destructive and should be avoided. Disagreement brings adverse outcomes such as violence, performance problems, and organizational downfall. It believes that conflict brings negative outcomes such as hatred, and disaffection among members, confusion, insecurity, anxiety, unhappiness, rivalry, miscommunication, Complaints, lowered motivation and decreased morale, tension at home or at work, erosion of strength, and satisfaction of relationships.[13,14]

b. *HR school of thought*: Conflict is natural and inevitable. This school of thought acknowledges individuals' differences, and the existence of these differences may lead to disagreement or conflict. Hence, it must be resolved amicably to achieve virtuous human relations. Conflict is harmful, and its resolution should be in the interest of the organization and the individual.[15]

c. *Interactionist approach*: This school of thought asserts that an optimum level of conflict is necessary to avoid static and obsolescence. Conflict is not only a positive force but is also necessary for the group to perform effectively. This approach emphasizes that conflict is functional as well as dysfunctional. The outcome can be dependent on how we manage it. The conflict which brings positive outcomes is good for the organization and should be encouraged. An optimum level of conflict can promote creativity and innovation and improve the decision's quality.[16]

1.4. Is Conflict Always Harmful?

A simple disagreement can easily develop into an exchange of emotionally charged personal attacks. Almost every individual will admit to having been involved in a disagreement that ended badly, leaving us furious, frustrated, or feeling horrible about ourselves. These are harmful types of disputes that include verbal and nonverbal abuse, ego attacks, rigidity, a revenge mindset, and the interchange of negative emotions. Such conflicts are characterized by adverse outcomes, often leading to a damaged relationship. Our fears, however justifiable, are often mislaid. Conflict itself does not need to be feared; our primary concern is ineffective dealing with conflict. Managers and social scientists have been aware of the conflict's positive elements since the 1960s.

Traditional views of conflict advocate legalistic forms of authority and fall short of recognizing the substance of conflict. Conversely, the current view is that disagreement is an essential component of transformation and change that can lead to enhanced trust, relational growth, and collaborative problem-solving. As a result,

---

[13]Bacal, R. (2004). Organizational conflict – the good, the bad, and the ugly. *The Journal for Quality and Participation, 27*(2), 21.

[14]Rahim, M. A. (1986). Referent roles and styles of handling interpersonal conflict. *Journal of Social Psychology, 125*, 79–86.

[15]Abiodun, A. R. (2014). Organizational conflicts: Causes, effects and remedies. *International Journal of Academic Research in Economics and Management Sciences, 3*(6), 118.

[16]Gaba, V., & Joseph, J. (2023). Content and process: Organizational conflict and decision making. *Frontiers in Psychology, 14*, 1227966.

conflict can be constructive, and an optimal degree of conflict in an organization is preferable to none. Arguments involving facts, information, ideas, or goals characterize constructive disputes, also known as cognitive conflicts or substantive conflicts. Better judgments, innovation, questioning the status quo, and creative solutions to problems are all benefits of optimal levels of constructive conflict. Conflict is neither good nor bad; it is efficiently it is handled.[17] Conflict can lead to destructive as well as creative and positive social change depending on how it is handled.[18]

Thus, based on the outcome, the conflict can be of two types:

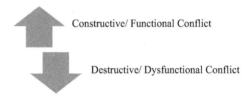

Constructive/ Functional Conflict

Destructive/ Dysfunctional Conflict

a. *Functional/constructive conflict*: A form of conflict that advances the objectives of the person or group or produces fruitful results. The functional outcomes demonstrate that conflict has good consequences. It can also improve performance, solve problems, or lead to creativity and innovation. It entails developing the ability to resolve conflicts in a sensible, balanced manner. The term "functional conflict" can refer to changes, innovation, and creativity. Enhanced procedures for making decisions, substitute approaches, cooperative answers to typical issues, improved performance on an individual and group level, and chances to look for novel ways to handle issues.[19]
b. *Dysfunctional/destructive conflict*: Conflict that hinders individual/group performance or brings negative outcomes. Disruptive results highlight the negative repercussions of conflict. It consists of disputes, arguments, fights, disagreements, etc. that can hinder performance or reduce productivity. Stress, exhaustion, and discontent, as well as decreased inter-personal and group communication, a culture of mistrust and suspicion, poor work performance, and heightened resistance to change, commitment, and loyalty, are all signs of dysfunctional conflict.[19] These differences are displayed in Table 1.

Thus, an optimum level of conflict can challenge the status quo, bring innovation and creativity, and solve problems, while a conflict that decreases productivity, output, profitability, or other desirable outcomes is harmful.

---

[17]Pondy, L. R. (1967). Organizational conflict: Concepts and models. *Administrative Science Quarterly, 12*(3), 296–320.

[18]Godwin, O. O., Godspower, A. K. P. O. Y. I. B. O., & Nelson, E. O. Human relations and organizational conflict resolution: A study of manufacturing firms in Nigeria. *IIARD International Journal of Economics and Business Management, 8*(6), 1–13. https://doi.org/10.56201/ijebm.v8.no6.2022.pg1.13

[19]Rahim, M. A. (2010). *Managing conflict in organizations* (4th ed.). Transaction Publishers.

Table 1.   Functional Versus Dysfunctional Conflict: A Comparison.

Dysfunctional Conflict	Functional Conflict
Upsurges rivalry	Enhanced cooperation
Involves emotions	Mostly cognitive
Comprises personal attacks	Separates the person from the problem
Reduces outcome quality	Improves outcome quality
Weakens relationships	Strengthens relationships
This leads to spiteful behaviors	Leads to personal and professional growth
It does not solve problems	Solves problems
Decreased performance	Increased performance
No role in innovation and creativity	Enhanced innovation and creativity

Source: Authors' creation in line with literature.

1.5. Diagnosis of Conflict

Conflict with obvious outcomes such as fights, arguments, strikes, and verbal and nonverbal abuse can easily be recognized. However, diagnosing latent conflicts through their symptoms is essential to avoid negative consequences. We all have been in conflicting situations, and we have confronted various ways through which parties or individuals concerned handle conflict. Before understanding the ways of managing conflict, the most momentous thing is to identify whether the individual or the parties are really in conflict. There are a few warning signs by which conflict can be recognized:

- Individuals experiencing guilt due to inner conflict often become depressed, irritable, and restless.
- When individuals within the organization disagree or differ in one or many ways like attitude, preferences, personality, values, goals, background, education experience, etc. It results in the attainment of goals needing improvement.
- An out-group hostility usually occurs because of cohesion, that is, sticking together within a group.
- Absenteeism, attrition, and the clash among employees.
- Low morale or job satisfaction level.
- Deviant behavior at the workplace.
- Stress, anxiety, and anger.
- Low quality in products or poor performance, etc.
- Politics and hatred.
- Decrease productivity.
- Lack of trust.
- Competition among individuals and lack of teamwork.

1.6. Sources of Conflict

Prevention of workplace conflict can be a critical tool to manage its consequences. Multiple factors can trigger conflict and are acknowledged as sources of conflict. Identifying these factors can help in the prevention of conflict.

1.6.1. Competition for Scarce Resources

Essential resources like money, human resources, time, materials, and equipment are limited and should be allocated to the people in the organizations prudently. The need for these resources among organizational members can cause conflict.

1.6.2. Incompatible Goals

When the goals of two parties are competitive or incompatible, and one party's gain can cause loss to the other party. For example, employers and employees and buyers and sellers. Individuals or groups often need help agreeing on action plans since they usually develop different competitive goals and objectives. Similarly, countless conflicts can take place since some believe that an accepted value should be applied to all circumstances, thus exceeding those whose values are different.

1.6.3. Inherent Conflict

Standardized procedures, rules, and policies that control actions tend to reduce the likelihood of conflict. Nevertheless, confrontation with their imposed control is promoted at the same time. Moreover, in a complex organization, the number of levels of authority may create problems that increase the potential for conflict.

1.6.4. Line–Staff Relationships

The difference in the task responsibilities of line and staff members, while enabling them to accomplish their respective tasks, also increases the likelihood of conflict. Line workers are involved in the core activities of a business, while staff workers support the core activities. A disagreement about their importance in the organization can lead to conflict.

1.6.5. Organizational Ambiguities

Happiness at workplace plays an important role in organizational effectiveness. However, various factors can create impediments for employees happiness.[20] When responsibility lines are unclear, role ambiguity leads to disagreement,

---

[20]Jaswal, N., Sharma, D., Bhardwaj, B., & Kraus, S. (2024). Promoting well-being through happiness at work: A systematic literature review and future research agenda, *Management Decision, Vol. ahead-of-print No. ahead-of-print.* https://doi.org/10.1108/MD-08-2023-1492.

Indiscipline, blame game, etc. Conflict may occur when goals are questionable and roles are not clearly defined also. Role ambiguity and unclear goals can lead to conflict. [Refer Case 1.1.]

1.6.6. Inter-dependence

It refers to the degree to which interaction among parties must be coordinated to perform their jobs adequately. The degree of inter-dependence can vary from total dependence to total independence. The degree of dependence on each other and misuse of this inter-dependence can lead to conflict.

a. *Total dependence*: This is a situation of dependence when one party can manipulate and control the other party's activities to the extent of affecting their outcomes.

b. *Total independence*: Two parties have no impact on each other's existence. Hence, both can work independently.

c. *Reciprocal inter-dependence*: When two parties involved share equal independence. The output of one party is an input for the other or vice versa. Example – sales and advertisement manager. If one will perform, the other will also perform better.

d. *Sequential inter-dependence*: In this type of dependence, the output of one party becomes the input for the other party.

e. *Pooled inter-dependence*: Two parties are independent but bring out a collective performance together.

1.6.7. Status Difference

Differences in status and position between two parties can trigger conflict. Example – superior and subordinate. Few organizations are trying to remove status differences and have evolved concepts such as reverse mentoring and boundary-less organizations.

1.6.8. Dispute Over Shared Success

Working in a team can lead to conflict if members start competing over their contribution over the success. Each member starts a race to get the maximum credit for shared success.

1.6.9. Different Interpretations of Facts

Perception and personality play an essential role in the interpretation of information by members. Facts and information, if interpreted differently, can bring differences and disagreements.

1.6.10. Communication Distortions

It is a known fact that communication is a two-way process, and encoding and decoding of messages play a critical role in effective communication. However, any error can lead to miscommunication and sometimes misunderstanding. Similarly, problems in the channel of communication can distort the message. The following problems in communication can be a source of conflict:

- Wrong interpretation of the message.
- Communication failure.
- Misunderstanding the language.
- Preconceived notion.
- Informational overload.
- Stereotypes.
- Halo effect.

1.6.11. Cultural Barrier

Sometimes, due to our ignorance, we behave in a particular manner in a cultural environment which can make other people feel offended. Particular acceptable behavior in one culture may be considered taboo in another culture. Example – in

Japan, maintaining eye contact with another person is rude and disrespectful to elders or seniors, while in the USA and India, it is treated as a sign of confidence.

1.7. Case 1.1: Role Clarity and Conflict

Rose and Gafoor are both working for HI-TECH, an AI-driven company. Astha, the product development manager, was the project team leader. Astha interviewed and hired Gafoor as a project team member. Rose, another project team member, interviewed Gafoor but strongly discouraged hiring him because she believed he was not a suitable candidate. Anyhow, he was hired by the company. Seven months later, Astha started her own business and left the project. Before leaving, she allocated Gafoor and Rose as joint project leaders. Rose was hesitant at first but consented to the proposal with the condition that she was not working for Gafoor. Within a month, the problems between them started taking place. Gafoor was portraying himself as the project manager and giving Rose the idea that she worked for him, which infuriated Rose. They each have reasons to defend themselves.

Rose says: Shortly after we decided on shared leadership, Gafoor called a project team meeting without consulting me beforehand about the time or agenda. He simply informed me of the meeting's date and time and invited me to attend. During the meeting, Gafoor went over everyone's responsibilities, including mine, line by line, treating me like just another member of his team. He sends out letters and marks himself as project director, implying that I work for him. I am not his subordinate neither I am working under his leadership.

Gafoor says: Rose is obsessed with titles and a sense of dominance. I did not indicate that she is employed by me only because I identified myself as the project director. Here's nothing that I can find fault with. What difference does it make? She is quite perceptive in all circumstances. She assumes right away that I'm trying to take over everything when I call a meeting. Additionally, Rose has several things to accomplish and projects to manage. As a result, she pays little attention to this one. She mostly laughs at stuff. When I make an effort to schedule a meeting, she begins yelling about how I am encroaching on her work and position.

Q1. Identify the factors triggering conflict in the above case.

Q2. Who should be blamed for the above problem?

Q3. Assume you are approached as a consultant to settle the abovementioned situation. How will you do it?

1.8. Part A (Self-assessment)

1. For every disagreement, there are usually _____ source or sources.
   a. One
   b. **Multiple**
   c. Sole
   d. Distinct

2. One can conclude attitudes and make judgments about people and things through _____.
   a. **Perception**
   b. Attribution theory
   c. Stimuli
   d. Learning

3. The meaning of language or words may be understood, causing a _____ conflict.
   a. Information
   b. Data type
   c. Resource
   d. **Communication**

4. Conflict acts as a challenge and could be transformed into _____.
   a. War
   b. System
   c. **Opportunity**
   d. Weakness

5. Conflict is largely considered as _____.
   a. Universal phenomenon
   b. **Perceived phenomenon**
   c. Negative phenomenon
   d. Positive phenomenon

6. Which of the following statements is correct?
   a. **Conflict doesn't always occur because of misunderstanding**
   b. Conflict can always be avoided
   c. Conflict is always bad
   d. Disagreement always signals that the relationship at stake

7. There is a contest among all employees of the organization about valuable suggestions for improving policies and productivity. What type of conflict may it be?
   a. Constructive
   b. **Competitive but constructive**
   c. Destructive
   d. Cooperative but destructive

8. Which of the following can be considered a functional conflict?
   a. When long-standing problems are confronted and resolved
   b. When it provides a chance for individuals to express their ideas and opinion
   c. When it challenges the status quo
   d. **All of the above**

9. According to _____ School of Thought, Conflict is inevitable. A minimum level of conflict is necessary to avoid static and obsolesce, and it can be managed to bring positive outcomes.
   a. Traditional school of thought
   b. **Integrationist school of thought**
   c. Human relation school of thought
   d. Avoidance school of thought

10. In which of the following situation the two parties share equal independence _____.
    a. **Reciprocal**
    b. Sequential
    c. Pooled
    d. All of above

11. Each statement is true about conflict except _____.
    a. Managing conflict involves both increasing and lowering conflict
    b. Organizational survival requires some conflict
    c. **Managing conflicts is basic management**
    d. Interactions in which one party opposes another party are considered conflicts

12. Which of the following statements is false about functional and dysfunctional conflict in organizations?
    a. Conflict is dysfunctional when it lowers productivity
    b. **Conflict management does not involve maintaining conflict at functional levels**
    b. Functional conflict in one group can be dysfunctional in another
    c. Dysfunctional conflict has the potential to undermine trust

1.9. Part B (Review Questions)

1. "Is conflict always negative?" Discuss.
2. Define various sources of conflict. Give example.
3. "Inter-dependence can be a source of conflict." Justify the statement with an example.
4. Differentiate functional versus dysfunctional conflict.
5. Discuss various factors that can trigger conflict in the workplace.
6. Discuss the nature of the conflict. How can we diagnose conflict in an organization?
7. Highlight propositions of various schools of thought on conflict.
8. Suggest guidelines for effective management of conflict.
9. Describe the three stages of conflict.

1.10. Part C (Glossary)

Functional conflict: Conflict that supports the goals of the individual/group or brings positive outcomes.

Dysfunctional/destructive conflict: Conflict that hinders individual/group performance or brings adverse outcomes.

Reciprocal inter-dependence: When two parties share equal independence. The output of two one party is an input for the other or vice versa.

Sequential inter-dependence: In this type of dependence output of one party becomes the input of the other party.

Halo effect: The halo effect occurs when our perception of someone or something is influenced by a single positive or negative feature.

Stereotypes: Stereotypes are generalized views or preconceived notions about a specific group of people based on their perceived qualities, attributes, or behaviors.

Culture: Culture refers to a certain group of people's common ideas, values, customs, traditions, behaviors, artifacts, and social practices.

Communication: Communication is a two-way process of transmitting information, ideas, thoughts, or feelings from one person, group, or entity to another.

Conflict: Conflict is an expressed struggle between two or more parties who perceive incompatible goals, scarce resources, and interference from others in achieving their goals.

1.11. Activity 1.1: Active Listening Game

Choose two partners for this game making a team of three members. Imagine a task you all must perform jointly as a team. Ask your partners to plan and develop two separate courses of action for the same task. Listen to Plan A carefully and attentively. Pay a little attention to Plan B. Now communicate with both your partners and observe the difference.

> *Q1.* In which case chances of conflict are more?

> *Q2.* Discuss the importance of active listening in rescuing chances of a conflict.

1.12. Activity 1.2: Group Discussion

Divide the groups into a team of 12–14 members. Conduct a group discussion on "Is Conflict always negative?"

Conclude the discussion by discussing the functional and dysfunctional outcomes of conflict.

1.13. Activity 1.3: Assessing Your Preconceived Notion

Recall the experiences of your life to develop a negative/positive attitude toward an individual who you have not met until now. Is it possible in an organization to develop a negative attitude toward a supervisor or anyone in a leadership role? What types of conflicts may arise in such a situation?

Chapter 2

Levels of Conflict: How Profound Can it Be?

> **Learning Objectives:**
>
> - Understanding the levels of conflict.
> - Dimensions of intra-personal conflict.
> - Inter-personal conflict.
> - Inter-group conflict.
> - Intra-organizational conflict,
> - Inter-organizational conflict.
> - International conflict.
> - Societal conflict.

Inter-personal relationships inherently involve conflict, which is neither inevitable nor inherently evil.[1] Contradictions lead to a situation of conflict and conflicts can occur at different levels based on their extent, intensity, and impact. By recognizing the various levels of conflict, effective strategies can be developed to maximize their benefits while minimizing negative repercussions. The concept of conflict is multidimensional and can exist at different levels. It is vital to recognize that disputes can occur at numerous levels simultaneously. Broadly, a conflict can occur at a personal, group, or organizational level and can be of the following types. Fig. 3 describes the various levels of conflict that can occur in an organization.

---

[1]Coleman, P., Deutsch, M., & Marcus, E. (2014). *The handbook of conflict resolution. Theory and practice.* John Wiley & Sons.

Managing and Negotiating Disagreements:
A Contemporary Approach for Conflict Resolution, 15–25
Copyright © 2024 by Bhawana Bhardwaj and Dipanker Sharma
Published under exclusive licence by Emerald Publishing Limited
doi:10.1108/978-1-83797-971-420241002

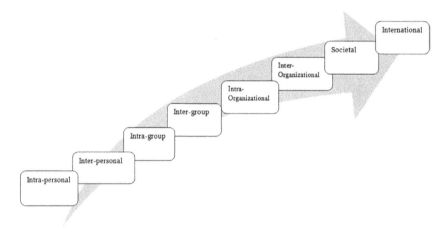

Fig. 3.   Levels of Conflict. *Source*: Created by authors.

2.1. Intra-personal Conflict

Intra-personal conflict is a form of conflict that occurs within an individual's mind or psyche. It is a psychological struggle when a person has opposing beliefs, emotions, values, or desires. An individual faces disagreement with himself/herself. It can ensue for multiple reasons, such as a person needing to be more explicit about his role or setting two mutually exclusive goals for himself.[2,3] When an individual is expected to execute a role and meet everyone's expectations, the incumbent begins to experience internal discomfort and anxiety. Intra-personal conflict arises from an individual's tension and frustration. There are different forms of intra-personal conflicts.

2.1.1. Role-related Intra-personal Conflict

a. *Intra-role conflict*: Intra-role conflict can be defined as "the concurrent appearance of two or more incompatible expectations for the behaviour of a person."[4,5] When someone is allocated to one role but has conflicting role

---

[2]Brown, J. S. (1957). Principles of intrapersonal conflict. *Conflict Resolution, 1*(2), 135–154.

[3]O'Connor, K. M., De Dreu, C. K., Schroth, H., Barry, B., Lituchy, T. R., & Bazerman, M. H. (2002). What we want to do versus what we think we should do: An empirical investigation of intrapersonal conflict. *Journal of Behavioral Decision Making, 15*(5), 403–418.

[4]Biddle, B. J. (1986). Recent developments in role theory. *Annual Review of Sociology, 12*(1), 67–92.

[5]Song, W., & Ai, W. (2023). Role conflict, its compromise, and the European Union's public diplomacy in China. *Journal of Contemporary European Studies, 31*(1), 35–49.

expectations. The incumbent must meet a variety of standards or expectations for the same function.[6,7] It is common in businesses with two bosses exhibiting dual authority framework, for example, in an organization, the project manager has different expectations, and the function manager also places performance pressure on the employee. A customer service person who deals with several customers and is expected to build a database of prospective consumers. Similarly, a struggle to keep both parents happy when while they have different expectations from us as sons or daughters lead to intra-role conflict.[8]

b. *Inter-role conflict*: Inter-role conflict can arise because of a person's multiple responsibilities or tasks. Opposing expectations are placed on an individual in the performance of their many social duties.[9] A common form of inter-role conflict is a person struggling to maintain a decent work–life balance. Clarity of roles and a balance of varied job expectations might help reduce the harmful consequences of such confrontations. A person who must attend an important office meeting while also attending his sibling's wedding, resulting in inter-role conflict.

c. *Person–role (for consistency) conflict*: Can you envision performing a job that is not your cup of tea or that goes against your personality? Would you be happy or miserable if you had this job? This is a kind of conflict that occurs when a person performs a role that contradicts his beliefs or value system.[10] Person–role conflict, also known as role–person conflict or role-incongruence, is a type of conflict that occurs when a person's personal values, views, attitudes, or qualities clash with the expectations, demands, or requirements of the role they are occupying.

There can also be an incompatibility between an individual's personality and his role. Placing the right person at the right job can reduce the chances of such conflict.[11] An ethical individual experiences this conflict when he has to offer bribes to get an order from a client. An introverted person performing a job that

---

[6]Kun, Z. Y., & Kim, V. W. E. (2023). Analysis and research on the role conflict of law teachers in five schools in Xi'an, China. *International Journal of Management, Accounting, Governance and Education, 3*(1), 59–68.

[7]Herman, J. B., & Gyllstrom, K. K. (1977). Working men and women: Inter-and intra-role conflict*. *Psychology of Women Quarterly, 1*(4), 319–333.

[8]Miles, R. H., & Perreault, W. D., Jr. (1976). Organizational role conflict: Its antecedents and consequences. *Organizational Behavior and Human Performance, 17*(1), 19–44.

[9]Behera, D. K., & Padhi, I. (1993). Role-conflict of working mothers in teaching profession. *Indian Anthropologist, 23*(1), 7–19.

[10]Pandey, S., & Kumar, E. S. (1997). Development of a measure of role conflict. *International Journal of Conflict Management, 8*(3), 187–215.

[11]Bhardwaj, B., & Kalia, N. (2021). Contextual and task performance: Role of employee engagement and organizational culture in hospitality industry. *Vilakshan-XIMB Journal of Management, 18*(2), 187–201. http://doi.org/10.1108/XJM-08-2020-0089

Fig. 4.   Role-related Conflicts. *Source*: Authors' creation.

demands a lot of social interactions and public speaking faces such a form of conflict. Thus, Fig. 4 exhibits the different types of role-related conflicts.

2.1.2. Goal-related Conflict

When there are two or more motives or goals to be achieved, conflict may arise. Lewin[12] has described three types of goal conflicts:

a. *Approach–approach conflict*: When an individual has two or more goals with positive valence that are equally important. Incumbent faces conflict as both goals are equally attractive but cannot be enjoyed together.[13] The dilemma of prioritizing goals causes anxiety, tension, and restlessness. For example, an individual has two well-paid job offers and must select one of them. This conflict is not negative, as the person will get a positive outcome with either decision. However, in some circumstances, selection will be very complicated. For example, a girl must choose loving parents or a man for her marriage. Such circumstances are analogous to saying, "You can't have your cake and eat it too." Similarly, a student being selected for admission to two reputed institutions is an approach–approach conflict.

b. *Avoidance–avoidance conflict*: This type of conflict occurs when a person is trapped between two antagonistic threats, fears, or situations. The individual is forced to pick between two awful goals. In such cases, both aims are undesirable, and one must be chosen.[14] The individual may attempt to flee the situation, but the repercussions of fleeing are even more severe. For example, continuing to work at a job one dislikes or remaining unemployed. Similarly, if an applicant has a choice between two jobs, one of which pays less and the other involves relocation.

c. *Approach–avoidance conflict*: This is a difficult problem to solve. A person in this situation of conflict is both fascinated and repulsed by the same purpose or objective. Goals can have both positive and negative valences. Positive

---

[12]Lewin, K. (2000). *Resolving social conflicts and, field theory in social science* (pp. 57–94). Harper and Row.
[13]Diederich, A. (2003). Decision making under conflict: Decision time as a measure of conflict strength. *Psychonomic Bulletin & Review, 10*(1), 167–176.
[14]Adomi, E. E., & Ozioma Anie, S. (2006). Conflict management in Nigerian university libraries. *Library Management, 27*(8), 520–530.

Fig. 5.   Goal-related Conflict.

valences attract an individual here. At the same time, the negative valence repels him. Conflict arises as a result of the goal's attractiveness and inability to reach it. Example – a job offer with an attractive salary is fascinating, but the candidate is repelled back as the job is hazardous.

d. *Multiple approach–avoidance conflict*: We may encounter situations involving both positive and negative valences of multiple natures. The goal brings out multiple positive and negative valences, and a person must analyze to make a final decision critically. The total of both valences determines the outcome of this dispute. Example – a woman is promoted to the position of senior manager. Promotion can have a favorable impact on her salary, respect, and quality of life. On the contrary, the promotion is repulsive because it requires her to travel frequently and work late at night. This may have an impact on her personal life and time spent with her children. Such circumstances result in numerous approach–avoidance conflicts. A brief framework is presented in Fig. 5.

2.2. Inter-personal Conflict

Inter-personal conflict materializes when two people's attitudes, behaviors, and actions clash. Personality incompatibilities or lack of clarity about one's role also lead to such conflicts. According to Ron Fisher (2000),[15] this level of conflict prevails when two persons have incompatibility of goals, needs, and approaches. Communication breakdown is another primary source of such conflicts. Sometimes genuine differences occur between people and any improved communication fails to resolve them. We can call them "personality conflicts," which refer to solid differences in motives, values, and style.

2.3. Intra-group Conflict

This form of conflict involves disagreement among group members over specific concerns causing ineffectiveness of group performance. It is a common aspect of

---

[15]Fisher, R. (2000). *Sources of conflict and methods of conflict resolution* (pp. 1–6). International Peace and Conflict Resolution, School of International Service, The American University, 1965.

family-run enterprises, especially when the argument turns heated. Mutual trust, transparent communication, and role clarity can reduce the chances of such conflicts. Example – conflict between the members of the marketing department in an organization.

2.4. Inter-group Conflict

Inter-group disputes are disagreements between teams or groups. They are the outcome of team antagonism and disagreements. A distinctive example of inter-group conflict is the management and the union disagreement. This conflict prevails in groups, departments, or ethnic or racial groups. Social–psychological processes are significant sources of inter-group conflict. Inter-group conflict can be destructive, especially when the group identities are threatened for which the cost can be extremely high, economically and socially.

2.5. Intra-organizational Conflict

This type of conflict prevails within the organization or a company and can generally be of four types:

2.5.1. Vertical Conflict

This refers to a conflict between hierarchical levels in an organization. In the context of organizational management, vertical conflict often refers to conflicts that emerge between different levels of the organizational structure. Conflicts can arise for a variety of reasons, including disagreements, differences in priorities, or conflicts of interest between persons or groups at various levels of authority within the organization. Goal misalignment, resource allocation, communication issues, cultural differences, and incentive decisions are some of the reasons behind this kind of conflict. Example – conflict between superior and subordinate.

2.5.2. Horizontal Conflict

Horizontal conflict, also known as lateral conflict, refers to disagreements that occur within an organization between people or departments at the same organizational level. Unlike vertical conflict, which occurs among different levels of authority, the horizontal conflict occurs when peers or colleagues with similar degrees of authority or influence disagree, compete, or are in conflict. The competition, overlap in responsibility, communication issues, and resource allocation could be some reasons for this form of conflict. Example – conflict between sales and accounts departments.

2.5.3. Line–staff Conflict

Line–staff conflict is a type of organizational conflict that occurs between an organization's line functions and staff functions. Staff functions are support

Fig. 6.   Intra-organizational Conflict.

functions that assist and advise the line functions in various ways. Line functions are those actively involved in carrying out the organization's essential activities and attaining its key goals. There can be a conflict between line and staff employees due to a struggle or competition to prove their worth in the organization. A brief framework is presented in Fig. 6.

2.5.4. Role Conflict

When individuals within an organization have unclear or hazy beliefs about their work responsibilities, expectations, or the extent of their tasks, this is referred to as role ambiguity. This lack of clarity can be caused by a variety of circumstances, including poorly specified job descriptions, frequent changes in job assignments, or contradicting supervisory orders. Role ambiguity can be harmful to both individuals and organizations, resulting in decreased job satisfaction, increased stress, and decreased productivity.

2.6. Inter-organizational Conflict

This type arises between two different organizations due to competition or rivalry in the business. Apart from the abovementioned organizational conflict, Ron Fisher (1990) explained that conflict can also occur at a multiparty and international level.

2.6.1. Multiparty Conflict

This type occurs when different interest groups and organizations have different priorities over resources and policy development. These are complex levels of conflict involving economic, value, and power resources. For resolving such conflict, traditional approaches may not be effective and thus demand collaborative approaches to build consensus (Cormick et al., 1996; Gray, 1989).

2.6.2. International Conflict

This type occurs at the global level between states. Competition for resources, value, and power can be significant sources of international conflict. They can range from diplomatic disagreements to armed conflicts and wars. International conflicts often have significant geopolitical implications.

2.6.3. Community or Societal Conflict

This level of conflict could be related to cultural differences, political disagreements, or socio-economic disparities.

2.7. Case 2.1: Sarah's Struggle

Sarah, a 35-year-old woman, works as a senior project manager at a high-tech firm. She is well-known for her job devotion and effectiveness. She also has two small children, ages 4 and 6. Sarah's spouse also has a tough career. Sarah's job entails managing complicated projects with short deadlines. Her employment frequently demands her to work late, attend numerous meetings, and occasionally travel for business. Meanwhile, her children have a full schedule of school activities, playdates, and extracurricular activities. Sarah's husband also travels for work on occasion. Sarah's employer wants her to be available and committed to her career, which frequently entails working late or from home to meet project deadlines. She is also urged to participate in networking events. Sarah aspires to be a hands-on mother, visiting her children's school events, assisting them with their schoolwork, and taking part in their extracurricular activities. On weekends, she also loves spending meaningful time with them. Sarah is frequently pulled between remaining late at work to meet her professional obligations and leaving on time to be present for her children's activities. Sarah feels bad when she is unable to attend her children's events owing to job obligations. She is concerned that her absence will have an effect on their emotional well-being and her relationship with them. Juggling professional commitments and family responsibilities exhausts and overwhelms Sarah, negatively hurting her overall well-being.

> *Q1*. Identify the type of conflict reflected in the above case.

> *Q2*. Put yourself in Sarah's shoes; how you would handle the situation?

> *Q3*. What can you do as the company's leader to aid employees like Sarah?

2.8. Activity 2.1

Create a small group of participants. Each participant must picture an issue that is still unresolved in his/her life. Request that each participant write down the specifics of the conflict on a piece of paper. Place all the events in a bowl and invite participants to pick up a piece of paper and offer strategies to resolve it.

2.9. Part A (Self-assessment)

1. A conflict which is purely internal and does not involve any other person is
   a. Inter-personal conflict
   b. Interpretive conflict
   c. **Intra-personal conflict**
   d. Not a conflict

2. If a person has a choice between two positive goals but is stressed because he can choose only one. This situation of intra-personal conflict can be referred as _____.
   a. Avoidance–avoidance conflict
   b. **Approach–approach conflict**
   c. Approach–avoidance conflict
   d. Multiple avoidance conflict

3. Many conflicting situations may have more than one
   a. Activity conflict
   b. **Inter-personal conflict**
   c. Agency conflict
   d. None of the above

4. Vertical channel conflicts refer to
   a. **A conflict between different levels within the organization**
   b. A conflict between the same levels within the organization
   c. A conflict between different levels within the organization
   d. None of the above

5. The conflict which takes place over the incompatibility of personal beliefs and role is _____.
   a. **Role conflict**
   b. Goal conflict
   c. Inter-personal conflict
   d. Conflicts over deeply held values

6. Horizontal conflicts are _____.
   a. Between members at the different levels
   b. **Between members at the same level within the organization**
   c. Between members at the same level but different organizations
   d. All of the above

7. Which of the following is/are a structural factor(s) that lead to conflict?
   a. **Policy and procedures**
   b. Communication error
   c. Perception
   d. None of the above

8. More than one boss in a company can lead to _____ conflict for an employee.
   a. Inter-role conflict
   b. Person–role conflict
   c. Inter-personal conflict
   d. **Intra-role conflict**

9. The conflict over content and goals of work is
   a. Process conflict
   b. Relationship conflict
   c. Purpose conflict
   d. **Task conflict**

10. Which style of management is most helpful in conflict resolution?
    a. **Participative**
    b. Authoritarian
    c. Bureaucratic
    d. Laissez-faire

11. Role conflict is an example for
    a. **Intra-personal conflict**
    b. Inter-personal conflict
    c. Inter-group conflict
    d. Intra-group conflict

12. Joy a state manager of a retail chain has just been offered a promotion to national manager of the company. At the same time, he has also been offered the position of state manager within the largest competitor in the industry. The latter position involves better pay but less autonomy. Both offers are appealing. What type of conflict is he experiencing?
    a. Avoidance–avoidance
    b. Avoidance–approach
    c. Approach–avoidance
    d. **None**

13. All of the following is a type of conflict except
    a. Intra-personal
    b. Inter-personal
    c. Intra-group
    d. **Manifest**

14. All but one of the following statements accurately describes aspects of levels and types of conflict in the organization. Which statement does not?
    a. **Intra-organization conflict includes all types of conflict between organizations**
    b. Inter-personal conflict is a conflict between two or more people
    c. Inter-group conflict is a conflict between two or more groups
    d. Intra-personal conflict is a conflict that occurs within a person

15. A situation when a decision can either bring a positive or negative outcome is which type of goal conflict?
    a. Approach–approach conflict
    b. **Approach–avoidance conflict**
    c. Avoidance–avoidance conflict
    d. Multiple approach conflict

2.10. Part B (Review Questions)

1. What is role conflict? What can be the role of time management in overcoming role conflict?
2. Explain various levels of conflict with examples.
3. What is role conflict? What can be the role of time management in overcoming role conflict?
4. Explain various types of goal conflicts. Give an example.
5. Elaborate various types of intra-organizational conflict. Give an example.
6. What is intra-personal conflict? Elaborate on various types of intra-personal conflicts.

2.11. Part C (Glossary)

Intra-personal conflict: A form in which an individual faces disagreement with himself/herself.

Intra-role conflict: The manifestation of two or more incompatible expectations for a person's behavior at the same time.

Work–life balance: This is defined as the amount of time spent on job versus time spent with friends and family.

Role-incongruence: It is a type of conflict that occurs when a person's personal values, views, attitudes, or qualities clash with the expectations, demands, or requirements of the role they are occupying.

Approach–approach conflict: When an individual has two or more goals with positive valence and are equally important.

Avoidance–avoidance conflict: When a person has two or more goals with negative valence and is forced to choose one.

Approach–avoidance conflict: This is a type of conflict when a person is fascinated and repelled by the same goal or objective.

Chapter 3

How Does a Conflict Occur? Genesis, Stages, and Process

Learning Objectives:

- Understanding the process of conflict.
- Exploring various stages of conflict.
- Incompatibility stage.
- Cognition and personalization stage.
- Intentions stage.
- Behavior stage.
- Outcome stage.

Management of shared resources frequently necessitates collaboration among stakeholders with significantly differing value systems and interests. Conflict arises when these parties have contradictory values, opinions, or opposing notions about resource allocation or when decision-making involves too few possibilities.[1,2] There are different contexts in which conflicts can occur, such as workplace, local communities, intimate partnerships, and world events. Variances in employees' personalities, goals, values, perceptions, preferences, and opinions can be a source of incompatibility, which further leads to conflict.[3,4] Thus,

---

[1]Condie, C. M., Alexander, K. A., Fulton, E. A., Vince, J., & Condie, S. A. (2022). Reducing socio-ecological conflict using social influence modelling. *Scientific Reports*, *12*(1), 22002.

[2]Lichbach, M. I., & Gurr, T. R. (1981). The conflict process: A formal model. *Journal of Conflict Resolution*, *25*(1), 3–29.

[3]Fraser, N. M., & Garcia, F. (1994). Conflict analysis of the NAFTA negotiations. *Group Decision and Negotiation*, *3*, 373–391.

[4]Deutsch, M. (1990). Sixty years of conflict. *International Journal of Conflict Management*, *1*(3), 237–263.

Managing and Negotiating Disagreements:
A Contemporary Approach for Conflict Resolution, 27–37
Copyright © 2024 by Bhawana Bhardwaj and Dipanker Sharma
Published under exclusive licence by Emerald Publishing Limited
doi:10.1108/978-1-83797-971-420241003

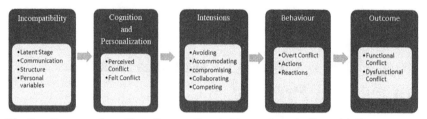

Fig. 7.   Process of conflict. *Source*: Created by authors in line with literature.

conflict can occur in five stages: potential opposition/incompatibility, cognition and personalization, intension, behavior, and outcome (Fig. 7).[5,6,7]

3.1. Stage I: Potential Opposition or Incompatibility

Stage I of conflict resolution is potential opposition or incompatibility. This phase represents the preliminary circumstances or elements that may allow conflicts to arise. While not all these elements usually result in conflict, they foster an environment where conflicts could occur. These elements may be referred to as antecedents or triggers. The following factors are considered as potential sources of conflict:

a. *Communication-related factors*: Communication is widely recognized as an effective method for resolving conflicts but can also act as a source for the same. Various factors including language barriers, miscommunication, misunderstandings, noise, and misperceptions can trigger conflict. Communication barriers, such as differences in word connotations, the use of technical terminology, excessive or insufficient communication, nonverbal cues, and cultural differences, can further increase the likelihood of conflicts (see Caselet 3.1).[8]

b. *Structural factors*: Structural elements such as the level of expertise, group size, leadership approaches, compatibility of group 'members' goals, clear delineation of roles and responsibilities, and the level of inter-dependence, and reliance between groups can significantly influence the occurrence of conflict within an organization.[9] It has been found that larger group sizes

[5]Robbins, S. P., & Judge, T. A. (2017). *Organizational behavior*. Pearson.

[6]Taylor, D., & Townsend, S. J. (Eds.). (2008). *Stages of conflict: A critical anthology of Latin American theater and performance*. University of Michigan Press.

[7]Thomas, K. (1992). Overview of conflict and conflict management. *Journal of Organizational Behavior (1986–1998)*, *13*(3), 263.

[8]Lindelow, J., & Scott, J. J. (1989). *Managing conflict*. Retrieved February 27, 2024, from https://files.eric.ed.gov/fulltext/ED309519.pdf

[9]Levine, M., Taylor, P. J., & Best, R. (2011). Third parties, violence, and conflict resolution: The role of group size and collective action in the micro regulation of violence. *Psychological Science*, *22*(3), 406–412.

and specialized activities are more likely to lead to conflict.[10] Additionally, a lack of clarity in defining roles and responsibilities can increase the likelihood of conflict. Unfair reward systems and competitive goals, where one group 'member's success comes at the expense of another, can also contribute to conflict. Moreover, the level of inter-dependence between groups can be a triggering factor for conflict (refer to Caselet 3.2).

c. *Personal variables*: In many instances, a person may develop aversion toward someone due to their personality or characteristics, such as their voice, smile, appearance, gender, or race. Collaborating with such individuals can result in frequent disagreements regarding their opinions or contributions. These conflicts arise due to personal variables, as mentioned in Caselet 3.3. Traits like disagreeableness, neuroticism, an authoritative style, and a dogmatic personality are predisposed to aggression and conflict.[11] Moreover, emotions and values also play a role in triggering conflicts.[12] For example, an individual who feels worried or depressed can create an environment that fosters conflict with coworkers. Similarly, anger has the potential to spark disputes in the workplace. It is evident that personal factors, including emotions, values, personality, education, and perception, can serve as significant sources of conflicts (see Caselet 3.4).

d. *Role ambiguity*: Uncertainty and disagreement can arise when there is ambiguity surrounding duties and responsibilities, creating a lack of clarity regarding which tasks should be assigned to whom.[13,14]

e. *Inter-dependence*: Task inter-dependence arises when activities are intertwined, leading to situations where one individual's actions impact others. Consequently, disagreements may arise concerning the appropriate execution of tasks.[15,16]

---

[10]Amason, A. C., & Sapienza, H. J. (1997). The effects of top management team size and interaction norms on cognitive and affective conflict. *Journal of Management*, *23*(4), 495–516.

[11]Nair, N. (2008). Towards understanding the role of emotions in conflict: A review and future directions. *International Journal of Conflict Management*, *19*(4), 359–381.

[12]Tehrani, H. D., & Yamini, S. (2020). Personality traits and conflict resolution styles: A meta-analysis. *Personality and Individual Differences*, *157*, 109794.

[13]King, L. A., & King, D. W. (1990). Role conflict and role ambiguity: A critical assessment of construct validity. *Psychological Bulletin*, *107*(1), 48.

[14]Tubre, T. C., & Collins, J. M. (2000). Jackson and Schuler (1985) revisited: A meta-analysis of the relationships between role ambiguity, role conflict, and job performance. *Journal of management*, *26*(1), 155–169.

[15]McMillan, S. M. (1997). Interdependence and conflict. *Mershon International Studies Review*, *41*(Supplement_1), 33–58.

[16]De Vries, M. S. (1990). Interdependence, cooperation and conflict: An empirical analysis. *Journal of Peace Research*, *27*(4), 429–444.

f. *Lack of trust*: Mistrust and hostility can escalate conflicts when a team lacks trust between individuals and management.[17,18]

g. *Differences in cultural and ethical convictions*: In cultural and ethical beliefs, conflicts can arise due to disparities in values and approaches. These clashes may occur due to variances in cultural backgrounds and moral convictions.[19]

h. *Perceived injustice*: Resentment and conflict can arise when people perceive unjust treatment, favoritism, or bias.[20]

i. *Power imbalances*: When those with less authority seek to challenge or modify the balance of power within an organization or relationship, it can lead to conflict.[21]

It is essential to remember that these attributes do not guarantee conflict but provide favorable conditions for disputes to arise if not dealt properly. In this phase, proficient communication, conflict resolution abilities, and mutual comprehension can all contribute to minimizing disputes.

3.2. Stage II: Cognition and Personalization

At this stage, incompatibility becomes manifested. The occurrence of conflict is dependent on the presence of triggering conditions that one or more individuals recognize. If A and B have a disagreement but do not feel tension or anxiety, then the conflict will not arise. It does not affect their bond or affection toward each other. Conflict occurs when both parties become emotionally invested and start experiencing hostility, anxiety, anger, or stress. The individuals participating may perceive and acknowledge the presence of a conflict, which is considered a perceived conflict. However, a conflict gets felt if the parties involved show emotional participation in it, which results in feelings of annoyance, irritation, or animosity. At this point, emotions and attitudes are also important.[22]

---

[17]Alon, I., & Bar-Tal, D. (2016). *Role of trust in conflict resolution.* Springer.

[18]Bhardwaj, B., & Kalia, N. (2021). Contextual and task performance: Role of employee engagement and organizational culture in hospitality industry. *Vilakshan-XIMB Journal of Management, 18*(2), 187–201. http://doi.org/10.1108/XJM-08-2020-0089

[19]Bhardwaj, B., Kalia, N., Chand, M., & Sharma, D. (2023). Engaged organizational culture as a precursor to job performance: An evidence from the hospitality industry of Himachal Pradesh. *International Journal of Hospitality and Tourism Systems, 16*(4), 48–57.

[20]Andrade, C., & Mikula, G. (2014). Work–family conflict and perceived justice as mediators of outcomes of women's multiple workload. *Marriage & Family Review, 50*(3), 285–306.

[21]Powell, L., & Hickson, M., III. (2000). Power imbalance and anticipation of conflict resolution: Positive and negative attributes of perceptual recall. *Communication Research Reports, 17*(2), 181–190.

[22]Jeanquart, S. A. (1991). *Felt conflict of subordinates in vertical dyadic relationships when supervisors and subordinates vary in gender or race.* Southern Illinois University at Carbondale.

3.3. Stage III: Intentions

Intentions play a great role in influencing the response or behavior. Disputes can arise when one party misinterprets or attributes incorrect meanings to the other party. Choices can be categorized into five different types:

a. *Avoiding intentions*: When parties have avoidance intentions, they attempt to prevent or postpone the confrontation. This can occur when parties are uncomfortable with confrontation or decide the conflict is not worth pursuing.
b. *Accommodating*: Involve one side conceding or giving in to the wants of the other, frequently to maintain harmony or to demonstrate kindness.
c. *Compromising*: Parties with compromise intents seek to achieve a middle ground by concessions on specific parts of the disagreement. This method attempts a balanced solution, which may only partially meet each party's initial aspirations.
d. *Collaborating*: Parties with collaborative intents aim to work together to discover solutions that meet the goals of all parties concerned. They seek a win–win situation.
e. *Competing intentions*: Both parties are motivated to attain their objectives, frequently at the expense of the other. This might escalate to open conflict and rivalry.

Furthermore, it is observed that intentions are flexible and may depend on situations.

3.4. Stage IV: Behavior

In this phase, the conflict is visible and manifests in the behavior. Different behaviors could be indicative of the opposing 'party's intentions. Such behaviors include silence, bickering, compromise, blame, strikes, riots, threats, etc. The behavior may vary with the intensity of conflict (Fig. 8). The bottom of the pyramid denotes an absence of conflict or a conflict of low intensity. The 'pyramid's base represents a low-intensity conflict, and as we move up, the intensity will rise. The bottom of the pyramid represents suggestive, hazy conflicts, and restrained energy. As we move upwards in the pyramid, the intensity of competition increases and the highest point is most damaging. Lower-level disputes that are handled to become functional conflicts can boost output, relationships, creativity, and innovation.

3.5. Stage V: Outcome

The action of conflicting parties can bring positive or negative outcomes. These consequences can either increase or decrease a group's performance. Thus, the outcome of conflict can be of two types:

a. Functional outcome.
b. Dysfunctional outcome.

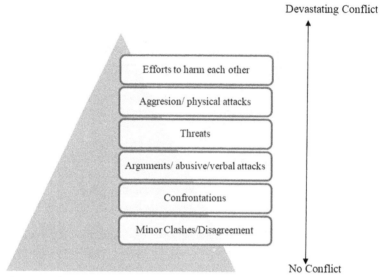

Fig. 8.   Conflict–Intensity Pyramid.

Functional outcome: Many people find it challenging to comprehend and embrace the idea that conflict may be beneficial. Nevertheless, many instances and examples support the claim that low to moderate levels of conflict enhance performance. Research has established that conflict may be productive and advantageous.[23,24] The following instances of conflict can be referred to as functional:

- Increased group performance.
- Innovation.
- Increase in inquisitiveness.
- Improved quality of decision.
- Increased productivity.
- Challenging the status quo.
- Reduces groupthink.
- Increased creativity.
- Change catalyst.
- Individual and organizational learning.
- Personal development.

Dysfunctional outcome: Dysfunctional outcomes refer to undesirable outcomes that may follow from unresolved or improperly handled conflicts. Conflicts

---

[23]Cosier, R. A., & Dalton, D. R. (1990). Positive effects of conflict: A field assessment. *International Journal of Conflict Management, 1*(1), 81–92.
[24]Vodosek, M. (2007). Intragroup conflict as a mediator between cultural diversity and workgroup outcomes. *International Journal of Conflict Management, 18*(4), 345–375.

that are not resolved successfully can have several detrimental effects on people, relationships, and organizations. The adverse effects of conflict include protest, resentment, opposition, strikes, and damage to the property or reputation of the opposing party. These effects eventually lower the opposing "party's performance and can result in the "organisation's collapse as a whole. Indicators of negative outcomes are:

- Reduces group effectiveness.
- Damaged relationship.
- Miscommunication.
- Reduced trust.
- Spoiled relationship.
- Reduced group member satisfaction.
- Threaten the group's survival.
- The downfall of the organization as a whole.
- Reduced productivity.
- Decreased morale.
- Loss of reputation.
- Stagnation.
- Group polarization.

Thus, conflict can be both productive and destructive. Accepting criticism and differing viewpoints is one way that can aid in fostering healthy conflict. Managers dislike receiving unfavorable comments. Managers should not perceive the differences of opinion as a threat. Encouraging employees to speak up and express their views is essential.

3.6. Caselet 3.1

Maruti Suzuki's violence at Manesar: One person was killed, and many were injured in the violence at Maruti Suzuki's Manesar plant. The court convicted 31 people for their involvement in the violence. The HR manager of the Manesar plant was burnt to death during the violence. The building of the plant was set on fire and he could not escape due to broken arms and legs. Other 94 managers and supervisors and some policemen were also injured. Around 145 workers were charged with various criminal cases.[25] Workers appealed to all unions across Gurugram to support them and join their protest.

> *Q1.* Looking at the above case, discuss the destructive outcome of the conflict.

---

[25]Dhankhar, L. (2017). Maruti factory violence verdict: A brief history of the case [Online]. *Hindustan Times.* https://www.hindustantimes.com/gurgaon/maruti-factory-violence-verdict-a-brief-history-of-the-case/story-hXMxAHf6I3DuJHCflV47YN.html

3.7. Caselet 3.2

Ruby has worked in 'EAS' – a logistics management company in Bangalore – for six years. During this period, she was very fond of her work and immensely enjoyed it, primarily due to her boss, Subodh. He was a great boss to work with. Three months back, Subodh got his promotion and was transferred to Delhi. Meera became Ruby's new boss. This is where the problem has started cropping up. Ruby feels that she says something but means something else, which has been like that since she joined. Not a day goes by when she doesn't scream at her.

> *Q1*. What do you think makes Ruby dislike the same work that she enjoyed so much before?

> *Q2*. How does communication become a source of conflict in the above case?

3.8. Caselet 3.3

Abha and Vibha are working in an insurance company. Abha is a salesperson, while Vibha is an operations manager. They stay in the same locality and are well-known to each other. They would have been best friends if they had been in different jobs if they had been in various positions, just like their kids are in their school. But they are always in conflict with each other. Abha's job is to sell insurance policies, and she is very good at her job. Vibha's job is to ensure all the required documentation is complete to issue an insurance policy; she keeps rejecting some of the applications. Abha and Vibha are constantly in conflict even when they have nothing personal against each other.

> *Q1*. What is the reason for conflict in the above case?

> *Q2*. How can you convert such situations into constructive conflict?

3.9. Caselet 3.4

Ms Mathew and Mr Ramesh work as teachers in a management institute. Both occupy dignified senior positions in the institute. Both have come from a reputed management institute in India. While Mr Ramesh looks and behaves maturely and professionally, Ms Mathew is naturally casual. Mr Ramesh developed a dislike for her. Her loud behavior, vibrant clothes, and too much make-up at work are the reason why Mr Ramesh dislikes her. To his surprise, their boss called them one day and asked them to work together on a combined project. Without thinking for a minute, Mr Ramesh rejected the proposal.

> *Q1*. Is Mr Ramesh's dislike for Ms Mathew justified?

> *Q2*. What is the source of conflict in the above caselet?

3.10. Part A (Self-assessment)

1. Using _____, one can infer sentiments and pass judgment on objects and people.
   a. **Perception**
   b. Attribution theory
   c. Inputs
   d. Mental framework

2. Misunderstandings of language or behavior could lead to a _____ dispute.
   a. Emotional
   b. Resource
   c. Cognitive
   d. **Communication**

3. There are _____ source(s) of a conflict.
   a. One
   b. **Many**
   c. Two
   d. Discrete

4. Disagreement can be seen as a prospect to grow and develop into _____.
   a. Menace
   b. **Opportunity**
   c. Goal
   d. profit

5. Which of the following outcomes of conflict might be regarded as positive?
   a. When long-standing problems are brought to the surface and resolved
   b. When it provides a chance for individuals to clarify their views
   c. When people are forced to search for new approaches
   d. **All of the above**

6. Which of the following is not a structural factor that leads to conflict?
   a. Group size
   b. **Perception**
   c. Policy and procedures
   d. Degree of dependence on each other

7. Second stage of the conflict comprises _____.
   a. Apparent and experienced conflict
   b. **Perceived and felt conflict**
   c. Expressed and perceived conflict
   d. Overt and covert conflict

8. Which of the following statement about conflict is true?
   a. **Conflict doesn't always occur because of misunderstanding**
   b. Conflict can always be avoided
   c. Conflict is always bad
   d. Disagreement always signals that the relationship is on the rocks

9. In an organization, there is a competition among all employees of organization about valuable suggestions for improving productivity. This type of conflict may be _____.
   a. **Constructive**
   b. Destructive
   c. Cooperative but destructive
   d. None of the above

10. If the meaning of language or behavior is misunderstood it can cause a _____ conflict.
    a. **Communication**
    b. Personality
    c. Data source
    d. Role

11. Which of the following is not structural factor that leads to conflict?
    a. Group size
    b. **Perception**
    c. Policy and procedures
    d. Degree of dependence on each other

3.11. Part B (Review Questions)

1. Explain the process of conflict in detail.
2. "Conflict does not arise until it is felt." Justify the statement.
3. Discuss sources of conflict in detail.
4. "It is not necessary that conflict leads to negative outcome only." Comment.
5. Explain the process of a conflict. Give an example for each stage of conflict.
6. What consequences might conflict at work have? Which professions are most likely to experience workplace violence? What makes you believe that is?
7. Discuss the effects of conflict that you have observed in your surroundings.
8. Highlight various stages of conflict. Give an appropriate example.

3.12. Part C (Glossary)

Latent conflict: The term "latent conflict" describes a scenario where there is a chance that conflict will develop between people, groups, or entities. However, it has not yet manifested as an outright or obvious conflict.

Felt conflict: Felt conflict is a phase in the conflict process where the individuals or parties involved begin to emotionally experience and recognize the conflict in addition to simply perceiving its existence.

Role ambiguity: Role ambiguity is a lack of clarity in the activities required to carry out a job. It is the absence of clearly formulated information on performance expectations, goals, duties, authority, responsibilities, obligations, and other working conditions related to role performance.

Group think: A phenomenon that occurs when a group takes a decision without considering all the options or ramifications. A common goal to keep the peace within the group is the basis of groupthink.

Chapter 4

Uncovering Styles of Conflict Management

Learning Objectives:

- Understanding various conflict management styles.
- Understanding the application, advantages, and disadvantages of various styles.
- Importance of conflict management styles.

Human capital and knowledge workers are the foundation of organizations and knowledge-based economies.[1] Post-COVID-19 era has caused a complete transformation in the workplace dynamics.[2] In such a scenario, engagement of employees in the workplace becomes challenging.[3] What is our propensity to handle conflict plays an important role in ensuring organizational effectiveness?[4] Do we prefer to run away from problems, face them head-on, compete to win, or try to find a workable solution to satisfy everyone? Conflict management styles are the diverse ways or strategies, people employ to address disagreements, disputes, or conflicts in various contexts. These techniques can differ based on an individual's personality, communication abilities, cultural background, and the nature

---

[1]Bhardwaj, B., & Sharma, D. (2022). Migration of skilled professionals across the border: Brain drain or brain gain? *European Management Journal*, *41*(6), 1021–1033. https://doi.org/10.1016/j.emj.2022.12.011

[2]Sharma, D., Chaudhary, M., Jaswal, N., & Bhardwaj, B. (2022). Hiding behind the SWOT: Gender equality and COVID-19. *Journal of Positive School Psychology*, *6*(6), 730–740.

[3]Kalia, N., & Bhardwaj, B. (2019). Contextual and task performance: Do demographic and organizational variables matter? *Rajagiri Management Journal*, *13*(2), 30–42. https://doi.org/10.1108/RAMJ-09-2019-0017

[4]Brewer, N., Mitchell, P., & Weber, N. (2002). Gender role, organizational status, and conflict management styles. *International Journal of Conflict Management*, *13*(1), 78–94.

Managing and Negotiating Disagreements:
A Contemporary Approach for Conflict Resolution, 39–49
Copyright © 2024 by Bhawana Bhardwaj and Dipanker Sharma
Published under exclusive licence by Emerald Publishing Limited
doi:10.1108/978-1-83797-971-420241004

of the issue itself.[5] Understanding and describing how others would react in a problematic scenario and how we would respond is required to cope with conflict. Each of us has a primary conflict resolution style.[6] Human resource managers often find themselves busy and devote much time to managing conflicts. However, understanding and analyzing conflict management style helps us better understand behavior of employees and determine the best approach to manage workforce.[7] It can also assist us in deliberately choosing how to react in a conflict and how to lessen stress and competition at work.

Most of the research on conflict management styles has focused on individual traits or inclinations. A person's behavioral orientation and general assumptions of how they handle conflict make up their conflict style. According to Kenneth Thomas and Ralph Kilmann (1974),[8] there are five dominant styles of conflict response: competition, collaboration, compromise, avoidance, and accommodation. Though no conflict style is inherently right or wrong, a few styles may be inappropriate for a given situation and result in an out-of-control situation.

4.1. Conflict Management Style

The dual concern model, initially developed by Blake and Mouton (1964)[9] and later adopted by various scholars and researchers, including Pruitt and Rubin (1986),[10] Rahim (2000),[11] and Thomas (1976),[12] has been used by most studies on conflict management style. Thus, conflict management styles are based on a person's behavior dimensions namely: cooperativeness and assertiveness. (1) Assertiveness is the propensity to satisfy own concerns and goals. (2) Cooperativeness refers to individual efforts to achieve the other person's concerns and goals. Fig. 9 explains the five distinct conflict-handling modes based on these two dimensions.

---

[5]Antonioni, D. (1998). Relationship between the big five personality factors and conflict management styles. *International Journal of Conflict Management, 9*(4), 336–355.
[6]Slabbert, A. D. (2004). Conflict management styles in traditional organisations. *The Social Science Journal, 41*(1), 83–92.
[7]Zartman, I. W. (2000). Conflict management: The long and the short of it. *SAIS Review of International Affair, 20,* 227.
[8]*Thomas-Kilmann Conflict Mode Instrument Profile and Interpretive Report.* http://www.kilmanndiagnostics.com/sites/default/files/TKI_Sample_Report.pdf
[9]Blake, R. A., & Mouton, J. S. (1964). *The managerial grid.* Gul.
[10]Pruitt, D. G., & Rubin, J. Z. (1986). *Social conflict: Escalation, stalemate.* Random House.
[11]Rahim, M., Magner, N., & Shapiro, D. (2000). Do justice perceptions influence styles of handling conflict with supervisors? What justice perceptions, precisely? *The International Journal of Conflict Management, 11,* 9–31.
[12]Thomas, K. W. (1976). Conflict and conflict management. In M. D. Dunnetee (Ed.), *The handbook of industrial and organizational psychology* (pp. 889–935). Rand McNally.

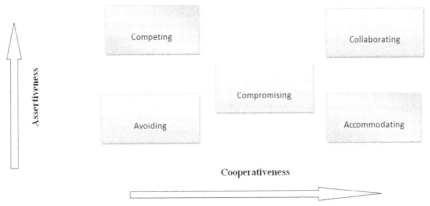

Fig. 9.   Conflict Management Styles.

4.1.1. Competing (Assertive, Uncooperative)

Competing conflict resolution styles aim to maximize personal gains. Here, individual prioritize his/her goal over relationship. This follows a fixed pie strategy in which the gain of one party is the loss of the other. It results in a win−lose situation. A person with this style tries to satisfy his/her own interest at the other person's expense. The basic premise of the disagreement is − I win, and you lose. The opposing parties attempt to utilize coercive power or dominance over the other. People who constantly adopt this approach might be hostile, oppressive, or threatening. Winning gives a person a sense of achievement and pride while loss imparts a sense of inadequacy and weakness.[13,14]

> *Example 1*: A conflict over wage hike between employer and employee, in which the employee wants to raise their compensation while the employer wants to reduce it as much as possible.

> *Example 2*: A confrontation between a superior and a subordinate in which the superior uses his power to execute his decision, such as demotion, dismissal, firing, or punishment. Similarly, employees threaten, resign, or strike for the same.

---

[13]Mukherjee, K., & Upadhyay, D. (2019). Effect of mental construals on cooperative and competitive conflict management styles. *International Journal of Conflict Management*, 30(2), 202–226.
[14]Tjosvold, D., Wong, A., & Chen, N. Y. F. (2014). Cooperative and competitive conflict management in organizations. In O. B. Ayoko, N. M. Ashkanasy, & K. A. Jehn (Eds.), *Handbook of conflict management research* (pp. 33–50). Edward Elgar Publishing.

When can we use competing styles?
A competing style can be appropriately applied in the following circumstances:

- Goals are critical, and conflicting parties must use power to implement them.
- When an unpopular decision must be put into practice.
- When given the choice between survival and satisfaction, the decision-maker selects survival over satisfaction.
- Make a quick decision, and time is short.
- In a crisis, the decision is critical.
- When we know we are correct, we must stand up for it.
- When we must advocate for our rights.

Advantages:

- This is a quick style of decision-making.
- Can be used in crisis.

Disadvantages:

- The relationships may be harmed because they can't be repaired.
- This can escalate the conflict further, leading to a worse situation.
- Losers may hit back or may not accept the decision.
- It can offend and hurt others' feelings.
- Does not bring out an optimum solution.

4.1.2. Avoiding (Unassertive, Uncooperative)

This approach entails avoiding the conflict entirely. In this style, a person stays away from competition by avoiding the entire situation by withdrawing, sidestepping, or postponing. Thus, pay no heed to disagreements or remain neutral. The avoidance approach is characterized by unassertive and uncooperative behavior, leading to aversion to tension and frustration and may let a conflict work itself out.[15] This conflict management style leads to a lose−lose situation and none of the party's benefit. The person has low value for his goal and less importance to the relationship as well, as the person does not care about own issue or the issue of others. When the problem is minor, emotions are high, or the time is not ideal to confront the conflict, this type of style is appropriate.[16]

> *Example*: Staying out of controversy and ignoring the disagreement of a peer group or subordinates.

---

[15]https://www.pon.harvard.edu/daily/conflict-resolution/conflict-management-styles-pitfalls-and-best-practices/
[16]Kim, M. S., & Leung, T. (2012). A multicultural view of conflict management styles: Review and critical synthesis. *Communication Yearbook*, 23, 227–269.

When can we use this style?

- When more information is needed and we need time to react.
- When the issue is a symptom of a deeper problem and we are not prepared to face it presently.
- When the relationships are at stake.
- When we are waiting to cool down and not react aggressively.
- When issues are not essential and we don't have time spare to deal with them.
- When individual power is less, and there is no chance of causing change.

Disadvantages:

- Deferring the matter may exaggerate the problem.
- Can lead to unresolved problems and resentment.
- Can lead to frustration and misinterpretation.
- It doesn't bring creativity or improvement.
- It doesn't give long-term solutions.

Advantages:

- Stay out of trouble for the time being.
- Some ignoring leads to settling down of the issue.

4.1.3. Accommodating (Unassertive, Cooperative)

In an accommodating style, an individual ignores his/her personal goals to protect other person's interest. There is an element of self-sacrifice to make the other person happy. The accommodating party feels that working toward a common goal is more important than any of the divergent concerns and confronting differences may damage relationships. This style of managing conflict leads to I lose–you win situation. This style refers to a high level of concern for others and a low level of assertiveness.[17]

> *Examples*: Selfless generosity or kindness, obeying another person's order, and accepting the demand of employees by the managers.

When can we use an accommodating style?

- When other person is more important than issue.
- When one party realizes his mistake and is willing to correct it.

---

[17]Saeed, T., Almas, S., Anis-ul-Haq, M., & Niazi, G. S. K. (2014). Leadership styles: Relationship with conflict management styles. *International Journal of Conflict Management*, 25(3), 214–225.

- When you are eager to let other party learn by their mistake.
- When you let other party win knowing that you cannot win.
- To earn social credit.
- When the timing is not appropriate, and you are more inclined to put it off for the future.
- When harmony is to be ensured.
- When the parties involved are more important than their differences.

Disadvantages:

- One great idea can get ignored.
- It is possible to lose credibility and influence.
- It can further lead to unresolved problems and resentment.
- It sometimes can create a competition to be nicer than other party – "I am nicer than you are." This further, may lead to increased power imbalances.

Advantages:

- Helps in maintaining peace and harmony.
- Accommodation can be useful when both parties are losing and want to minimize their losses.

4.1.4. Compromising (Midway Between Assertiveness and Cooperativeness)

This approach seeks a solution in which both parties give up as well as gain something. The compromising style demonstrates belief in a give-and-take relationship with give-a-little and get-a-little approach. The outcome of this style leads to a half-win, half-lose situation.[18,19]

> *Example*: An organizational conflict where the managers accept some of the demands of the works and some of the terms of managers are accepted by the employees.

Advantages:

- It helps in sustaining relationships.
- It is less time-consuming than collaboration.

---

[18]Lim, J. H., & Yazdanifard, R. (2012). The difference of conflict management styles and conflict resolution in workplace. *Business & Entrepreneurship Journal*, *1*(1), 141–155.
[19]Munduate, L., Ganaza, J., Peiro, J. M., & Euwema, M. (1999). Patterns of styles in conflict management and effectiveness. *International Journal of Conflict Management*, *10*(1), 5–24.

- Saves relationships.
- Avoids lose–lose situation.
- Ready to lend a hand if the issue is composite.

Disadvantages:

- The optimum solution still needs to be achieved.
- The dark side of compromising is that it can be an easy way out and reduces new creative options.
- The needs of both parties need to be met.

When can we use compromising style?

- In a circumstance of dead lock/no agreement.
- When a total win–win is not possible.
- When both parties are not willing to accommodate.

4.1.5. Collaborate (Assertiveness-Cooperativeness)

In this style, both assertiveness as well as concern for others are high. Collaboration occurs when conflicting parties team up and try to recognize a solution that protects everybody's interest. A person sees conflict as natural, helpful, and creative. The conflict is viewed as a problem that must be solved by finding an innovative solution. It involves recognizing the primary concerns of the conflicting parties and identifying a way to meet everyone's concerns. It leads to a win–win situation of problem-solving. This style tenets that the satisfaction of both parties brings long-term results.[20,21]

This technique necessitates researching a problem to understand the underlying concerns of the two persons and then devising a resolution that satisfies both the parties. Resolving a conflict to understand each other's perspectives, and finding a creative solution to an inter-personal problem to create win–win situation is an example of collaborative conflict management.

> *Example*: when employers and employees mutually find a way where workers' demands are met and organizational well-being is also not compromised.

When can we use the collaborative style?

- When long-term relationship is anticipated.

---

[20]Mattessich, P. W., & Johnson, K. M. (2018). *Collaboration: What makes it work* (3rd ed.). Fieldstone Alliance.
[21]Nguyen, G., & Kumar, V. (2021). Impact of different conflict levels on culturally diversified Japanese organisations' performance under a collaborative conflict management style. *International Journal of Organizational Business Excellence*, 4(2), 71–94.

- When inter-dependence is immense.
- When there is time and energy to sort out the prevalent issue.
- When top management value participation and happiness of all.

Advantages:

- Create mutual trust.
- Builds long-term relationship.
- Brings creativity.
- Builds commitment.
- Reduce conflict.

Disadvantages:

- It takes time and energy.
- It is not always feasible to find a win–win outcome.
- Demands active participation of parties involved.

4.2. Importance of Understanding Conflict Management Styles

Understanding the styles of conflict can help in multiple ways. Understanding them in a more harmonious work environment can lead to improved relationships and enhanced performance. It is important to remember that conflict is a natural part of human interaction, and having a range of strategies to manage it can lead to more positive outcomes.[21]

1. *Impact on behavior*: Recognizing one's preferred conflict resolution style and understanding how it influences behavior in different contexts is essential. Various approaches can produce different results, and awareness of this impact can help individuals modify their systems for better results.
2. *Effective management of time and resources*: Individuals and organizations can select the best solution for a given situation by knowing the various conflict management styles. For example, a collaborative method may be better suited for complex projects that require multiple viewpoints, whereas a compromising approach may be better served when time is tight.
3. *Conflict reduction*: Understanding conflict resolution styles can also help reduce workplace conflict and stress. Conflicts can be resolved to bring win–win situations through good communication, active listening, and the appropriate conflict resolution strategy, reducing friction, and tension in the workplace.
4. *Relationship building*: Certain dispute resolution techniques, such as collaboration and accommodation, place a premium on relationship building. When

people approach issues with respect for the ideas and needs of others, it can build a more positive and collaborative work environment.

5. *Improving leadership skills*: Understanding conflict resolution types benefits leaders and managers. They may adjust their approach to the issue and the individuals involved, enhancing team chemistry, morale, and production.
6. *Adapting to diversity*: Different cultures and personalities may favor different conflict resolution strategies. Individuals can change their approach to work effectively with varied groups and avoid misunderstandings by being aware of these variations.
7. *Stress reduction*: Unmanaged conflict can cause stress. By utilizing proper conflict resolution approaches, the stress and anxiety can be managed to a great extent.

4.3. Case Study 4.1

The case study centers on "Innovation for You," a mid-sized technology firm. Joy and Rose are the main protagonists in this case study. Joy is a seasoned software developer with over 10 years of industry experience. He is well known for his technical expertise and direct, no-nonsense communication approach. He values efficiency and wants others to do the same. Rose, on the other hand, is a recent addition to the organization, having joined six months ago. She is a creative thinker who embraces her work enthusiastically. Rose is also approachable and loves developing strong relationships with her coworkers.

When Rose is assigned to work alongside Joy on a key project that requires inventive ideas within a short timeframe, the conflict erupts. Joy favors a disciplined approach and is more comfortable working individually, whereas Rose believes in brainstorming and collaborative problem-solving. Joy is concerned with attaining his objectives by allocating target-based jobs to all the project members. Joy becomes impatient with Rose's brainstorming sessions in this situation, viewing them as a waste of time. He expresses his displeasure clearly and is unwilling to assist Rose. Rose believes in involving others in order to produce fresh ideas. However, to avoid more confrontation, she agreed to implement Joy's idea and decided to drop her brainstorming idea.

Q1. Analyze the conflict management styles of Rose and Joy.

Q2. Was Rose's decision to get along with Joy correct?

4.4. Part A (Self-assessment)

1. Ability of an individual to see things from others' point of view is called ____.
   a. Sympathy
   b. **Empathy**
   c. Emotional maturity
   d. Emotional stability

2. Which of the following style leads to the lose–lose situation?
   a. Competition
   b. Accommodating
   c. **Avoidance**
   d. Collaborating

3. Which of the following conflict management style tries to bring win–win situation to the problem?
   a. Competition
   b. **Collaboration**
   c. Avoidance
   d. Compromise

4. The workers in ABC Pharmaceutical went on strike as they demanded a 10% hike in their salary. To run the business smoothly, the management of the company decided to accept all the demands of the employees without terms and conditions. Which style of conflict management is highlighted in the above example?
   a. Competition
   b. **Accommodating**
   c. Avoidance
   d. Compromise

5. A style that indicates a high level of assertiveness and cooperation is _____.
   a. Competition
   b. Accommodating
   c. Avoidance
   d. **Collaborating**

6. Which of the following styles of conflict management brings an optimum solution?
   a. Competition
   b. Accommodating
   c. Avoidance
   d. **Collaborating**

7. The five styles of management or conflict mode instrument has been developed by _____.
   a. **Thomas-Kilman**
   b. Kurt Lewin
   c. Robert Oven
   d. None of the above

8. A person holds_____ power when he gets things done through others by forcing, intimidating, hurting, and irritating.
   a. Reward
   b. Normative
   c. Expert
   d. **Coercive**

4.5. Part B (Review Questions)

1. "There can be various ways of handling conflict." Comment. Explain multiple conflict management styles with examples.
2. Explain various types of situations where different styles of conflict management are appropriate.
3. What are the various styles of conflict management? Give example.
4. Discuss the merits and demerits of different conflict management styles.
5. "Collaborative styles preserve the relationship and trust." Justify the statement.

4.6. Part C (Glossary)

Collaboration: Collaboration is an approach which involves when conflicting parties team up and try to recognize a solution so that no one is at a loss.

Compromising: It is a midway situation in which the parties sacrifice something for the other party's profit.

Accommodating: Style of conflict management one party sacrifices its interest to make the other party happy.

Avoidance: Staying away from the conflict by withdrawing, sidestepping, or postponing.

Fixed pie strategy: When the gain of one party is the loss of the other. An individual tries to satisfy his/her own interest at the other 'person's expense.

4.7. Activity 4.1

Form a team of 4–5 people from your group. Request each team to visit one company from a different industry. Inquire with the staff about their dispute resolution styles. Ask each team to make a presentation. Discuss and compare how conflict management styles of employees differ depending on the nature of the industry.

Chapter 5

Personality and Conflict: How are They Inter-connected?

Learning Objectives:

- Role of personality in conflict management.
- Big five personality traits and conflict management.
- The role of transactions and transactional analysis in conflict management.

Personality refers to the pattern of behaviors and qualities that can assist in anticipating and explaining a person's behavior. Multiple factors can influence personality, ranging from hereditary, environment, and experience.[1] Personality, in general, is a complicated and varied part of conflict resolution. Understanding one's personality traits and those of others involved in a conflict can be crucial for effective conflict resolution.[2] The conflict management style and negotiation skills are influenced by personality. Personality traits of an individual may affect conflict resolution strategies in the following ways:

1. *Communication styles*: Miscommunication is a critical factor in the emergence of a dispute.[3] Personality factors can also have an impact on how people interact during conflicts. Extrovert and forceful people tend to be

---

[1]Cervone, D., & Pervin, L. A. (2022). *Personality: Theory and research*. John Wiley & Sons.

[2]Gokoglan, E., & Ozen Bekar, E. (2021). The relationship between nurse managers' personality traits and their conflict management strategy preferences. *Journal of Nursing Management*, 29(5), 1239–1245.

[3]Katz, N. H., Lawyer, J. W., Sosa, K. J., Sweedler, M., & Tokar, P. (2020). *Communication and conflict resolution skills*. Kendall Hunt Publishing.

Managing and Negotiating Disagreements:
A Contemporary Approach for Conflict Resolution, 51–64
Copyright © 2024 by Bhawana Bhardwaj and Dipanker Sharma
Published under exclusive licence by Emerald Publishing Limited
doi:10.1108/978-1-83797-971-420241005

more direct and vocal, whereas introverted and pleasant people may struggle assertively and resort to passive–aggressive communication.[4]

2. *Emotional regulation*: Emotionally intelligent individuals are better at being calm and composed, whereas those who are disposed to emotional volatility may struggle with rage or frustration during conflicts.[5]

3. *Perceptions and biases*: Personality traits can influence how individuals see conflicts and the persons involved in them.[6] For example, people with high levels of openness are more willing to consider different points of view, whereas those with solid confirmation biases may be antagonistic to new ideas.

4. *Personality traits*: Personality traits in leadership positions can significantly impact how conflicts are managed within teams or organizations. Leaders with charismatic and compelling personalities may have considerable authority in conflict resolution techniques.[7]

5. *Conflict triggers*: Certain personality traits or qualities may be more likely to cause conflicts. Highly competitive individuals, for example, may clash with others with similar characteristics.

5.1. Conflict Management: Role of Big Five Personality Traits

Five factor model (FFM) is a widely accepted framework for assessing and understanding personality. These characteristics can influence numerous elements of conflict management, including how individuals approach and resolve disagreements.[8,9] The role of personality traits in influencing dispute resolution is discussed in Fig. 10.

---

[4]Antonioni, D. (1998). Relationship between the big five personality factors and conflict management styles. *International Journal of Conflict Management*, *9*(4), 336–355.

[5]Mayer, J. D., Salovey, P., & Caruso, D. (2000). Models of emotional intelligence. *Handbook of Intelligence*, *2*, 396–420.

[6]Jensen-Campbell, L. A., & Graziano, W. G. (2001). Agreeableness as a moderator of interpersonal conflict. *Journal of Personality*, *69*(2), 323–362.

[7]Utley, M. E., Richardson, D. R., & Pilkington, C. J. (1989). Personality and interpersonal conflict management. *Personality and Individual Differences*, *10*(3), 287–293.

[8]Soomro, B. A., Saraih, U. N., & Ahmad, T. S. T. (2022). Personality traits and conflict management styles: building the relationship through leadership effectiveness. *Kybernetes*, *52*(12), 6251–6278.

[9]Gokoglan, E., & Ozen Bekar, E. (2021). The relationship between nurse managers' personality traits and their conflict management strategy preferences. *Journal of Nursing Management*, *29*(5), 1239–1245.

Low Score	Factor	High Score

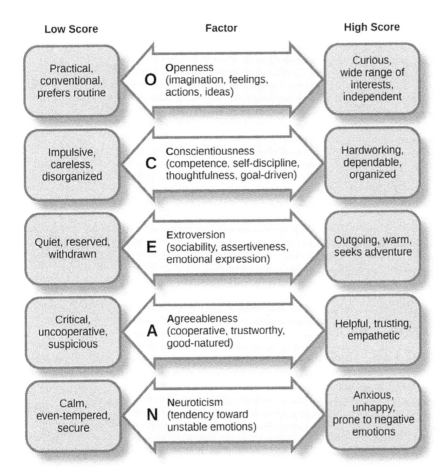

Fig. 10.   FFM of Personality. *Source*: Adopted from *Psychology* (2nd ed., Rice University, CC BY-NC-SA 4.0).

5.1.1. Openness to Experience

Individuals with high levels of openness are more open-minded, creative, and eager to explore various points of view. This attribute can lead to a higher willingness to seek new alternatives and compromise in conflict resolution.[10] Thus, people with a high level of openness bring new viewpoints to situations and are more adaptable in creating creative solutions. Thus, this trait develops a propensity to identify creative and functional outcomes to the conflict.

---

[10]Xu, X., Xia, M., Zhao, J., & Pang, W. (2021). Be honest, open, and creative: How openness to experience and to change mediates the authenticity–creativity association: *Thinking Skills and Creativity*, *41*, 100857.

5.1.2. Conscientiousness

People with high conscientiousness are organized, responsible, and detail-oriented. A high level of consciousness can reduce the chances of conflict.[11] With this trait, they may excel at planning and structuring discussions, ensuring that agreements are upheld. Conscientious individuals can maintain order and accountability in conflict management processes. However, their perfectionist tendencies can sometimes lead to inflexibility or a focus on rules at the expense of inter-personal relationships.[12]

5.1.3. Extraversion

Extraversion is a broad personality trait that includes a variety of subtypes such as friendliness, assertiveness, a high activity level, pleasant emotions, and impulsivity.[13] Extraverts are gregarious, forceful, and friendly, which makes them good conflict-resolution candidates. They may excel at starting conversations and openly addressing conflicts. Extraverts can facilitate communication and engage others in dispute-resolution initiatives.

5.1.4. Agreeableness

Agreeableness is described as the desire to maintain pleasant inter-personal connections. Agreeable people are recognized as friendly, warm, helpful, and tolerant.[14] Agreeableness has been connected to cooperation, adaptive conflict resolution, mood control, and having fewer prejudices. These people are cooperative, empathic, and attentive to the sentiments of others. They prefer to avoid conflict and seek harmony. As a result, agreeable people can aid in maintaining positive connections amid conflicts and may prioritize compromise. However, it is noteworthy that person high on agreeableness find it challenging to be assertive and express their point of view with incredible difficulty.[15,16]

---

[11]Bazana, S., & Dodd, N. (2013). Conscientiousness, work-family conflict and stress amongst police officers in Alice, South Africa. *Journal of Psychology*, 4(1), 1–8.

[12]McGuigan, R., & Popp, N. (2012). Consciousness and conflict (explained better?). *Conflict Resolution Quarterly*, 29(3), 227–260.

[13]Lucas, R. E., & Diener, E. (2001). Extraversion. *International Encyclopedia of the Social & Behavioral Sciences*, 5202–5205.

[14]Graziano, W. G., & Tobin, R. M. (2017). Agreeableness and the five-factor model. In T. A. Widiger (Ed.), *The Oxford handbook of the five-factor model* (Vol. 1, pp. 105–131). Oxford University Press.

[15]McGuigan, R., & Popp, N. (2012). Consciousness and conflict (explained better?). *Conflict Resolution Quarterly*, 29(3), 227–260.

[16]Jensen-Campbell, L. A., & Graziano, W. G. (2001). Agreeableness as a moderator of interpersonal conflict. *Journal of Personality*, 69(2), 323–362.

5.1.5. Neuroticism (Emotional Stability)

Emotional intelligence (EI) is the ability to monitor own emotions as well as the emotions of others, to correctly discern and categorize different emotions, and to utilize emotional information to steer one's own thoughts and behavior as well as to influence the behavior of others.[17] Individuals with low neuroticism (high emotional stability) stay calm and composed under stressful situations. They have fewer chances of emotional outbursts. Emotionally stable people can be a calming influence in emotionally heated situations and make sensible decisions. Similarly, people with strong neuroticism may struggle to successfully manage their emotions during confrontations, potentially exacerbating the individuals with low neuroticism (high emotional stability) who tend to remain calm and composed during conflicts. They are less prone to emotional outbursts. Emotionally stable individuals can provide a stabilizing influence in emotionally charged conflicts and make rational decisions. However, those with high neuroticism may find it challenging to manage their emotions effectively during conflicts, potentially escalating the situation.

Thus, no single personality attribute is intrinsically good or bad for conflict resolution. The success of a person's conflict resolution style is determined by the unique setting, the personalities of those involved, and the nature of the disagreement itself. Furthermore, people are not restricted by their personality features, and they may learn and improve their conflict-resolution skills over time. Effective conflict resolution frequently involves a combination of qualities and talents from the Big Five personality traits, and individuals' approaches may need to be adjusted based on the circumstances of each conflict. Furthermore, awareness of one's and others' personality traits can be beneficial in encouraging constructive conflict resolution and maintaining positive relationships.

5.2. Role of Personality in Influencing Conflict Management Styles[18,19]

People have diverse personalities, and these characteristics can influence how they approach and resolve problems in various settings, including personal relationships, the workplace, and groups. Here are some prevalent personality qualities and how they relate to dispute-resolution methods.

---

[17]Goleman, D. (1995). *Emotional intelligence* (p. 262). Bantam Books, Inc..
[18]Barbuto, J. E., Jr., Phipps, K. A., & Xu, Y. (2010). Testing relationships between personality, conflict styles and effectiveness. *International Journal of Conflict Management*, *21*(4), 434–447.
[19]Tehrani, H. D., & Yamini, S. (2020). Personality traits and conflict resolution styles: A meta-analysis. *Personality and Individual Differences*, *157*, 109794.

5.2.1. Collaborative Style

Individuals with an open, cooperative, and aggressive attitude are likely to collaborate. They seek win−win solutions and are eager to collaborate with others to achieve mutually beneficial results.

5.2.2. Competitive Style

People try to maximize their benefits in a competitive style. People with aggressive and influential personalities may choose a competitive conflict style. They work hard to succeed and attain their goals, often at the expense of others.

5.2.3. Avoidance

Avoidance can be a preferred style of an introverted person. Introverted, shy, or anxious individuals may prefer to withdraw from conflict, avoiding confrontation and difficult conversations. They may avoid a condition that needs much communication and interaction with people.

5.2.4. Accommodating

Accommodating personalities prioritize relationship maintenance and may give in to others' wishes to avoid conflict. They are frequently more concerned with maintaining the peace than pursuing their interests.

5.2.5. Compromising style

A person with a pragmatic personality may use compromising as their conflict style. They make concessions to reach a middle ground or settle a conflict to avoid further complications. To achieve this, they may largely compromise.

5.3. Unraveling the Role of Transactions and Transactional Analysis in Conflict Management

The concept of transactional analysis (TA) was propounded by Dr. Eric Berne a prominent psychiatrist.[20] TA plays a role in understanding inter-personal interactions and disputes. Understanding the notions of "life positions," "ego states," "strokes," and "transactions" is critical in TA. Here is how they are related to one another.

5.3.1. Role of Life Positions in Conflict Management

Life positions are fundamental beliefs or attitudes people have about themselves and others. There are four prominent life positions:

---

[20]Ramaraju, S. (2012). Psychological perspectives on interpersonal communication. *Journal of Arts, Science & Commerce, 3*(4), 68–73.

a. *I'm OK, you're OK*: People in this life position see themselves and others as equally valuable and capable.[21] It implies that one respects oneself and others, accepts all people's inherent worth and value and is confident in expressing and hearing diverse points of view. Individuals in this life situation have a good attitude toward themselves and others. They believe both parties in a conflict are valuable and capable of reaching a mutually beneficial agreement. People in this position approach conflict with a collaborative and open communication mindset. They are more inclined prone to seek win–win solutions and concentrate on problem resolution rather than blaming or criticizing. It is regarded as the best, healthiest, and most practical stance for problem-solving and communicating with others in a courteous and understanding manner. It also means that one accepts all people's inherent worth and value.

b. *I'm OK, you're not OK*: Individuals with this position perceive themselves as competent and worthy while they view others as inadequate or problematic. They think they are capable while others as imperfect or insufficient. This type of life position might lead to disagreements and judgmental attitudes. This life position can lead to a condescending attitude to conflict resolution, in which one person believes they have all the answers and the other side is the source of the problem. Conflict resolution style in this position may include attempts to control or dominate the opposing party, which can intensify disagreements.

c. *I'm not OK, you're OK*: People with this life position have a low self-image yet have a favorable outlook on others. Individuals in this life position feel insufficient or inferior, while others are seen as competent and worthy.[22] This might lead to feelings of inadequacy or reliance. They may believe they are faulty or insufficient, which causes them to be passive or subservient during disagreements. Conflict resolution in this position may entail avoiding or accommodating the other party's demands and desires to maintain harmony. This, however, might result in one-sided compromises and discontent.

d. *I'm not OK, you're not OK*: Individuals in this life situation have a lousy self-image and regard others negatively. This is a negative life perspective in which people regard themselves and others as imperfect, incompetent, or unworthy. This can lead to prolonged dissatisfaction and conflict. Conflict resolution in this situation can be complicated since both parties may participate in a blame game or defensive behaviors. Conflict resolution becomes difficult because neither party believes they can successfully handle the issue.

Thus, understanding the life position can help managers in conflict management to a great extent. An awareness of life positions can help conflict managers

---

[21]Harris, T., & Harris, T. A. (2012). *I'm OK, you're OK*. Random House.
[22]Harris, A. B., & Harris, T. A. (2011). *Staying* OK. Random House.

choose appropriate strategies and interventions to promote constructive conflict resolution and improved relationships.

1. Conflict managers can focus on developing collaborative problem-solving in confrontations with "I'm OK, you're OK" positions in order to identify mutually satisfying.
2. Mediating parties may modify their approaches if one or both parties have opposing life positions. The conflict manager can focus on developing trust and increasing communication by creating a secure, non-judgmental environment.
3. Encouraging people to grasp the other person's point of view can be especially helpful when dealing with life problems typified by negative self- or other perceptions.
4. When one party dominates (e.g., "I'm OK, You're not OK"), conflict managers may need to address power imbalances to ensure fair and successful conflict resolution.

5.3.2. Role of Ego States in Conflict Management

Ego states also play an important role in conflict management. According to Eric Berne, every person, regardless of age, has three ego states: parent, adult, and child.[23] Each ego state represents a different set of thoughts, feelings, and behaviors, and understanding these ego states can help manage conflicts effectively.

Parent ego state: This ego state comprises thoughts, feelings, and behaviors learned through parental and authority sources. It is classified into two sub-states: nurturing parent (positive and compassionate) and critical parent (critical and controlling).[24]

Adult ego state: The reasonable, logical, and objective adult ego state. It is in charge of processing data and making judgments based on facts and analysis.

The Child's ego state: This ego state comprises emotions, feelings, and behaviors developed as a youngster. It is separated into two sub-states: the adapted child (compliant and conforming) and the free child (free and spontaneous).[25]

5.3.3. What Is a Transaction?

Transaction occurs when a person (A) communicates/interacts with another person (B) (See Fig. 11), and a transaction occurs between the ego states of

---

[23]Berne, E. (2016). Transactional analysis in psychotherapy: A systematic individual and social psychiatry. Pickle Partners Publishing.

[24]Thomson, G. (1972). The identification of ego states. *Transactional Analysis Journal*, *2*(4), 46–61.

[25]Stewart, I. (2001). Ego states and the theory of theory: The strange case of the little professor. *Transactional Analysis Journal*, *31*(2), 133–147.

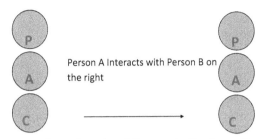

Person A Interacts with Person B on the right

Fig. 11. How transaction takes place? *Source*: Author's creation.

the persons.[26] When people communicate, there is communication between their ego states as well. Transactions are how people communicate using both spoken and non-verbal signs.[27] They are characterized by the interchange of strokes across ego states. Two important transactions that can affect the conflict between two individuals are:

Complementary transactions: In complementary transactions, one person's ego state matches or complements the other person's ego state. This usually results in excellent communication and little disagreement.[28] Fig. 12 exemplifies a complementary transaction, which occurs when the person fits into the ego states he is expected by the other person. If the transaction is complementary, the chances of conflict are negligible.

Crossed transaction: As depicted in Fig. 13, a crossed interaction is one in which the person being addressed refuses the ego state ascribed to them by the first speaker. The conflict occurs when the transaction is crossed.[29]

Apart from these two transactions, there can be angular and ulterior transactions that can impact conflict. Thus, in order to manage conflict between understanding and managing transactions between two parties is essential. It has been identified that staying in an adult ego minimizes conflict chances.

How to apply the concept of ego states in conflict management?

a. *Self-awareness*: During a disagreement, individuals should be aware of the ego state(s) they are functioning from. Self-awareness allows individuals to understand why they are reacting in a certain way and to adopt a more acceptable ego state for conflict resolution.

b. *Communication*: Recognizing the ego states of others is essential for effective communication. Individuals can alter their communication style to create

---

[26]Tudor, K. (2018). The neopsyche: The integrating adult ego state. In K. Tudor (Ed.), *Co-creative transactional analysis* (pp. 29–67). Routledge.

[27]Rath, I. (1993). Developing a coherent map of transactional analysis theories. *Transactional Analysis Journal, 23*(4), 201–215.

[28]Vinella, P. (2013). Transactional analysis counseling groups: Theory, practice, and how they differ from other TA groups. *Transactional Analysis Journal, 43*(1), 68–79.

[29]Wadsworth, D., & DiVincenti, A. (2003). Core concepts of transactional analysis: An opportunity born of struggle. *Transactional Analysis Journal, 33*(2), 148–161.

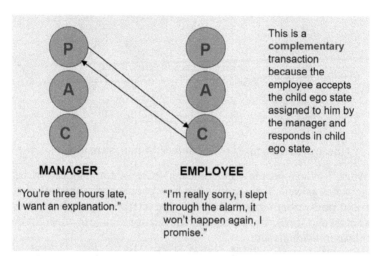

Fig. 12. Complementary Transaction. *Source*: Developed by authors.

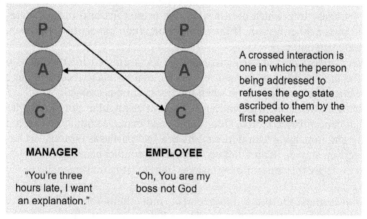

Fig. 13. Crossed Transactions. *Source*: Developed by authors.

better understanding and collaboration by recognizing the ego state from which the other person operates.

c. *Conflict resolution tactics*: Conflict resolution tactics are influenced by ego states. For example, if both sides engage their Critical Parent ego state, the conflict may become more combative. Encouraging people to engage their adult ego state for reasonable dialogue and problem-solving can result in more constructive conflict resolution.

5.3.4. Role of Stroke in Conflict Management

Strokes are units of acknowledgement or communication conveyed between individuals in TA. The term "strokes" is used in TA to refer to any type of social interaction in which another person's presence is acknowledged.[30] Broadly, there are types of strokes:

a. *Positive strokes*: These are gestures, words, or behaviors that convey appreciation, affirmation, or support. Positive strokes are essential for building and maintaining healthy relationships.[31]
b. *Negative strokes*: These are critical, disapproving, or undermining gestures, words, or behaviors. Negative strokes can lead to conflicts and emotional distress.[32]

They can further be divided into verbal and non-verbal strokes.

a. *Communication and miscommunication*: Miscommunication and misconceptions are common causes of conflict. Strokes are a kind of communication, and how they are delivered and perceived can impact the outcome of a disagreement. Positive strokes can help to clarify goals and foster greater understanding, but negative strokes or a lack of strokes can lead to confusion.
b. *Understanding the stroking patterns*: Individuals involved in a conflict can assist conflict managers or mediators assess the underlying dynamics. For example, if one party repeatedly uses negative language (criticizing or demeaning), it might aggravate the conflict. Recognizing and resolving negative stroking patterns can be critical in conflict resolution.
c. *Emotional regulation*: Strokes can influence emotional states during a conflict. Positive strokes have a calming effect and can help individuals manage their emotional reactions. On the other hand, a lack of positive or an abundance of negative strokes can lead to increased emotional distress and reactivity.
d. *Strokes*: Allow people to validate and recognize one another's presence, feelings, and contributions. Positive strokes can help de-escalate tensions in a conflict setting. For example, recognizing someone's point of view or sentiments might indicate respect.
e. *Building rapport*: Offering positive strokes can aid in developing rapport and trust between conflicting parties. This is especially true in more complex or long-running situations where trust has been destroyed. Building rapport with positive strokes, helps establish a more conducive environment for conflict resolution.
f. *Active listening*: Listening and sympathetic communication, which are significant conflict resolution tactics. Individuals can establish a more collaborative environment to work together to discover mutually accepted solutions by actively listening to each other and delivering positive strokes.

---

[30]Berne, E. (2011). Games people play: The basic handbook of transactional analysis. Tantor eBooks.
[31]Barrow, G., Bradshaw, E., & Newton, T. (2012). Improving behaviour and raising self-esteem in the classroom: A practical guide to using transactional analysis. Routledge.
[32]Kahler, T., & Capers, H. (1974). The miniscript. *Transactional Analysis Bulletin*, 4(1), 26–42.

5.4. Caselet 5.1

Davis is Lucy's supervisor, and she works in the Information Department. She has having trouble getting to work on time and is constantly apologizing, but Davis believes she is just making excuses. As the subject stays unsolved after multiple heated meetings, anger and resentment grow. It is tough for the two to talk without disagreeing. Davis does not want to terminate Lucy because, as a single mother, she realizes how important the job is to her. Lucy makes every effort to arrive at work on time, but getting three young children ready for school is a challenge.

> *Q1.* Assess the personality type of Lucy and David in the above situation.

> *Q2.* What can be solution for the above stated problem?

5.5. Activity 5.1

Form a group of 8–10 members and ask each member to rate themselves on five dimensions of personality traits.

5.6. Part A (Self-assessment)

1. A problematic assignment was given to Roma and Reeta. Before even starting the project, Roma was confident that she would complete the assignment and was also sure that Reeta did not have the potential to complete such an assignment. Which type of ego state Roma has displayed in the above example?
   a. I'm not OK–You are OK
   b. **I'm OK–You are not OK**
   c. I'm not–You are not OK
   d. Any of these, depending on the situation

2. A neurotic is more prone to believe ———.
   a. I'm not OK–You are OK
   b. **I'm not OK–You are not OK**
   c. I'm OK–You are not OK
   d. Depending on the circumstances, any of these

3. Child ego state statements usually sound something like this ———.
   a. I want to be happy
   b. I need help
   c. I love you
   d. **All of the above**

4. Which of the following transactions has parallel stimulus and response?
   a. Cross transactions
   b. **Complementary transactions**
   c. Social transactions
   d. All the above

5. Involve two ego states in the initiator and responder and two messages – a verbalized social message and an implied psychological message.
   a. **Ulterior transactions**
   b. Cross transactions
   c. Complementary transactions
   d. Angular

6. According to TA, when a person is rational and logical, he is in which ego state
   a. Parent ego state
   b. **Adult ego state**
   c. Child ego state
   d. Rational ego state

7. In TA, what are the three basic ego states?
   a. Parent, adolescent, adult
   b. Parent, child, sibling
   c. Teacher, student, parent
   d. **Parent, adult, child**

8. Which of the following ego states represents rational and objective thinking?
   a. **The adult ego state**
   b. The child ego state
   c. The sibling ego state
   d. The parent ego state

9. What is a crossed transaction in TA?
   a. A transaction in which two parties are completely in sync
   b. A transaction in which four ego states are involved
   c. **A transaction in which the two individuals engaged' ego states do not align as planned**
   d. A transaction that exclusively involves the parent ego state.

5.7. Part B (Review Questions)

1. Explain:
   a. Ego states and transactions.
   c. Johari windows.

2. Explain the role of strokes and life positions in conflict management.
3. Discuss how ego states can make or mar a relationship.
4. Discuss strokes and types of strokes. How positive and negative strokes affect conflict?
5. Discuss various types of life positions and their role in conflict management.
6. Elaborate the importance of personality in negotiation with the help of the big five model.

5.8. Part C (Glossary)

Conscientiousness: Being conscientious implies willingness to do a task right and taking one's obligations to others seriously. Those who are conscientious are more productive and well-organized than those who are carefree and haphazard.

Openness to experience: Willingness to seek new alternatives and learn new things.

Extrovert: The eminent psychologist C. G. Jung coined the term in the early 20th century. An extrovert is a person whose motives and actions are directed outwards. This personality trait encompasses qualities like friendliness, assertiveness, a high activity level, positive emotions, and impulsivity.

Introvert: A person who is preoccupied with their own ideas and feelings rather than with outward objects. They prefer to be alone or in low-stimulation surroundings because they find social interactions exhausting.

Agreeableness: Agreeableness is described as the desire to maintain pleasant interpersonal connections.

Complementary transaction: In complementary transactions, one person's ego state matches or complements the other person's ego state.

Crossed transactions: Crossed transaction is one in which the person being addressed refuses the ego state ascribed to them by the first speaker.

Positive Stroke: Gestures, words, or behaviors that convey appreciation, affirmation, or support.

Negative stroke: Critical, disapproving, or undermining gestures, words, or behaviors.

Chapter 6

Conflict Resolution: Initial Reactions and Strategies

> **Learning Objectives:**
> - Surfacing the cognitive, emotional, and behavioral dimensions of conflict.
> - Strategies to manage inter-personal and intra-personal conflict.

In the era of globalization, expanding a firm internationally has become important. International organizations now operate in complex environments where
staff members are exposed to a variety of strange and cultural circumstances.
These variations in culture and intercultural components can cause disputes
and performing business functions more challenging.[1] Conflict management
entails a variety of strategies and approaches that can be used depending on
the scenario, the nature of the dispute, and the individuals involved. There is
no one-size-fits-all approach to conflict resolution. Different types of conflict
may necessitate other tactics, and the efficacy of these strategies may vary significantly.[2] Different dimensions can be taken into consideration while resolving
conflict. These dimensions offer a complete framework for comprehending and
resolving disputes. Within each dimension, below are some frequent conflict
resolution strategies.

---

[1]Bhardwaj, B. (2022). Short-term foreign trips correlates of the four factors model of
cultural intelligence. *Rajagiri Management Journal*, 16(3), 213–225.
[2]Ohbuchi, K. I., & Suzuki, M. (2003). Three dimensions of conflict issues and their
effects on resolution strategies in organizational settings. *International Journal of
Conflict Management*, 14(1), 61–73.

Managing and Negotiating Disagreements:
A Contemporary Approach for Conflict Resolution, 65–76
Copyright © 2024 by Bhawana Bhardwaj and Dipanker Sharma
Published under exclusive licence by Emerald Publishing Limited
doi:10.1108/978-1-83797-971-420241006

6.1. Dimensions of Conflict Resolution

Resolution of conflict can involve three dimensions.

6.1.1. Cognitive Dimension

This represents how conflicting parties understand and view the conflict. Cognition is the way one party perceives another contradictory party.[3,4] The following strategies can be adopted for managing cognitive conflict:

a. *Communication*: Addressing cognitive components of conflict requires open and effective communication. Encouraging participants to voice their opinions, issues, and points of view can aid in mutual understanding.[5]
b. *Empathy*: Encouraging folks to see the problem through the eyes of the opposing party can foster empathy and aid resolution. This is carefully listening and attempting to comprehend the other person's point of view.[6]
c. *Negotiation*: Finding common ground and mutually accepted solutions is the goal of negotiation. Parties can hold discussions to create consensus and agreements that consider each other's interests. This also improves mutual understanding.[7]
d. *Mediation*: A mediator, a neutral third party, can assist in enabling conversation and establishing common ground. Mediation helps parties in exploring viable ideas and reaching a mutually acceptable agreement.

6.1.2. Emotional Dimension

This represents the way conflicting parties feel about the conflict. The emotional dimensions of conflict include anger, jealousy, hatred, stress, depression, etc. Emotional dimension can be managed through the following strategies[8,9]:

---

[3]Sacco, K., & Bucciarelli, M. (2008). The role of cognitive and socio-cognitive conflict in learning to reason. *Mind & Society*, *7*, 1–19.
[4]Kahneman, D., & Tversky, A. (2004). Conflict resolution: A cognitive perspective. In E. Shafir (Ed.), *Preference, belief, and similarity: Selected writings by Amos Tversky* (pp. 729–746). Boston Review.
[5]Spaho, K. (2013). Organizational communication and conflict management. *Management Journal of Contemporary Management Issues*, *18*(1), 103–118.
[6]De Wied, M., Branje, S. J., & Meeus, W. H. (2007). Empathy and conflict resolution in friendship relations among adolescents. *Aggressive Behavior: Official Journal of the International Society for Research on Aggression*, *33*(1), 48–55.
[7]Nadler, J. (2003). Rapport in negotiation and conflict resolution. *Marquette Law Review*, *87*, 875.
[8]Jones, T. S. (2001). Emotional communication in conflict. In M. Coulthard, J. Cotterill, & F. Rock (Eds.), *The language of conflict and resolution* (pp. 81–104). Routledge.
[9]Bramsen, I., & Poder, P. (2018). *Emotional dynamics in conflict and conflict transformation*. Berghof Foundation.

a. *Emotional regulation*: It is critical to assist folks in managing their emotions during conflict. Deep breathing, awareness, and pausing to cool off can all help in controlling emotional reactions.
b. *Emotional intelligence*: Encourage parties to empathize with each other's emotional experiences to humanize the issue and lessen negative emotions. This can be accomplished by actively listening to each other and acknowledging each other's sentiments.[10]
c. *Coaching*: A coach can work with individuals to address the emotional aspects of conflict, assisting them in developing emotional regulation and self-awareness.[11]

6.1.3. Behavior Dimension

This represents how conflicting parties act or respond in a contradictory situation. The following strategies can be helpful in managing behavior dimension:

a. *Assertiveness training*: "Assertive behavior is defined as any action that reflects an individual's own best interest, including standing up for oneself without significant anxiety."[12,13] Teaching people how to assert their demands and concerns courteously and effectively will improve their behavior during conflict.[14]
b. *Conflict resolution workshops*: Such training and workshops can be used to equip people with practical skills for managing disagreements positively.
c. *Starting clear ground rules*: Clear ground rules and guidelines for communication and behavior during confrontations can prevent escalation and maintain a respectful environment.
d. *Apology and forgiveness*: In some circumstances, a genuine apology or forgiveness can help to resolve problems and heal relationships.
e. *Behavioral modification*: Identifying and correcting specific problematic behavior such as passive-aggressiveness or avoidance can contribute to conflict resolution.[15]

---

[10]Zhang, S. J., Chen, Y. Q., & Sun, H. (2015). Emotional intelligence, conflict management styles, and innovation performance: An empirical study of Chinese employees. *International Journal of Conflict Management, 26*(4), 450–478.

[11]Caruso, D. R., & Salovey, P. (2008). Coaching for emotional intelligence. In S. Palmer & A. Stough (Eds.), *Psychometrics in coaching: Using psychological and psychometric tools for development* (pp. 151–170). Kogan Page.

[12]Alberti, R., & Emmons, M. (1970). *Your perfect right: A guide to assertive behavior.* Impact Press.

[13]Alberti, R., & Emmons, M. (2008). *Your perfect right: A guide to assertive behavior* (9th ed.). Impact Press.

[14]Speed, B. C., Goldstein, B. L., & Goldfried, M. R. (2018). Assertiveness training: A forgotten evidence-based treatment. *Clinical Psychology: Science and Practice, 25*(1), e12216.

[15]Eelen, P. (2018). Behaviour therapy and behaviour modification background and development. *Psychologica Belgica, 58*(1), 184.

6.2. Managing Different Levels of Conflict

The following strategies can help in the prevention and resolution of conflict at various levels.

6.2.1. Intra-personal Conflict

When an individual is facing a conflict within him/herself, the following strategies may be helpful:

a. *Positive attitude*: Attitude represents the general tendency of a person to respond positively or negatively to an event, a person, or a situation. Since conflict is a perceived phenomenon, a positive attitude may minimize the chances of misunderstanding misperception. Conflict is a natural part of life and cannot be avoided.[16] The attitude of an individual plays a vital role in conflict management. Believing in you and having a positive attitude can prevent and help manage intra-personal conflict. A person who stays positive experiences less stress and conflict.[17]

b. *Minimizing and prioritizing roles*: An individual must play multiple roles in an organization and society. Diversified demands from these roles can lead to discomfort. Accepting multiple roles beyond one's potential capability can create role conflict. "Saying no when you should say no" can help minimize the roles that may overburden him. Setting priorities and putting important tasks first can also help an individual to avoid role conflict.[18,19]

c. *Rational decision-making*: Decision-making is part and parcel of personal and organizational activities and can lead to conflicts where numerous options or alternatives are available. Emotions are one of the most significant intervening factors in decision-making. The chances of getting trapped into emotional decision are when something personal is at stake.[20,21] In such cases,

---

[16]Mohanty, M. S. (2009). Effects of positive attitude on happiness and wage: Evidence from the US data. *Journal of Economic Psychology*, *30*(6), 884–897.

[17]Salim, L., Shariff, M. N. M., & Arshad, D. A. (2016). Attitude toward conflict and family business succession. *Journal of Business Management and Accounting*, *6*(1), 75–89.

[18]Kline, S. L., & Floyd, C. H. (1990). On the art of saying no: The influence of social cognitive development on messages of refusal. *Western Journal of Speech Communication*, *54*(4), 454–472.

[19]Shrivastava, A., Dhole, K., Bhatt, A., & Raghunath, S. (2020). *Saying no is an art: Contextualized fallback responses for unanswerable dialogue queries*. ArXiv./abs/2012.01873

[20]Bodtker, A. M., & Katz Jameson, J. (2001). Emotion in conflict formation and its transformation: Application to organizational conflict management. *International Journal of Conflict Management*, *12*(3), 259–275.

[21]De Neys, W. (2010). Heuristic bias, conflict, and rationality in decision-making. In B. Glatzeder, V. Goel, & A. von Müller (Eds.),*Towards a theory of thinking: Building blocks for a conceptual framework* (pp. 23–33). Springer.

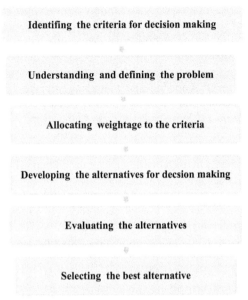

Fig. 14.   Rational Decision-making. *Source*: Created by author.

adopting a rational decision-making process can be helpful.[22] Fig. 14 depicts the possible stages that can be included in a rational decision-making process. This approach can be adopted in goal-related conflicts such as approach–approach, avoidance–approach, avoidance–avoidance, etc.

d.   *Time management*: Time management is one of the most demanded skills in the contemporary world. We all are into a juggling act of satisfying demands from social life, work life, family, personal interest, etc. The struggle to give our best in each such dimension and balancing each role that we are performing can cause stress. It is known that time is fixed and cannot be changed. The best approach is to maximize the overall benefit of these activities within the boundary of a limited amount of time. Time management is the process of planning and exercising cognizant control of time on specific activities, to enhance efficiency, productivity, and effectiveness.[23]

e.   *Work–life balance*: Balancing work and family demands is a significant challenge faced by employees in the current world. Literature on work–life balance

---

[22]Martínez-Tur, V., Peñarroja, V., Serrano, M. A., Hidalgo, V., Moliner, C., Salvador, A., González-Bono, E., & Molina, A. (2014). Intergroup conflict and rational decision making. *PLoS One*, *9*(12), e114013.

[23]Claessens, B. J., Van Eerde, W., Rutte, C. G., & Roe, R. A. (2007). A review of the time management literature. *Personnel Review*, *36*(2), 255–276.

has largely focused on how work and family roles conflict can be balanced.[24] However, recent studies focus on the idea that individuals improve their quality of life by participating in both roles. Work–life balance has six essential components,[25] namely:

1. *Self-management*: Knowing and managing yourself is essential. It also involves understanding emotions, interests, goals, etc.
2. *Time management*: Managing time can help devote appropriate time for facility, social, and work-related commitments.
3. *Stress management*: Stress can lead to a decrease in the efficiency of an individual. Stress management helps an individual utilize his potential at work and in the family.
4. *Change management*: Accepting and getting adjusted to change.
5. *Technology management*: Use of technology to improve the quality of work and professional life.
6. *Leisure management*: Planning and managing time for leisure activities.

f. *Yoga, meditation, and exercise*: Meditation and exercise help the body and mind to keep fit. They also help an individual manage and keep calm in difficult situations. Available reviews on yoga exercises, meditation, and relaxation practices propose that they can lessen the impact of stress responses, anxiety, and depression. In this regard, yoga works similarly to other self-soothing practices such as meditation, relaxation, exercise, or even socializing with friends. Yoga appears to alter stress response systems by lowering perceived stress and anxiety. This, in turn, reduces physiological arousal, such as lowering heart rate and blood pressure and easing respiration. Yoga practices have also enhanced heart rate variability, measuring the body's ability to respond to stress more flexibly.

6.2.2. Resolving Inter-personal, Inter-group Conflict

The following strategies can be adopted for resolving inter-personal and inter-group conflicts:

1. *Communication*: Much pointless conflict can be avoided with apparent, transparent, written, and verbal communication. Presuming that others already know something and not communicating can create resentment. Losing a single mail or message can fail a project or plan and point fingers. Communication, being a two-way process, also seeks active listening. Active listening can avoid many conflicts and win the hearts of people. Pay attention to what is being conveyed to avoid misinterpretation and misunderstanding.

---

[24]Jang, S. J., & Zippay, A. (2011). The juggling act: Managing work–life conflict and work–life balance. *Families in Society*, *92*(1), 84–90.
[25]Kalliath, T., & Brough, P. (2008). Work–life balance: A review of the meaning of the balance construct. *Journal of Management & Organization*, *14*(3), 323–327.

2. *Developing complementary transactions*: Ensuring complementary transactions and avoiding crossed transactions can help reduce conflict. Maintaining adult ego states also reduces the incidences of conflict. Adult-to-adult communication/transactions result in the most effective and healthy communication and relationships with others.[26]

3. *Emotional intelligence (EQ)*: EQ is an individual's ability to understand and manage their feelings and those of others; people with high EQ are good at recognizing and fulfilling the needs of others. They can also control their damaging emotions, such as anger, jealousy, worries, etc., and establish good inter-personal relationships to avoid conflict. The significant components of EQ include self-awareness, self-regulation, internal motivation, empathy, and social skills.[27]

4. *Empathy*: Sometimes, understanding anothers' point of view or perspective can results in lesser occurrence of conflict. Empathy means putting yourself in other's shoes and feeling what others may feel. Observing a circumstance from someone else's viewpoint and understanding their viewpoint, needs, motivation, etc., is crucial for effective conflict management. Only some people are naturally blessed with being empathic; others can develop this skill. Empathy can build up good workplace relationships and help manage conflicts well.[28]

5. *Creative problem solving*: Conflict may happen when no one can come up with a feasible solution, and the benefit of one can be the loss of another, so resolving the conflict may depend on creating a solution. Finding a creative solution that leads to a win–win situation may settle down a disagreement.

6. *Addressing problems rapidly before reaching a crisis stage:* Small problems if ignored in infancy stage can lead to big crises if ignored in infancy. A vigilant and quick action against little problems that can lead to significant issues is a wise act against conflict.

7. *Being assertive without blaming*: Being assertive is expressing yourself and putting up your point of view. Simultaneously, it includes respecting the rights and beliefs of others. Assertiveness helps in boosting self-esteem and earn respect. However, assertiveness is effective when it is based on mutual respect. During conflict management, assertiveness is essential, but it should also demonstrate awareness of the other party's rights and interests.

---

[26]Murray, H. (2023). Transactional analysis theory & therapy: Eric Berne. Retrieved October 5, 2023, from simplypsychology.org

[27]Jordan, P. J., & Troth, A. C. (2021). Managing emotions during team problem solving: Emotional intelligence and conflict resolution. In N. M. Ashkanasy, W. J. Zerbe, & C. E. J. Härtel (Eds.), *Emotion and performance* (pp. 195–218). CRC Press.

[28]Rahim, M. A., Psenicka, C., Polychroniou, P., Zhao, J. H., Yu, C. S., Chan, K. A., Anas, A. A., Dong, K., Alves, M. G., Lee, C. W., Rahman, S., & Van Wyk, R. (2002). A model of emotional intelligence and conflict management strategies: A study in seven countries. *The International Journal of Organizational Analysis*, 10(4), 302–326.

Expressing yourself and blaming others may demean the importance of assertiveness and further spoil the situation.

8. *Conflict dynamics profile*: This technique provides feedback about a person's behavior. This tool assesses how a person understands his behavior, and the answers are then compared with the feedback from peer groups and managers. Behavior is measured by using a questionnaire. The following characteristics may be used as a competent leader's reference point (Runde & Flanagan, 2012):[29]

   a. Ability to stay cool and calm.
   b. Accepting and utilizing constructive/functional conflict.
   c. Ability to separate personal issues from criticism and criticize ideas and not people.
   d. Focus on bringing the best outcomes rather than winning the argument.
   e. To recognize and understand all aspects of issues.
   f. She was listening carefully and encouraging fairness.

9. *Logical argument mapping* (LAM): LAM is a technique for improving communication, encouraging contemplation, and sharing perspectives (Hoffmann, 2005).[30] LAM's primary idea is that everybody who wants to accomplish something should have a cause to do it. As a result, the goal of LAM is to organize argumentation. LAM is a powerful tool for improving communication, stimulating critical thinking, and sharing perspectives. It aids individuals and businesses in organizing and structuring logical arguments. As you mentioned, the fundamental premise of LAM is that anyone who intends to declare a claim or make a point must offer arguments to back it up.

   a. *Improving communication*: LAM helps people communicate their ideas more effectively. When the framework of an argument is visually portrayed, it is easier for others to understand the main point and supporting grounds.
   b. *Encourages critical thinking*: LAM helps people to examine their arguments critically. Consider the strength of the reasons and their relationship to the central assertion while developing a logical argument map. This approach promotes introspection and self-evaluation.
   c. *Sharing points of view*: LAM has the potential to be a powerful tool for facilitating discussions and debates. It enables participants to evaluate the structure of multiple arguments, making it easier to compare and

---

[29]Runde, C. E., & Flanagan, T. A. (2012). *Becoming a conflict competent leader: How you and your organization manage conflict effectively*. John Wiley & Sons.
[30]Hoffmann, M. H. (2005). Logical argument mapping: A method for overcoming cognitive problems of conflict management. *International Journal of Conflict Management, 16*(4), 304.

contrast various points of view. This exchange of ideas has the potential to lead to more constructive and informed debates.

   d. *Argumentation organization*: LAM's primary purpose is to organize argumentation. It requires visually representing the primary, sub-claims, and supporting reasons clearly and orderly. This form prevents confusion and ensures that the argument proceeds logically.

10. *Vaaland's improvement model*: This conflict resolution model is helpful for both recognizing and analyzing the problem. Furthermore, according to Vaaland (2004),[31] while utilizing this approach, a third party should oversee and organize the process to avoid confusion and dysfunctional disputes. The benefits of employing this technique are that it involves both parties and helps them understand and address the problem in order to develop healthier relationships. The Vaaland improvement model is a conflict resolution paradigm that identifies and analyses underlying issues to address and resolve conflicts. This technique, according to Vaaland (2004), involves several vital ideas and steps:

   1. *Identifying the issue*: This stage aims to identify the roots of conflict and collect many perspectives on conflict to create a clear picture. It is necessary to comprehend the fundamental reasons, underlying issues, and many facets of the dispute.

   2. *Deciding assessment criteria*: The second stage employs a set of evaluation criteria that link the outcome of a conflict in team relationships. The disagreement can also be associated with formal procedures such as poor routines, inflexibility, and poor time management.[31]

   3. *Creating a shared understanding*: The next stage is to make the conflict participants aware of what has to be done to improve their relationship. Parties can offer the following actions, but they must also be prepared for the opposing party's potential to reject their proposals.

   4. *Balancing and resolution*: The final stage involves balancing and disclosing the causes of the issues. It means resolving the disagreement reasonably and rationally by addressing the root reasons.

   5. *Negotiation*: Negotiation is a communication process that involves interactions with two or more parties who have competing interests, goals, or points of view and are attempting to reach a mutually acceptable agreement or resolution to a particular topic or conflict. Negotiations can occur in various circumstances, such as business, diplomacy, legal difficulties, inter-personal interactions, etc. The procedure will be covered in depth in the following chapters.

   6. *Third-party conflict resolution*: When the conflict cannot be solved at a bipartite level, a neutral third party may be involved to resolve the

---

[31]Vaaland, T. I. (2004). Improving project collaboration: Start with the conflicts. *International Journal of Project Management*, 22(6), 447–454.

dispute, referred to as third-party conflict resolution. The various forms of third-party conflict resolution may be involved in mediation, counseling, arbitration, and adjudication. The details of these approaches will be discussed in the subsequent chapters. These methods offer diverse approaches to settling disputes, and choosing one to apply is determined by criteria such as the nature of the conflict, the preferences of the persons involved, and the desired outcome. Each technique has advantages and limitations, and the procedure's efficiency frequently depends on the dispute's specifics. In practice, depending on the complexity of the disagreement, some conflicts may involve a combination of these strategies or numerous steps of resolution.[32,33,34]

6.3. Case 6.1

David teaches Management at the Institute of Management Development. Jane is a graduate assistant in the same department. They have been working on a project that, if successful, will result in numerous options for publication. Jane is looking forward to the publication component of her research because she wants to teach at a university. She is convinced she will be credited as a co-author in any publication dealing with their findings because she conducted most of the experiments. Imagine her surprise when she read the departmental newsletter and discovered that an article about their research did not mention her name. On the other hand, David was regularly mentioned as the primary investigator and sole author of any resulting papers. No satisfactory results were attained after repeated visits to Bob, the department heads, and the dean's offices. Jane decided to contact a member of the alternative dispute resolution committee.

Q1. Can David be blamed for the above situation?

Q2. What kind of personality traits are depicted in Jane's and David's personality?

Q3. What strategies can be opted for conflict resolution in the above case?

---

[32]Birkeland, S. (2013). Negotiation under possible third-party resolution. *The Journal of Law and Economics, 56*(2), 281–299.

[33]Arunachalam, V., Dilla, W., Shelley, M., & Chan, C. (1998). Market alternatives, third party intervention, and third party informedness in negotiation. *Group Decision and Negotiation, 7*, 81–107.

[34]Lewicki, R. J., Weiss, S. E., & Lewin, D. (1992). Models of conflict, negotiation and third party intervention: A review and synthesis. *Journal Of Organizational Behavior, 13*(3), 209–252.

6.4. Part A (Self-assessment)

1. Which inter-personal conflict resolution technique is essential?
   a. Avoidance
   b. Passive listening
   c. **Active listening**
   d. Ignoring the problem

2. What role does EQ play in resolving disputes between people?
   a. By stifling feelings
   b. By denying feelings
   c. **By comprehending and controlling feelings**
   d. By avoiding feelings

3. What role does active listening have in resolving disputes?
   a. Interrupting the speaker
   b. **Showing empathy**
   c. Disregarding the speaker's viewpoint
   d. Offering unwanted advise

4. Why is empathy regarded as such an effective strategy for resolving conflicts? It does the following:
   a. Increase conflict
   b. **Promote understanding and connection**
   c. Encourage rivalry
   d. Encourage blaming

6.5. Part B (Review Questions)

1. In what ways can self-awareness contribute to effective intra-personal conflict management?
2. Describe the role of EQ in conflict resolution.
3. Provide a list of three techniques for self-reflection that can be used to determine the underlying causes of intra-personal conflict.
4. How meditation and mindfulness be useful techniques for handling inter-personal conflicts?
5. Think back to a time in your life when you had an intra-personal quarrel. What lessons did you take away from the experience, and how did you handle it?
6. Enumerate and explain three successful communication techniques for settling disputes between people.
7. In what ways may active listening aid in the settlement of disputes between people?

6.6. Part C (Glossary)

Assertive behavior: Any action that represents a person's own best interest, such as standing up for oneself without experiencing significant anxiety, is defined as assertive behavior.

Rational decision-making: Rational decision-making is an approach of considering logic and objectivity rather than intuition and subjectivity to make a decision. Identifying a problem, selecting a solution from a range of options, and finding an answer are the objectives of rational decision-making.

Work–life balance: Engaging in several roles with roughly equal attention, time, involvement, or commitment is known as work–life balance.[35]

Critical thinking: Reflective and reasonable thinking that is focused on deciding what to believe or do.[36]

---

[35]Greenhaus, J. H., Collins, K. M., & Shaw, J. D. (2003). The relation between work–family balance and quality of life. *Journal of Vocational Behavior, 63*(3), 510–531.
[36]Ennis, R. H. (1985). A logical basis for measuring critical thinking skills. *Educational Leadership, 43*(2), 44–48.

Chapter 7

Resolving Interpersonal and Intergroup Conflict Through RAT and RNT

Learning Objectives:

- Understanding role analysis technique (RAT).
- Process of RAT.
- Process and objective and role negotiation technique.

The organization's potential resource for gaining a competitive edge and improving performance is its human capital. Selecting qualified applicants is not enough to ensure the incorporations' long-term success but their retention is correspondingly important. The relationship between employer and employee plays an important role in employee retention and organizational effectiveness.[1,2,3] Problem-solving techniques of conflict management aim to prevent conflict and strengthen the relationships. Role analysis technique (RAT) and role negotiation technique (RNT) are essential techniques for conflict resolution. They are the methodical approach to clarifying responsibilities and expectations, which can

[1]Anshima, Bhardwaj, B., & Sharma, D. (2024). Artificial intelligence: Shifting the landscape of the human resources ecosystem. In D. Sharma, B. Bhardwaj, & M. C. Dhiman (Eds.), *Leveraging AI and emotional intelligence in contemporary business organizations* (pp. 371–381). IGI Global.
[2]Sharma, D., Salehi, W., Bhardwaj, B., Chand, M., & Salihy, H. (2023). Dovetailing the human resource management with the cloud computing in the era of industry 4.0: A review. *Frontiers in Management and Business*, 4(2), 340–351.
[3]Bhardwaj, B., Kalia, N., Chand, M., & Sharma, D. (2023). Engaged organizational culture as a precursor to job performance: An evidence from the hospitality industry of Himachal Pradesh. *International Journal of Hospitality and Tourism Systems*, 16(4), 48–57.

Managing and Negotiating Disagreements:
A Contemporary Approach for Conflict Resolution, 77–84
Copyright © 2024 by Bhawana Bhardwaj and Dipanker Sharma
Published under exclusive licence by Emerald Publishing Limited
doi:10.1108/978-1-83797-971-420241007

lead to enhanced efficiency, production, and general satisfaction among individuals and teams.

7.1. Role Analysis Technique

This technique was proposed by Ishwar Dayal and John. M. Thomas.[4] The technique is used to clarify team members' role expectations and obligations, reducing the chances of conflict.[5,6,7,8] Fig. 15 exhibits the process of RAT. It includes the following stages:

1. *Role identification*: The first step is determining the specific jobs within a given setting. This can include formal organizational responsibilities, such as job titles, informal roles within a group, or societal roles based on gender, age, or other demographics. In this stage, the focal role individual is identified. The individual performing the role to be analyzed is also called the focal role individual. In this stage, the focal role individual defines the role, its place in the organization, the rationale of its existence, its place in achieving the organizational goals, and specific duties to be performed under this role.
2. *Role description*: Once roles have been determined, each is given a full description. This involves describing the role's responsibilities, expectations, tasks, and behaviors. This can be accomplished in organizational contexts through job descriptions or role profiles.
3. *Role expectations*: It is critical to understand the expectations that come with each role. This includes thinking about what others expect of people in specific roles and what they expect of themselves. Focal role Individuals examine the perceived expectations of others from the role and list expectations they perceive others have from their role. It also involves discussion, clarification, and modification.
4. *Examining others' expectations*: The group members describe what they want from the incumbent. The expectation is discussed, clarified, modified, and agreed upon.[9]

---

[4]Dayal, I., & Thomas, J. M. (1968). Operation KPE: Developing a new organization. *The Journal of Applied Behavioral Science*, 4(4), 473–506.

[5]Golembiewski, R. T. (2019). Role analysis technique. In R. T. Golembiewski (Ed.), *Handbook of organizational consultation* (2nd ed., pp. 661–663). Routledge.

[6]Dayal, I. (1969). Role analysis technique in job descriptions. *California Management Review*, 11(4), 47–50.

[7]Dayal, I., & Thomas, J. M. (1968). Operation KPE: Developing a new organization. *The Journal of Applied Behavioral Science*, 4(4), 473–506.

[8]Kerrin, M., Mossop, L., Morley, E., Fleming, G., & Flaxman, C. (2018). Role analysis: The foundation for selection systems. In F. Patterson & L. Zibarras (Eds.), *Selection and recruitment in the healthcare professions: Research, theory and practice* (pp. 139–165). Palgrave Macmillan.

[9]Lyons, P. (1993). Developing expectations with the role analysis technique (RAT). *Journal of Management Education*, 17(3), 386–389.

Fig. 15. The Process of RAT. *Source*: Developed by authors.

5. *Role performance*: Evaluate how people are currently functioning in their roles. Are they living up to the roles' expectations and responsibilities? Is there anything missing links that could be improved?
6. *Role conflict*: Examine any potential conflicts or overlaps between positions. Individuals may have conflicting duties in some instances, causing tension or confusion. Effective role analysis requires identifying and resolving role conflicts.
7. *Role satisfaction*: Determine how satisfied people are with their jobs. Are they happy with their current positions, or do they believe their skills and abilities could be more utilized or overburdened?
8. *Role modification*: Based on the analysis findings, roles may need to be updated or redefined to match better the group's, organization's, or department's goals and objectives.
9. *Conclusion and role profile*: The focal role individual is responsible for making a written report and summary of the role, which is called a "Role Profile."

Role profile includes:

a. Set of activities classified as prescribed and discretionary.
b. Obligation of the role.
c. Expectations of the role form other roles.

Advantages of RAT:
1. RAT is a process that brings role clarity among team members.
2. It helps develop the competency and skills needed to perform a job.

3. It reduces the chances of role conflict.
4. It also acts as a tool for self-development and career planning.
5. Clarity of goals removes job ambiguity and enhances job satisfaction.
6. It also improves organizational climate and improves interpersonal relationships.

7.2. Role Negotiation Technique

The RNT is a systematic and collaborative strategy developed by Roger Harrison to help organizations and teams clarify and negotiate over roles and responsibilities, resolve conflicts, and increase overall productivity and satisfaction. It underlines the importance of clear communication, attentive listening, and flexibility in changing situations. The process may involve the following stages:

1. *Initiation*:
   Determine the need for a role negotiation. It could be due to organizational changes, team restructuring, or conflicts resulting from unclear roles and duties.
2. *Preparation*:
   Self-reflection: Each party should consider their current duties and responsibilities and what they hope to achieve through the discussion.
   Gather information: Gather relevant data, such as job descriptions, performance metrics, and any historical background connected to the roles under consideration.
   Parties involved: Decide who should be involved in the role negotiation. Team members, managers, and other essential stakeholders may be included.
3. *Initial meeting*:
   Agenda setting: Establish the purpose and objectives of the negotiation meeting.
   Roles and expectations: Discuss any challenges or concerns that have led to the need for negotiation and the current responsibilities and expectations.
   Active listening: Encourage all parties to express their perspectives and concerns while actively listening to each other.
4. *Role analysis*:
   Role mapping: Create a visual representation of the parties' roles, responsibilities, and relationships. This can be accomplished through diagrams, charts, or other visualization tools.
   Identify overlaps and gaps: Examine the job map for areas of overlap or ambiguity and gaps in responsibilities.
5. *Negotiation*:
   Collaborative discussion: Engage in open and collaborative discussions about how roles and duties might be modified or clarified to solve the highlighted concerns.
   Interests and needs: Discover each party's interests and needs. Discuss what adjustments or concessions might be necessary to meet these interests.

Brainstorm solutions: Encourage brainstorming and creativity to discover viable solutions. Consider several scenarios and their consequences.

Trade-offs and concessions: Be prepared to make trade-offs and concessions to reach a mutually acceptable agreement.

Document agreements: Agreements should be documented in writing when they are achieved to ensure a clear record of what has occurred. As agreements are established, make a written record to guarantee a clear record of what was agreed upon.

6. *Follow-up*:

Implementation plan: Create an implementation strategy outlining how the agreed-upon modifications will be implemented.

Review and evaluation: Establish regular review periods to evaluate the efficacy of the new positions and responsibilities. Make any necessary changes.

Continuous communication: Maintain open lines of communication during the implementation phase to resolve any difficulties or concerns that may arise.

Resolution and closure: The role negotiation can be resolved and closed whenever all parties are satisfied with the negotiated roles and responsibilities, and the changes have been successfully implemented (see Fig. 16).

Fig. 16.　The Process of RNT. *Source*: Created by authors based on available literature.

Thus, RAT and RNT can help create organizational structures that are important techniques for enhancing team member well-being and conflict management, leading to enhanced individual performance.

7.3. Activity 7.1

Divide your class into two groups based on gender, for example, boys and girls. Now, invite each group to use RAT and RNT to explain and negotiate their roles. Discuss how this practice can help reduce conflict and increase collaboration between the two groups.

7.4. Part A (Self-assessment)

1. Which of the following is a necessary stage in the RAT?
   a. Performing a SWOT analysis
   b. Identifying employee strengths and shortcomings
   c. **Defining employee roles and tasks**
   d. Creating a marketing plan

2. What is the advantage of precisely outlining the roles and responsibilities of persons within an organization in the RAT?
   a. **It aids in lowering employee turnover**
   b. It improves consumer satisfaction
   c. It boosts the company's brand
   d. It makes tax reporting more straightforward

3. Which of the following is an essential aspect while conducting role analysis?
   a. Employee dress and personal grooming
   b. The company's historical heritage
   c. **The precise abilities and competencies required for each function**
   d. Employee political affiliations

4. What is one possible result of a successful RAT implementation?
   a. An increase in customer complaints
   b. A decrease in employee morale
   c. **An increase in organizational efficiency and production**
   d. A decrease in sales revenue

5. What does the term "role ambiguity" mean in the context of the RAT?
   a. **Condition in which individuals have excessive power and a lack of clarity regarding**
   b. The obligations and expectations associated with a particular function
   c. A situation in which employees have clearly defined tasks and responsibilities
   d. Staff turnover

6. What is the primary goal of the RNT?
   a. To impose your perspective on the other party
   b. To avoid communication and compromise
   c. **To find mutually acceptable solutions and agreements**
   d. To prove your point of view is the only correct one

7. Which of the following best describes a significant principle of role negotiation strategies?
   a. Stressing inflexible roles and demands
   b. Strictly focusing on short-term gains
   c. **Actively listening and seeking common ground**
   d. Avoiding communication with the other side

8. What is a critical part of effective RNTs when dealing with a conflict?
   a. Adherence to a single solution
   b. Turning down any concessions
   c. **Investigating various options and alternatives**
   d. Refusal to speak with the opposing party

9. Who proposed the RNT?
   a. **Roger Harrison**
   b. Douglas McGragire
   c. Roger Harris
   d. Tom Harris

10. Who proposed the RAT?
    a. **Ishwar Dayal and John. M. Thomas**
    b. Roger Harrison
    c. Tom Harris
    d. None of the above

11. What is the primary goal of the RAT in the context of organizational development?
    a. Recognizing market trends
    b. Examining employee job satisfaction
    c. **Understanding individual roles and duties within an organization**
    d. Evaluating financial performance

12. Who typically participates in the RAT within an organization?
    a. Only top-level executives are eligible
    b. Only human resources personnel
    c. **Employees at all organizational levels**
    d. Only external consultants

7.5. Part B (Review Questions)

1. Discuss the process of the RAT.
2. What are the objectives of RAT?
3. What is a role profile and its importance? What is the information contained in the role profile?
4. Define the RNT and its application in conflict management.
5. Explain the essential steps in doing a role analysis within a company.
6. Describe how role analysis benefits both employees and the organization.
7. "Role analysis is a must-have tool for organizational development." Discuss the importance of role analysis in conflict management. Give specific examples of how role analysis has helped you achieve your goals.
8. "Role negotiation techniques are critical for conflict resolution and achieving mutually beneficial agreements." Discuss the significance of role negotiation in conflict resolution, providing examples of instances where it can be instrumental and outlining the procedures involved in a successful role negotiation.

7.6. Part C (Glossary)

Focal role: The role that is considered for analysis in RAT.
Focal role individual: The person who plays the focus role.
Role profile: A written explanation of the role's functions and responsibilities.
Role negotiation technique: This is a systematic and collaborative strategy that can help organizations and teams clarify and negotiate over roles and responsibilities, resolve conflicts, and increase overall productivity and satisfaction.

Chapter 8

Negotiation: Bringing Conflict to a Negotiation Table

Learning Objectives:

- Understanding the concept of negotiation.
- Objectives of negotiation.
- Process of negotiation.
- Types of negotiators.

The COVID-19 pandemic has caused pandemonium in the world economy due to which people's attention has driven for the best in their lives.[1] Though, partnerships and teamwork are essential components of organizational effectiveness, conflict may arise in such partnerships due to inter-dependence. This sometimes makes conflict unavoidable and needs a conscious resolution. Negotiation is the most widely and effectively used approach for conflict resolution. It is generally defined as a discussion aimed at reaching an agreement. This provides a way of settlement between two or more conflicting parties. Furthermore, negotiation also provides a platform to find a mutually acceptable solution in a congenial way.

8.1. Definition

"Negotiation is a dialogue between two or more people or parties intended to reach a beneficial outcome over one or more issues." Negotiation is also defined

---

[1]Bhardwaj, B., Balkrishan, P., & Sharma, D. (2023). Fostering creative entrepreneurship through self-help group: Post-COVID resilience. In I. Hill, S. R. S. T. A. Elias, S. Dobson, & P. Jones (Eds.), *Creative (and cultural) industry entrepreneurship in the 21st century* (Contemporary Issues in Entrepreneurship Research, Vol. 18A, pp. 91–104). Emerald Publishing Limited. https://doi.org/10.1108/S2040-72462023000018A007

Managing and Negotiating Disagreements:
A Contemporary Approach for Conflict Resolution, 85–96
Copyright © 2024 by Bhawana Bhardwaj and Dipanker Sharma
Published under exclusive licence by Emerald Publishing Limited
doi:10.1108/978-1-83797-971-420241008

as "Interaction and process between entities who aspire to agree on matters of mutual interest while optimizing their utilities" (Adnan et al., 2016).[2] It is "A discussion among conflicting parties with the aim of reaching agreement about a divergence of interest."[3] Negotiation may occur daily in our routine life in personal situations such as marriage, divorce, parenting, etc. It may also happen in/among organizations (private/public), businesses, legislators, diplomats, and politicians.

8.2. Objectives of Negotiation

It is crucial to remember that precise negotiation objectives can vary greatly depending on the setting, the parties involved, and the nature of the negotiated issues. A thorough knowledge of the objectives and a planned strategy to achieve them are frequently required for successful negotiation.[4,5] Broadly, negotiation can be organized to achieve the following objectives:

1. *To resolve points of difference or disagreement*: Point of difference or disagreement occurs between parties for multiple reasons. Negotiation provides them a platform to sort out these differences or disagreements.[6]
2. *To gain an advantage*: Negotiation provides an advantage for individual or a group to satisfy diverse needs of people.[7]
3. *Maximizing value*: The goal of business negotiations may be to maximize the value or benefits each party can derive. This may entail negotiating favorable terms, pricing, or conditions.[8]
4. *Sustaining relationship*: In some circumstances, preserving a long-term relationship is the primary goal. In business, for example, negotiators may seek to secure a transaction while simultaneously building a positive connection between the parties in preparation for future interactions. Negotiation

---

[2]Adnan, M. H. M., Hassan, M. F., Aziz, I., & Paputungan, I. V. (2016, August). Protocols for agent-based autonomous negotiations: A review. *2016 3rd international conference on computer and information sciences (ICCOINS)* (pp. 622–626), Kuala Lumpur, Malaysia. IEEE.

[3]Pruitt, D. G. (1998). Social conflict. In D. T. Gilbert, S. T. Fiske, & G. Lindey (Eds.), *Handbook of social psychology* (4th ed., pp. 470–503). Academic Press.

[4]Weiss, J. (2016). *HBR guide to negotiating* (HBR Guide Series). Harvard Business Review Press.

[5]Nwlebuff, B., & Brandenburger. (2021). *It's a smarter way to split the pie. Rethinking Negotiation*. Rethinking Negotiation (hbr.org). Accessed on 2 November, 2023.

[6]Musambachime, M. G. (2001). Review of *the negotiation process and the resolution of international conflicts*, by P. T. Hopmann. *International Journal on World Peace*, 18(2), 76–81. http://www.jstor.org/stable/20753308

[7]Latz, M. (2004). Gain the edge!: Negotiating to get what you want. St. Martin's Press.

[8]Urdy, J. M. (2011). Negotiation approaches: Claiming and creating value. In M. A. Benoliel (Ed.), *Negotiation excellence: Successful deal making* (pp. 57–77). World Scientific Publishing.

may help settle the issue and facilitate mutual understanding and long-term relationships.[9]

5. *Risk management*: In a few circumstances, negotiation can be used as a strategy to minimize or mitigate risks. To safeguard their interests, parties may utilize negotiation to allocate risks and duties under negotiation contracts or agreements.[10]

6. *Information exchange:* Parties frequently exchange information during negotiations to obtain a better understanding of each other's needs and concerns. This might be a strategic goal because more knowledge leads to improved decision-making.[11]

7. *Balancing the power*: Negotiation can balance power dynamics and achieve a fair resolution in a significant power imbalance between parties. It provides a common platform for communication between people of different power positions.[12]

8. *Legal compliance*: Ensuring that the negotiation and ensuing agreements comply with applicable rules and regulations is a critical goal, particularly in business and international talks. Negotiations between agencies and affected parties determine the actual obligations which result from regulatory policies.[13]

8.3. Types of Negotiation

In many business relationships, negotiations are an essential component. Numerous variables affect how the negotiation process is implemented, and the success of the process depends on the design that is selected. The process of negotiation is shaped by the qualities and characteristics of negotiation. The result of the negotiation is determined by the parties' ability to negotiate, the information at hand, and their selected strategy and conduct.[14] Based on objective, negotiation can be of two types:[15]

---

[9]Salacuse, J. W. (1998). So, What is the deal anyway, contracts and relationships as negotiating goals? *Negotiation Journal*, *14*, 5.

[10]Oliveira, A. I., & Camarinha-Matos, L. M. (2013). Negotiation support and risk reduction in collaborative networks. In L. M. Camarinha-Matos, S. Tomic, & P. Graça (Eds.), Technological innovation for the internet of things: 4th IFIP WG 5.5/SOCOLNET doctoral conference on computing, electrical and industrial systems, DoCEIS 2013, Costa de Caparica, Portugal, April 15–17. Proceedings 4 (pp. 15–24). Springer.

[11]Inayaturrahmah, R., Barkah, C. S., & Novel, N. J. A. (2022). Analysis the role of negotiation as communication skills in conflict management. *JBTI: Jurnal Bisnis: Teori dan Implementasi*, *13*(3), 217–227.

[12]Massengale, J. D., & Sage, G. H. (1995). Shared power through negotiation in higher education. *Quest*, *47*(1), 64–75.

[13]Langbein, L., & Kerwin, C. M. (1985). Implementation, negotiation and compliance in environmental and safety regulation. *The Journal of Politics*, *47*(3), 854–880.

[14]Kersten, G. E. (2001). Modeling distributive and integrative negotiations. Review and revised characterization. *Group Decision and Negotiation*, *10*, 493–514.

[15]Fisher, R., Ury, W. L., & Patton, B. (2011). *Getting to yes: Negotiating agreement without giving in*. Penguin.

1. Integrative negotiation.
2. Distributive negotiation.

8.3.1. Integrative Negotiation

This type of negotiation is based on the "Expand the Pie" principle and is also called collaborative negotiation. This is a joint problem-solving that focuses on mutual gain. In this approach, people focus on sharing information, building relationships, and separating people from problems. Transparent and open sharing of information forms a basis for bargaining. The objective is to invent multiple options to create a win−win outcome and build relationships. Integrative negotiation, often known as "collaborative" or "win−win" negotiation that emphasizes creating value. The goal is to uncover shared interests, trade-offs, and creative solutions to increase the negotiation's value so that both parties profit.[16]

8.3.2. Distributive Negotiation

This approach is based on the "Cut the Pie" principle. In this approach of negotiation, each party focuses on maximizing their gain and views other parties as opponents. Here, people attack people rather than problems. Negotiating parties may hide or guard the information. The outcome of this type of negotiation leads to a win−lose situation and may sacrifice relationships. Distributive negotiation, sometimes referred to as "competitive" or "zero-sum" negotiation, usually includes the parties sharing a specific issue or resources. In this method, the benefit of one party is the loss of the other. In this lose−lose strategy, each partner aims to maximize their share while the overall value stays constant.[17,18]

8.4. Negotiation Versus Bargaining

Both bargaining and negotiating are commonplace activities that can be seen in marketplaces, at roadside stands, and even in upscale establishments. However, negotiation and bargaining are different from each other. Table 3 elaborates on the difference between bargaining and negotiation.

8.5. Process of Negotiation

A formal negotiation is a process that comprises various stages (Fig. 18).

---

[16]Alavoine, C. (2012). You can't always get what you want: Strategic issues in negotiation. *Procedia-Social and Behavioral Sciences, 58*, 665–672.
[17]Thompson, L., Peterson, E., & Brodt, S. E. (1996). Team negotiation: An examination of integrative and distributive bargaining. *Journal of Personality and Social Psychology, 70*(1), 66.
[18]Barry, B., & Friedman, R. A. (1998). Bargainer characteristics in distributive and integrative negotiation. *Journal of Personality and Social Psychology, 74*(2), 345.

Table 3.   Difference Between Negotiation and Bargaining.

Negotiation	Bargaining
It is a discussion aimed at reaching an agreement	Bargaining is haggling for prices
Negotiation is not just for money; it embraces other objectives such as quality, relationship building, etc.	People use bargaining to pay less for a thing or a service
It is a broader concept	It is a subset of negotiation
Negotiation can include a wide range of topics such as contracts, disagreements, deals, and any other situation in which parties must make a decision together can all be negotiated	Bargaining entails offers and counteroffers to reach an agreement
The goal of negotiation is to find a solution that meets the interests and needs of all parties concerned, which typically results in a win–win situation	The goal of bargaining is to establish an agreement on specific terms or prices acceptable to all sides, even if it requires some compromise

8.5.1. Preparation Stage

The availability of relevant information plays a vital role in the effectiveness of a negotiation process. It also supports and reinforces the validity of the negotiating party's arguments. The preparation stage is the first stage of the negotiation process. Negotiating parties collect all information that is relevant and important for effective negotiation.[19,20] Four essential areas for ordering information, as depicted in Fig. 17, are as follows:

Know yourself: This involves knowing your own interests and alternatives. It also comprises anticipating the alternatives available to opponent parties.
Understand another party: This involves collecting information to understand the expectations, possible interests, and leverage of opponents.
Negotiate climate and set up: This involves preparing for meeting arrangements, ensuring appropriate time, location, and people to be included.
Identify context: This is an effort to understand situations, agenda, actual decisionmakers, reputation, and the importance of relationships.

---

[19]Fells, R. (1996). Preparation for negotiation: Issue and process. *Personnel Review*, *25*(2), 50–60.
[20]Liu, M., & Chai, S. (2011). Planning and preparing for effective negotiation. In M. Benoliel (Ed.), *Negotiation excellence: Successful deal making* (pp. 15–37). World Scientific.

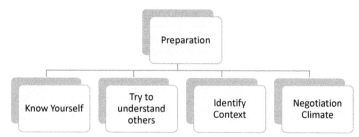

Fig. 17.   Preparation for Negotiation. *Source*: Created by authors.

8.5.2. Negotiation Meeting and Entering the Negotiation

Members of both parties gather at this point to negotiate. The meeting may start with an introduction of participants. The objective of the introduction phase is rapport building and giving a positive start to the negotiation process. Furthermore, this phase has the following objectives:

1.   Agenda setting in which a glimpse of discussion will be given on which discussion will take.
2.   Both parties also decide the break time, time limitation of the discussion, etc.
3.   Entering the negotiation process.

8.5.3. Communication and Generating Alternatives

This stage involves putting individual concerns and expectations before another party. This stage requires communication and expression; negotiation is not part of this stage. After each party has communicated, the individual party may start finding alternatives.

8.5.4. Information Gathering and Exploration

At this stage, both parties indulge in the information exchange process. For clarity in information gathering process, one should be an active listener. Parties should listen to each other and frequently ask questions if they have queries. The more one speaks, the more information will be gathered, giving new insight into the problem. This will also help them to understand each other, their vision, and their thinking. Brain streaming is an integral part of this stage.

8.5.5. Opinion Generation

After information gathering, both parties get to know their actual aspirations and the status of the opposition parties to the negotiation deal. Following that, both sides discuss the issue at hand and develop a potential solution that will work for both of them. Alternative solutions are identified, parties present their opinions and tentative solutions. They may write and offer their opinion in written form.

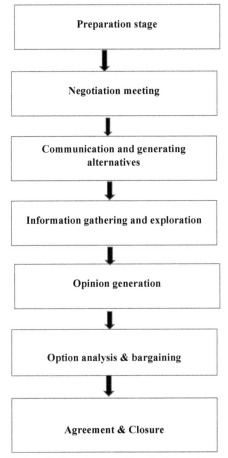

Fig. 18.   Process of Negotiation. *Source*: Created by authors.

8.5.6. Option Analysis and Bargaining:

After presenting different options, the next step is to analyze available alternatives. While exploring the options, each party tries to match the options with their set limits; if they are up to their set limit or expectations, they accept the proposals. If they still need to, they can start with the bargaining process. Before the negotiation, every party set its negotiation limits. A few suggestions for effective negotiation are as follows:

✓ Tackle one issue at a time.
✓ Stay focused.
✓ Patience and peace are essential.
✓ Objectives evaluation criteria are also critical.
✓ Remember your as well as other parties' interest.

8.5.7. Agreement and Closure

Agreement is the phase of negotiation where negotiating parties reach a point of decision that is acceptable to both parties.

✓ The agreement should be specific, clear, and detailed.
✓ Mentioning clear responsibilities and roles.
✓ Other components will also be mentioned.
✓ Potential incentives to comply.
✓ Identify procedures for disputes.

Closure: This involves bringing negotiation to an end. Norms for closure are as follows:

1. Be gracious.
2. The end of the affirmative role means appreciation.
3. Use ceremony or publicity if required.

8.6. Types of Negotiators

8.6.1. Hard Negotiator

These negotiators are competitive in their approach and see any situation as a contest of wills. They perceive any situation as a battle of interest and most extreme positions and hold out the longest wins. They may act mentally against the other person to frighten them. Since they anticipate the same behavior from their rivals, competitive negotiators have mistrust for them. A high initial demand, restricted disclosure of information about facts and preferences, and few and tiny concessions, threats, and arguments are common tactics used by competitive negotiators. They put pressure on others to compromise, make threats, and show mistrust toward others. Their ultimate objective is triumph, and they view everyone else as their enemies. They also look for a single solution and demand that you accept it. They find it difficult to separate people from the problem and are hard on both the people involved and the problem.[21,22]

These negotiators use psychological warfare on their opponents by acting in a way that makes them feel uneasy. Negotiators frequently use a method that consists of making a large initial demand, disclosing just a limited amount of information about the facts and their preferences, making few, little concessions, threatening, and arguing. There is a strong correlation between a negotiator's first

---

[21]Kirgis, P. F. (2012). Hard bargaining in the classroom: Realistic simulated negotiations and student values. *Negotiation Journal, 28*(1), 93–115.
[22]Hüffmeier, J., Freund, P. A., Zerres, A., Backhaus, K., & Hertel, G. (2014). Being tough or being nice? A meta-analysis on the impact of hard-and softline strategies in distributive negotiations. *Journal of Management, 40*(3), 866–892.

demand and payoff.[23,24] These people use contentious strategies to influence, such as "this is my final offer" and "take it or leave it."

8.6.2. Soft Negotiator (Cooperative)

The cooperative or soft negotiator begins by establishing a relationship based on trust and compromises to generate a moral obligation to reciprocate. The collaborative negotiator sees concessions and believes in a collectivistic approach to reach a fair solution.[25,26] The advocates of the cooperative strategy are better than a competitive technique that leads to anger between parties leading to opponents to respond with similar-sized concessions. Furthermore, cooperative strategies include techniques that build trust between the parties and are based on the hope that the opponent will make ungrudging compromises. Soft negotiators surrender to 'others' demands to avoid conflict.[27]

8.6.3. Principled Negotiator

They are problem-solving and adopt integration methods. Issues are resolved on their merits. They are grounded on the notion of mutual gains wherever possible. They prefer a solution that is based on some fair standards and independent of either side's will. The style is authoritarian on merit but kind to people. It makes no use of trickery or posturing.[28,29] There is no war mindset to determine who wins and who loses, and not a concession-based strategy aimed at dividing a fixed pie. Furthermore, it tries to maximize the benefit.[30] Principled negotiators concentrate on the problem rather than the people involved intents, objectives, and needs. They make decisions based on objective standards rather than power,

[23]https://www.pon.harvard.edu/tag/hard-bargaining-tactics/

[24]Weiss, J. (2016). *HBR guide to negotiating* (HBR Guide Series). Harvard Business Review Press.

[25]Crawford, A. R. (2008). Licensing and negotiations for electronic content. *Resource Sharing & Information Networks*, *19*(1–2), 15–38.

[26]Zhao, W. (2021). A multi-hatted expert: Exploring possible roles of the interpreter in business negotiations with specifics of Sino-German negotiations. In R. Moratto & M. Woesler (Eds.), *Diverse voices in Chinese translation and interpreting: Theory and practice* (pp. 219–241). Springer Singapore.

[27]Ashcroft, S. (2004). Commercial negotiation skills. *Industrial and Commercial Training*, *36*(6), 229–233.

[28]Lens, V. (2004). Principled negotiation: A new tool for case advocacy. *Social Work*, *49*(3), 506–513.

[29]Whitford, A. B., Bottom, W. P., & Miller, G. J. (2013). The (negligible) benefit of moving first: Efficiency and equity in principal-agent negotiations. *Group Decision and Negotiation*, *22*, 499–518.

[30]Fisher, R., Ury, W., & Ertel, D. (1986). *Principled negotiation. Psychology and the prevention of nuclear war*. New York University Press.

influence, self-interest, or an arbitrary decision-making system. These criteria may be based on moral norms, fairness ideals, professional standards, or tradition.[31]

8.7. Case Study 8.1: Labor Dispute

The XYZ Company, a major manufacturing firm, was embroiled in a labor dispute. Employees at the company, who were represented by a labor union, had demanded higher wages and better working conditions, even though the company was facing financial difficulties due to increased production costs and severe market competition. Negotiations between management and the labor union had reached a crossroads, and a resolution was required to avoid potential strikes and production delays. The XYZ Company had a long history of fruitful labor-union negotiations, but recent market shifts have strained their relationship. The union sought a 10% pay rise, more incredible healthcare benefits, and reduced necessary overtime hours. According to the company's financial statistics, meeting the union's demands would put the company at a competitive disadvantage and jeopardize its profitability.

8.7.1. Key Demands

Wage increase: The main issue was the union's desire for a 10% wage increase, which the corporation thought was unsustainable given their financial restrictions.

Working conditions: The union advocated for better working conditions, such as reducing mandated overtime hours and improving safety measures.

Market competition: The corporation stressed the importance of maintaining cost competitiveness to compete in a highly competitive market.

As the manager of the company, draft the strategy to negotiate as the manager of the company to generate a win–win outcome.

8.8. Part A (Self-assessment)

1. Negotiation in which the disputants are the only participants is called_____.
   a. **Simple negotiation**
   b. Adjudication
   c. Mediation
   d. Facilitated negotiation

2. A trust among disputants make_____.
   a. Disputants less responsive
   b. **Negotiation more efficient**
   c. Workplace friendship
   d. A competitive conflict

---

[31]Hak, F. R., & Sanders, K. (2018). Principled negotiation: an evidence-based perspective. *Evidence-based HRM: a Global Forum for Empirical Scholarship*, 6(1), 66–76. https://doi.org/10.1108/EBHRM-03-2017-0014

3. The stage of negotiation in which the negotiating parties try to collect the information and documents related to negotiation and understand the other party's demands and expectations is_____.
   a. **Preparation stage**
   b. Confrontation
   c. Meeting
   d. Bargaining

4. This is a type of negotiation in which interest is divided into two parties, and one has to sacrifice for the other_____.
   a. **Distributive negotiation**
   b. Differentiate negotiation
   c. Integrative negotiation
   d. BATNA

5. What exactly is negotiation?
   a. One-sided communication method
   b. **Reaching mutually acceptable agreements**
   c. Imposing one's will on the other party
   d. Conflict resolution procedure

6. Which of the following is an important negotiation principle?
   a. Refraining from any compromise
   b. Withholding information from the opposite party
   c. **Creating win–win situations**
   d. Making rash, unilateral judgments

7. In negotiating, what is a win–win situation?
   a. A solution in which one party gains much more than the other
   b. **Solution in which both parties achieve their objectives and are pleased with the outcome**
   c. A solution in which one party gains supremacy over the other
   d. A compromise arrangement that provides no true satisfaction to either party

8.9. Part B (Review Questions)

1. Write a short note on the process of negotiation.
2. "Is it ethical to lie or bluff in negotiation?" Support your answer with any of the case studies discussed in the class.
3. Differentiate between bargaining and negotiation.
4. Can you describe a recent negotiation you participated in, personally or professionally? What were the main issues, and how did the negotiation go?
5. What, in your opinion, are the primary distinctions between distributive and integrative negotiation? Can you give instances from your personal experiences?

6. How do you approach the negotiating preparation phase? What research, knowledge, or tactics have you found most helpful?
7. How do you handle difficult negotiators or those who use aggressive or combative tactics? What methods or tactics have you found helpful in dealing with such situations?
8. Explain briefly the significance of negotiation abilities in various sectors of life.
9. Highlight the essential elements of effective negotiation.
10. Define negotiation and its importance in both personal and business settings.

8.10. Part C (Glossary)

Negotiation: Negotiation is a dialogue between two or more people or parties intended to reach a beneficial outcome over one or more issues where a conflict exists concerning at least one of these issues.

Bargaining: A process in which parties attain an agreement through the exchange of offers and counteroffers.

Distributive negotiation: A competitive negotiation in which parties haggle over a predetermined value quantity, frequently resulting in a win−lose outcome.

Integrative negotiation: A cooperative negotiation in which all parties engaged attempt to create value and develop mutually beneficial solutions.

Impasse: A point in a negotiation where progress has stalled, and the parties cannot agree.

Principled negotiating: A strategy for negotiating that emphasizes justice, integrity, and reaching solutions based on objective criteria rather than positional bargaining.

Chapter 9

Negotiation Temperaments: An Overview

Learning Objectives:

- Personality dichotomies.
- Key negotiating temperaments:
  Harmonizer;
  Controller;
  Pragmatist; and
  Action seeker.

9.1. Introduction

Negotiation temperament plays a significant role in determining participants' behavior during the negotiation process. The word "temperament" is derived from the Latin word "temperare," which means to temper or moderate a process, manner of thought and action. John T. Cocoris (2016)[1] states, "Temperament is a cluster of inborn traits that causes you, in part, to do what you do." These four temperaments are characterized by four discrete "traits" or tendencies groups. Each cluster of "traits" yields a discrete behavior. Thus, temperament characterizes traits apparent in day-to-day behavior and depicts how a person interacts with others. Temperament and personality sometimes need to be clarified. Personality is the sum of a person's characteristics, whereas temperament is a subset

[1]Cocoris, J. T. (2016). *Born with a creative temperament: The Sanguine-Melancholy (I-C)*. Profile Dynamics.

Managing and Negotiating Disagreements:
A Contemporary Approach for Conflict Resolution, 97–106
Copyright © 2024 by Bhawana Bhardwaj and Dipanker Sharma
Published under exclusive licence by Emerald Publishing Limited
doi:10.1108/978-1-83797-971-420241009

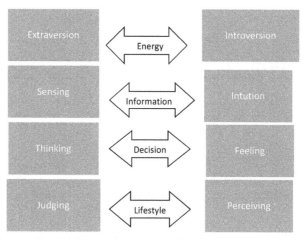

Fig. 19.   Personality Dichotsomies. *Source*: Created by the authors.

of personality.[2,3,4] Negotiation temperaments are based on Carl Jung's personality dimension. Carl Jung (1921) has identified four areas of personality that further form the basis of temperament. This is expanded in Fig. 19.

9.1.1. Extraversion (E) Versus Introversion (I)

Introverts are people who acquire energy by spending time alone and are more reserved in social situations. They are preoccupied with their inner world of ideas, feelings, and reflections.[5] Extraverts are drawn to the outside world, social connections, and activities. They acquire energy from being with others and become more outgoing.[6,7]

---

[2]Ekstrand, D. W. (2015). *The four human temperaments*. Retrieved March 2024 from https://docpid.s3.amazonaws.com/media/the-four-human-temperaments-by-dr-d-w-ekstrand.pdf

[3]Bennett, A., & Bennett, L. (2005). *The temperament god gave you*. Sophia Institute Press.

[4]Childs, G. (2013). *Understand your temperament!: A guide to the four temperaments-choleric, sanguine, phlegmatic, melancholic*. Rudolf Steiner Press.

[5]Itani, O. S., El Haddad, R., & Kalra, A. (2020). Exploring the role of extrovert–introvert customers' personality prototype as a driver of customer engagement: does relationship duration matter? *Journal of Retailing and Consumer Services, 53*, 101980.

[6]Walker, D. L. (2020). Extraversion–introversion. In B. J. Carducci, C. S. Nave, & A. Di Fabio (Eds.), *The Wiley encyclopedia of personality and individual differences: Models and theories* (pp. 159–163). Wiley.

[7]Jung, C., & Beebe, J. (2016). *Psychological types*. Routledge.

9.1.2. Sensing (S) Versus Intuition (N)

Sensors: These people seek the importance of details and like to give and receive facts and data. Individuals who want to gather information with their five senses and concentrate on concrete, practical aspects. They are detail-oriented and fact-based people.[8]

Intuitors: Intuitors look at the big picture and look for concepts and connections. They enjoy giving and receiving bigger pictures. Individuals who rely on patterns, possibilities, and insights beyond immediate sensory information are said to have intuition. They are frequently more concerned with the larger picture and abstract concepts.[9]

9.1.3. Thinking (T) Versus Feeling (F)[10]

Thinking: Individuals base their conclusions on logical analysis, objective criteria, and rationality. They may appear more objective, preferring fairness over empathy.[11]

Feeling: People make decisions based on their personal beliefs, emotions, and consideration for others. In their interactions, they frequently prioritize harmony and empathy.

9.1.4. Judging Versus Perceivers[12]

Judgers and perceivers approach and interact with the world in a distinctive way

Judgers: Judgers seek closure, believe in deadlines, and prefer things in order. They reveal their positions and thoughts. They may predict and anticipate decisions. Individuals who value structured organization, and a planned approach to life are being judgers. They are more inclined to make decisions and adhere to deadlines.

Perceivers: Perceivers prefer randomness and are not worried about deadlines. They keep postponing things; for perceivers, a solution is more important than

[8]Ma, L., Guo, H., & Fang, Y. (2020). Analysis of construction workers' safety behavior based on the Myers–Briggs Type Indicator Personality Test in a bridge construction project. *Journal of Construction Engineering and Management, 147*(1), 04020149.

[9]Ertemel, A. V., & Çaylak, G. (2021, August). The effect of personality traits on credit score using Myers–Briggs Type Indicator (MBTI) personality types. In M. H. Bilgin, H. Danis, E. Demir, & C. D. García-Gómez (Eds.), *Eurasian business and economics perspectives: Proceedings of the 32nd Eurasia Business and Economics Society conference* (pp. 185–189). Springer International Publishing.

[10]Stricker, L. J., & Ross, J. (1964). Some correlates of a Jungian personality inventory. *Psychological Reports, 14*(2), 623–643.

[11]Kamal, A., & Radhakrishnan, S. (2019). Individual learning preferences based on personality traits in an E-learning scenario. *Education and Information Technologies, 24*(1), 407–435.

[12]McCannon, B. C., & Stevens, J. (2017). Role of personality style on bargaining outcomes. *International Journal of Social Economics, 44*(9), 1166–1196.

time. Perceivers do not anticipate decisions. People who are more adaptable, receptive to new information, and flexible in their approach to life are perceived. They like to leave their options open and may need to make decisions.

9.2. Four Key Negotiating Temperaments

The four types of temperaments are[13,14,15]:

9.2.1. Harmonizer (Pacifier)

Harmonizer is the combination of intuitive-perceiving (N/P) dimensions. These types of people perceive and understand the bigger picture and confront problems with a broad outlook. Harmonizers include all those people who know the relatedness in things and always focus on the overall big picture of the issue. As these people do not focus on minor details, it is always easy to distract them if a mistake occurs. They never give the judgment; instead, they give their perception. They share their point of view openly but cannot accept the criticism.

Since they never focus on details, the only way to catch their focus on details is showing their importance in the big picture. Harmonizers have the outstanding convincing ability and capacity to generate creative alternatives. Deadline is of utmost importance and to get along with harmonizers, the key is to admire their original notions and alternatives and give an equally comprehensive alternative. Harmonizers simply be identified at the negotiation table by their broad, theoretical, and open-ended attitudes. Fig. 20 highlights the features of harmonizers. Harmonizer can become the pacifier when gets out of control. If such a situation arrives, there is unlikely to be a resolution at the negotiation table.

Recognizing a harmonizer:

- Contacts and interacts well with others.
- Makes favorable impressions.
- Creates a motivating environment.
- Group or team participant.
- Concerned about the needs of others.
- Values harmony.
- Motivates others.
- Broad viewpoint, discussion of numerous subjects concurrently, resistance to time constraints, and an open-ended, broad, and theoretical outlook.

---

[13]Cocoris, J. T. (2024). *Temperament model of behavior: Identifying your natural temperament*. Profile Dynamics.
[14]Corvette, B. A. B. (2007). *Conflict management: A practical guide to developing negotiation strategies*. Pearson Prentice Hall.
[15]Kalé, S. (1996). How national culture, organizational culture and personality impact buyer–seller interactions. In P. Ghauri & J. C. Usunier (Eds.), *International business negotiations* (pp. 21–37). Pergamon.

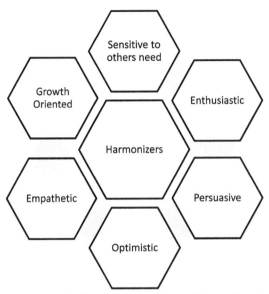

Fig. 20.   Characteristics of a Harmonizer. *Source*: Created by the authors.

9.2.2. Controller (Bull)

The combination of the intuitive-judging (N/J) personality dimension forms these types of temperament. They have intuitive inclination, see the bigger picture and grips tasks from a broad viewpoint. Controllers always remain focused on the topic because closure is their primary concern. Thus, they are impatient for decisions and resolutions but always have an organized plan. As a controller, they gather knowledge and observe the interconnectedness of matters in pursuit of significance.

They are firm, decisive, and deliberate and thus always want things in their way. Controllers believe in structure and order. Despite their domineering demeanor, these people wish for harmony rather than conflict. They hold strong beliefs and may become or seem to be contentious. Due to their strong opinions, they may be perceived as argumentative. The best way to manage them on the negotiation table is to reveal a desire to agree. When out of control, they may become the bull characterized by rigidity, and there will likely be no resolution. Fig. 21 exhibits the significant characteristics of a controller.

Recognizing a controller:

- Standard-setter.
- Visionary.
- Perfectionist.
- Explores all alternatives while making a decision.
- Systematic in approach.
- Conscientious.
- Knowledgeable.

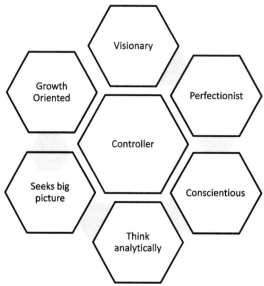

Fig. 21.   Key Characteristics of a Controller. *Source*: Created by the authors.

- Analytical.
- Intrusive and intellectual.
- Look for a "big picture."
- Broad perspective.
- Can discuss multiple issues.

9.2.3. Pragmatist (Street Fighter)

The pragmatist is a personality dimension depicting an amalgamation of the sensing-judging (S/J). Such people understand details, concentrate on specifics, and deal with things sequentially.

They believe in numbers and prefer facts and concentrate on tangible results. They are realistic and focused on the bottom line. They are well-organized and eager to resolve the issue. Furthermore, they are firm, decisive, deliberate in negotiation and can be stubborn.

Pragmatists focus only on details of minor topics and thus need help to see the big picture and make decisions with the purpose of being right (Fig. 22). They usually find small reasons for accepting decisions or giving proposals. During disagreements, they can become intense and argumentative. The best way to manage them is to present facts and figures and establish a concern for the bottom line. If uncontrolled during a negotiation, they may turn into street fighters who perceive the negotiation as a win/lose proposition, want to win at any cost, and can potentially hurt someone.

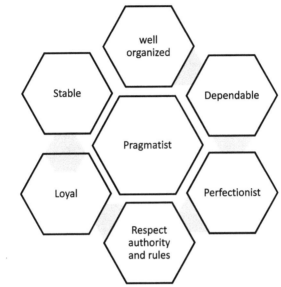

Fig. 22.   Key Characteristics of a Pragmatist.

Recognizing a Pragmatist:

- Organized.
- Consistent and predictable.
- Specialized.
- Generates a steady work environment.
- Dependable and loyal.
- Value organization.
- Quibbler.
- Always come prepared.
- Shows loyalty.
- Seek detail and service oriented.
- Respect rules as well as authority.

9.2.4. Action Seeker (High Roller)

Such people combine sensing-perceiving (S/P) personality traits. They notice details, examine particulars, and address problems progressively. Action seekers avoid both theory and planning and interpret situations conceptually. They are not anxious for resolution, yet their enthusiasm might overpower meticulous thought, causing these people to win or lose significantly.

As the name shows, these people are action-oriented and seek a thrill. They can postpone decisions and acclimate to new set of information. Fig. 23 highlights the key characteristics of an action seeker. In communication, the action

Fig. 23.   Key Characteristics of an Action Seeker. *Source*: Created by authors.

seeker shares perceptions, *not* judgments or decisions. The appropriate way to negotiate with the action is to use facts and figures and sometimes allow them to reveal their interests. They do not prefer order or deadlines and can be distracted easily. If they go out of control, they are the high rollers, who are significant risk-takers and bring huge losses.

Recognizing Action seeker:

- Confident and accept challenges.
- Quick decisionmaker.
- Problem solver.
- Demands change.
- Competitive.
- Quick and spontaneous.
- Can act in a crisis.
- Great and clear negotiator.
- Witty and humorous.
- Enjoys tangible rewards.

9.3. Activity 9.1

Observe your group members critically and divide them into four groups according to their temperaments. Allow each group to negotiate over an issue. Notice the approach of each group based on their temperament. Discuss at the end of the activity.

9.4. Part A (Self-assessment)

1. Harmonizers are a combination of types of personality characters
   a. **Intuitive–perceiving**
   b. Intuitive judging
   c. Sensing judging
   d. Sensing perceiving

2. Action seekers are a combination of types of personality characters
   a. Intuitive–perceiving
   b. Intuitive judging
   c. Sensing judging
   d. **Sensing perceiving**

3. Harmonizers are a combination of types of personality characters
   a. **Intuitive–perceiving**
   b. Intuitive judging
   c. Sensing judging
   d. Sensing perceiving

4. Which temperament is marked by a lot of energy, spontaneity, and a love of new things and excitement?
   a. Contemplator
   b. Planner
   c. Harmonizers
   d. **Action seeker**

5. What kinds of challenges are usually appealing to action seekers?
   a. Tasks that are predictable and usual
   b. Complicated problem-solving
   c. **Competitive, high-stakes scenarios**
   d. Cooperation among groups and team-building

6. An action seeker in a group context is more likely to be
   a. Observing and evaluating from a distance
   b. **Taking the initiative and leading the group**
   c. Concentrated on fostering harmony
   d. Methodically allocating tasks and resources.

7. Which of the following types of negotiators are highly unpredictable and even can disdain the rules of negotiation?
   a. Harmonizers
   b. **Controllers**
   c. Pragmatist
   d. Action seeker

9.5. Part B (Review Questions)

1. What are key negotiation temperaments? What can be the extreme and uncontrolled form of these temperaments? In your opinion, which temperament is best during negotiation?
2. Which of the four significant temperaments do you believe your words and actions most clearly demonstrated?
3. Consider a recent interaction in which you participated. Consider yourself through the eyes of the opposing party. Which bargaining style did you exhibit?
4. Discuss the critical characteristics of action seekers and how we should deal with them.
5. Give two examples of activities that an action seeker would find appealing.
6. How can an action seeker go about fixing problems in a group context? Give a succinct justification.

9.6. Part C (Glossary)

Sensors (S): A sensor is a personality type that favors using their five senses to gather information about the outside world. They are realistic, firm, and practical.
Judging (J): Judgers seek closure, believe in deadlines, and prefer things in order.
Intuitors (N): Intuitors look at the big picture and look for concepts and connections
Thinker (T): Individuals who base their conclusions on logical analysis, objective criteria, and rationality.

Chapter 10

Rules for Effective Negotiation: Do's and Don'ts

Learning Objectives:

- Definition and forms of negotiation failure.
- Reasons of negotiation failures.
- Do's and don'ts of effective negotiation.

The inability of parties involved in a negotiation process to obtain a mutually acceptable agreement or conclusion is referred to as negotiation failure.[1,2] It occurs when the negotiation process fails to provide a satisfying outcome for one or more sides, frequently leading to a breakdown of negotiations or an impasse. Negotiation failure can occur for a variety of reasons, including a lack of agreement on terms, communication failures, unmet expectations, cultural differences, or unsolved conflicts of interest. Changing strategy and enhancing communication can raise the likelihood of future successful negotiations. In essence, negotiation failure indicates that the parties were unable to identify common ground or achieve an agreement on the problems at hand.[3]

10.1. Negotiation Failure

It usually takes careful planning, a well-thought-out approach, and a skillful maneuver to feel comfortable presenting ideas during a negotiation and reach

---

[1]https://www.pon.harvard.edu/daily/negotiation-skills-daily/why-negotiations-fail/

[2]Mnookin, R. H. (1992). Why negotiations fail: An exploration of barriers to the resolution of conflict. *Ohio State Journal on Dispute Resolution, 8*, 235.

[3]Underdal, A. (1983). Causes of negotiation 'failure'. *European Journal of Political Research, 11*(2), 183–195.

Managing and Negotiating Disagreements:
A Contemporary Approach for Conflict Resolution, 107–116
Copyright © 2024 by Bhawana Bhardwaj and Dipanker Sharma
Published under exclusive licence by Emerald Publishing Limited
doi:10.1108/978-1-83797-971-420241010

a mutually agreeable conclusion. Conventional negotiation literature typically focuses only on tactics and methods, excluding psychological communication and emotional intelligence components like empathy and non-verbal communication, which are crucial for successful negotiation.[4] Walking away from the negotiation is just one form of negotiation failure. Failed negotiation also includes regret over time and failure to implement. Broadly, negotiation failure can be of the following types.[5]

10.1.1. Negotiation Impasse

In some situation, the negotiators reach a deadlock even when the best alternative to a negotiated agreement, or BATNA, is worse (or expected to be worse) than the deal on the table. Such deadlock is also referred to as a negotiation impasse and can be defined as "Negotiation in which one or two parties discontinue the interaction, either because one or both parties prefer no agreement, or because they could not reach an agreement despite them benefitting from doing so."[6] The impasses can be of three types:

a. *Wanted impasse*: If negotiators perceive that an impasse can be beneficial, they willingly create a deadlock.
b. *Forced impasse*: If impasse is beneficial to one negotiator and he/she creates a situation of deadlock, it can be referred to as force impasse.
c. *Unwanted impasse*: When an impasse is undesirable for both parties.

Major factors that can cause the negotiation impasse include:

1. Structural factors such as bargaining zone and communication channels.
2. Inter-personal factors which may include factors such as tough tactics and emotions.
3. Intra-personal factors such as biases, filtering of information, and framing.

To be successful in business negotiation, we must be confident that we will be able to resort to our BATNA if the other party refuses to accept our requests. Through consideration of BATNA, comparing it to the offer on the table, and then making the most sensible decision can help avoid a deadlock.

---

[4]Sokolova, M., & Szpakowicz, S. (2007). Strategies and language trends in learning success and failure of negotiation. *Group Decision and Negotiation, 16,* 469–484.
[5]Shonk, K. (2023). *Why negotiations fail? Common pitfalls to avoid in business negotiations.* https://www.pon.harvard.edu/daily/negotiation-skills-daily/why-negotiations-fail/#We%20Walk%20Away%20from%20A%20Good%20Deal.
[6]Schweinsberg, M., Thau, S., & Pillutla, M. M. (2022). Negotiation impasses: Types, causes, and resolutions. *Journal of Management, 48*(1), 49–76.

10.1.2. Accepting a Deal and Regretting It Later

Accepting a deal that is worse than BATNA is the inverse of rejecting an offer that is better than BATNA. It is typical to regret a decision made during a negotiation. However, if the negotiating parties regret the deal post-acceptance, the negotiation cannot be treated as successful. Such regret if gets intensified may lead to non-compliance with the agreement. For example, automobile buyers frequently believe they got a good deal at the dealership. But at the later stage, we experience buyer's or seller's remorse.[4] This remorse could be caused by a variety of circumstances, including obtaining better deals elsewhere, uncovering hidden costs, or simply second-guessing the decision.

Effective negotiation entails not just achieving an agreement but also ensuring that the parties are satisfied with the conditions and are committed to following through on their commitments. Monitoring and controlling post-agreement regret are critical components of the negotiating process since they can affect the deal's success and long-term viability.

10.1.3. We Close a Deal That Is Too Feeble to Sustain

Closing the negotiation at the negotiation table cannot be reckoned as a success. Negotiation can be treated as a failure that concludes with an agreement but rapidly falls apart during the implementation phase. Such negotiations commonly fail due to a failure to handle disputes during negotiations or to provide a solid structure for the contract. The finest corporate negotiators establish rapport and trust throughout the process and extensively set the parameters of implementation.

Negotiation extends beyond the act of obtaining an agreement at the negotiation table. Its success is determined not only by achieving an agreement; but also includes the effective implementation of the agreed-upon terms. Negotiating a deal is only one phase in a larger process, and the ultimate success of the negotiation is frequently assessed in the successful execution and implementation of the agreement.

The importance of developing rapport and trust throughout the negotiation process cannot be overstated. Successful negotiation entails more than simply the terms on paper; it also entails the parties developing a positive and productive relationship. Because parties are more willing to work together to address problems and manage issues that may occur, trust and rapport can contribute to a smoother implementation phase. In practice, the best negotiators recognize the necessity of early consideration of the implementation phase. They strive to negotiate not just the substantive contents of the agreement, but also the implementation procedures such as setting explicit expectations, defining roles and responsibilities, and providing procedures for monitoring and addressing difficulties that may develop during implementation.

To summarize, the success of a negotiation is decided not only by the ability to reach an agreement at the table, but also by the effectiveness of the implementation phase. Addressing potential conflicts during negotiations, creating a solid

structure for the transaction, and developing rapport and trust all contribute to
the negotiation process's overall success.

10.2. Reasons for Negotiation Failure[7,8,9,10]

There are many reasons why negotiations fail, and most of the time it is due to a
complex web of inter-related events. The following are some of the most common
causes of failed talks:

a. *Insufficient preparation*: It is impossible to exaggerate the value of preparation in any negotiation. It is essential for helping negotiators accomplish their
   objectives, forging strong bonds with one another, and overcoming the challenges posed by the negotiation process.
b. *Ineffective communication*: The negotiation process can be significantly
   impacted by poor communication, unclear terminology, and miscommunication. Inaccurate assumptions, a damaged connection, a failure to establish
   common ground, and a lack of trust can all result from poor communication.
   Negotiators should prioritize open and honest communication, aggressively
   seek clarification when needed, and make sure to allay these worries.[11,12]
c. *Lack of trust*: Trust is an essential component of any discussion. When parties
   trust one another, a favorable climate is created that promotes collaboration
   and effective communication. Here are some of the reasons why trust is so
   important in negotiations. Building trust in negotiations needs regular and
   dependable behavior, shared interests, and fairness. Building trust takes time,
   but it is an investment that pays dividends in the shape of smoother negotiations and stronger inter-personal relationships.[13,14,15]

[7]Bazerman, M. H., & Chugh, D. (2006). Bounded awareness: Focusing failures in negotiation. In L. Thompson (Ed.), *Negotiation theory and research* (pp. 7–26). Psychology Press.
[8]Sokolova, M., & Szpakowicz, S. (2007). Strategies and language trends in learning
success and failure of negotiation. *Group Decision and Negotiation, 16,* 469–484.
[9]Kesner, I. F., & Shapiro, D. L. (1991). Did a failed negotiation really fail. *Negotiation
Journal, 7,* 369.
[10]Opresnik, M. O. (2014). *Hidden rules of successful negotiation and communication.*
Springer International Publishing.
[11]Spangle, M. L., & Isenhart, M. W. (2002). *Negotiation: Communication for diverse
settings.* Sage Publications.
[12]Adair, W. L., & Loewenstein, J. (2013). Talking it through: Communication sequences in
negotiation. In M. Olekalns & W. L. Adair (Eds.), *Handbook of research on negotiation*
(pp. 311–331). Edward Elgar Publishing.
[13]Lewicki, R. J., & Polin, B. (2013). Trust and negotiation. In M. Olekalns & W. L. Adair
(Eds.), *Handbook of research on negotiation* (pp. 161–190). Edward Elgar Publishing.
[14]Gunia, B., Brett, J., & Nandkeolyar, A. K. (2014). Trust me, I'm a negotiator: Diagnosing trust to negotiate effectively, globally. *Organizational Dynamics, 43*(1), 27–36.
[15]Song, Y. J., Hale, C. L., & Rao, N. (2004). Success and failure of business negotiations for South Koreans. *Journal of International and Area Studies, 11*(2), 45–65.

d. *Emotional factors*: Emotions play a significant role in the negotiation process, and strong emotions such as anger, frustration, or ego can indeed interfere with rational decision-making and compromise. Parties can establish a more constructive and collaborative environment throughout the negotiating process by acknowledging and resolving emotions. This increases the possibility of reaching a mutually beneficial agreement.[16,17]

e. *Rigid positions*: Lack of flexibility and a refusal to compromise can indeed lead negotiations to reach an impasse. An impasse occurs when parties are unable to find common ground or reach an agreement. Successful negotiations require a willingness to be flexible and compromise. Finding a solution becomes difficult when parties are locked into hard stances, and negotiations may grind to a halt. Open communication, innovation, and a focus on underlying interests can all aid in overcoming hurdles and moving toward a mutually beneficial solution.[18,19,20,21]

f. *Power imbalance*: Significant power imbalances in talks can indeed pose difficulties and potentially lead to failure. Economic strength, political influence, legal authority, and even inter-personal dynamics can all appear as power imbalances. Power inequalities must be addressed in negotiations to establish a fair and constructive process. Failure to resolve these disparities can result in perceived injustices, animosity, and, eventually, failed negotiations.[22,23]

g. *Hidden agendas*: Transparency is a key factor in building and maintaining trust in any relationship, including business or inter-personal relationships. When one party is not open about their goals or has hidden agendas, it can

---

[16]Luomala, H. T., Kumar, R., Singh, J. D., & Jaakkola, M. (2015). When an intercultural business negotiation fails: Comparing the emotions and behavioural tendencies of individualistic and collectivistic negotiators. *Group Decision and Negotiation, 24*, 537–561.

[17]Sokolova, M., & Szpakowicz, S. (2007). Strategies and language trends in learning success and failure of negotiation. *Group Decision and Negotiation, 16*, 469–484.

[18]Druckman, D. (1993). The situational levers of negotiating flexibility. *Journal of Conflict Resolution, 37*(2), 236–276.

[19]Spector, B. (2006). Resiliency in negotiation: Bouncing back from impasse. *International Negotiation, 11*(2), 273–286.

[20]Ozaki, M. (Ed.). (1999). *Negotiating flexibility: The role of the social partners and the state.* International Labour Organization.

[21]Marschik, A., Kydd, A., John, A. W. S., Boyer, B., Tinsley, C., Albin, C., Jönsson, C., Fridl, D., Cede, F., Zartman, I. W., & Littlewood, J (2012). *Unfinished business: Why international negotiations fail* (Vol. 16). University of Georgia Press.

[22]Ünal, A. F., & Emel, G. G. (2009, April). The effect of framing and power imbalance on negotiation behaviors and outcomes. In B. Fleischmann, K.-H. Borgwardt, R. Klein, & A. Tuma (Eds.), *Operations Research proceedings 2008: Selected papers of the annual international conference of the German Operations Research Society (GOR), University of Augsburg, September 3–5, 2008* (pp. 407–412). Springer.

[23]Zartman, I. W., & Rubin, J. Z. (Eds.). (2000). *Power and negotiation.* University of Michigan Press.

lead to several negative consequences. Transparency and open communication establish a favorable climate in which trust may blossom, collaboration can thrive, and group goals can be attained more successfully. It is critical for all people concerned to be open and honest about their intentions.[24,25]

h. *Cultural differences*: Cultural misunderstandings and communication style variations can considerably hinder negotiations, especially in multinational contexts where people from various cultural backgrounds come together. Negotiators can improve their efficacy in international contexts and develop better, more productive partnerships across cultures by understanding and addressing cultural differences.

i. *Overestimating BATNA*: A BATNA is crucial in negotiations, and overestimating it can have significant implications for the negotiation process. If a party believes its BATNA is extremely strong, it may be less reluctant to make concessions during discussions.[26]

j. *Incomplete information*: Information plays a critical role in negotiation, and a lack of access to relevant or complete data and information about the other party's constraints, needs, or alternatives can indeed hinder the negotiation process. Negotiators can increase the possibility of obtaining fair, mutually advantageous, and durable agreements by addressing information asymmetry and actively trying to ensure a fuller understanding of each party's needs and restrictions.

10.3. Rules for Effective Negotiation

Effective negotiation may follow various rules. We discuss them as do's and don'ts of negotiation.

10.3.1. Do's for an Effective Negotiation

1. *Common Goals*: One needs to think in partnership terms, that is, common goals, and not focusing only on individual benefits.
2. *Time management*: Don't waste time; get right to the point. Bring up the underlying problems. Take them on head-on and resolve issues in person.
3. *Be empathetic*: Individuals usually ignore information that deviates from preconceived notions and instead look for facts to support their own beliefs. The other party's perspective must be understood to negotiate successfully.

---

[24]Hagemann, S., & Franchino, F. (2016). Transparency vs efficiency? A study of negotiations in the Council of the European Union. *European Union Politics*, *17*(3), 408–428.

[25]Kolb, D., & Williams, J. (2001). *The shadow negotiation: How women can master the hidden agendas that determine bargaining success*. Simon and Schuster.

[26]Diekmann, K., & Galinsky, A. D. (2006). Overconfident, underprepared: Why you may not be ready to negotiate. *Negotiation*, *9*(10), 6–9.

It is important to be receptive to different viewpoints and try to understand others' perspectives.

4. *Discuss each other's perspectives*: Discussing each other's perspectives is an additional direct method of getting to know the other person. It is important for everyone to express their opinions honestly and freely, without passing judgment or placing blame on others.
5. *Speak with a purpose*: Information overload can be just as harmful as information scarcity. Before bringing up a crucial topic, decide exactly what you want to say to the other person. Ascertain the exact purpose for which this shared data will be put to use.
6. *Active listening*: It takes more than just hearing what the other person is saying to truly listen. Active listening involves paying great attention to what is stated, both vocally and nonverbally. It means consistently seeking an explanation from the person. The person may realize you are taking them seriously and are not just going through the motions if you ask them what they mean.
7. *Prepare well*: Preparing well will make negotiation effective and systematic.

10.3.2. Don'ts of an Effective Negotiation

1. Don't waste time complaining, focus on finding solutions.
2. Avoid letting little disagreements linger or go unnoticed.
3. Always have an agenda in mind before a meeting begins.
4. Don't try to bluff each other during the negotiation process, as it is never a good idea. There is always someone willing to do it cheaper to gain the business. You must treat the relationship as a marriage. Communication and compromise are key.
5. Don't enter a negotiation without conducting adequate investigation and comprehension of the problems at hand.
6. Don't be a poor listener. Failure to listen to other party's needs and opinion causes negotiation failure.
7. Don't adopt a win–lose mindset in which the purpose is to "win" at the expense of the opposing party.
8. Don't focus entirely on the immediate transaction without regard for the long-term relationship with the other party. Strong relationships can lead to better terms in future talks and build a collaborative workplace.
9. Don't share sensitive information without understanding the implications of the negotiation.
10. Don't rush the negotiation process and settle for a deal prematurely.

10.4. Case Study 10.1: The Lodi Corporation Labor Dispute

Background: The global manufacturing corporation Lodi Corporation was embroiled in a labor dispute with its unionized workforce. Negotiations for a new collective bargaining agreement were started because the current agreement between the union and the corporation was about to expire.

Factors that caused negotiations to fail:

1. *Communication failure*: Throughout the negotiation process, there was a communication breakdown. No one was able to convey their priorities to the other party in an effective manner.
2. *Trust issues*: Over time, trust eroded between the union representatives and the management of Lodi Corporation. Past grievances and perceived unfair labor practices fueled suspicion and made it difficult for the parties to collaborate.
3. *Unrealistic expectations*: The company was having financial difficulties, which made it impossible for the union to meet their demands for better benefits and pay raises. It was challenging to balance the exaggerated expectations that both parties brought into the talks.
4. *Failure to address key interests*: Both parties stuck to their arguments rather than concentrating on underlying interests. The union was determined to win significant wage increases, while the firm was obsessed with cost-cutting measures. The creation of innovative solutions was hampered by this failure to recognize and address important interests.
5. *External pressure*: Without focusing on underlying interests, all parties adhered to their positions. While the company was fixated on cost-cutting initiatives, the union was eager to obtain large wage increases. This failure to identify and address key interests impeded the development of creative solutions.
6. *Inadequate preparation*: The union and the business did not fully prepare for the talks. Informed decision-making was hampered by a lack of information on industry benchmarks, market trends, and the 'company's financial situation.
7. *Lack of mediation*: In this case, there was no neutral mediator involved to facilitate the negotiation process. The absence of a third party to guide the discussions and help bridge the gap between the two sides allowed tensions to escalate.
8. *Emotional factors*: The negotiations were significantly influenced by emotional elements. Anger, frustration, and old grudges got in the way of making thoughtful decisions and productively solving problems.

Ultimately, talks collapsed, leading to a damaging walkout and a stop to work. The failure to reach a mutually agreeable solution resulted in financial losses for the company and damage to the employees' reputations. Because the parties failed to build a foundation of trust and address the root reasons for the disagreement, the labor conflict continued.

> *Q1*. Please discuss the above situation in light of the negotiation failure.

> *Q2*. Discuss strategies to avoid the above situation.

> *Q3*. Discuss the implications of failed negotiation for employees and employers.

10.5. Part A (Self-assessment)

1. What is a common result of bad negotiation communication?
   a. Increased trust
   b. Clear understanding
   c. **Misperception**
   d. Prompt resolution

2. Why could negotiators who have unrealistic expectations have difficulty reaching an agreement?
   a. Realism encourages creativity
   b. Realistic expectations develop trust
   c. **Unrealistic expectations may lead to disappointment and frustration**
   d. Unrealistic expectations encourage compromise

3. What consequences might a lack of confidence between negotiation parties have?
   a. Efficient teamwork
   b. Greater flexibility
   c. **Difficulty in obtaining agreements**
   d. Timely resolution

4. Why is it critical to concentrate on underlying interests in negotiations?
   a. It lengthens the negotiation process
   b. It facilitates rigid positions
   c. **It enables creative problem-solving**
   d. It enhances emotional intelligence

5. How do cultural differences affect negotiations?
   a. They have little effect on talks
   b. **They can complicate negotiations, particularly in multinational contexts**
   c. They foster understanding
   d. They result in speedy resolutions

6. How might power differentials influence negotiations?
   a. They encourage collaboration
   b. They facilitate talks
   c. **They can create difficulties for the weaker side**
   d. They lead to transparency

7. What consequences might poor negotiation preparation have?
   a. Sound decision-making
   b. Clear communication
   c. Informed decision-making
   d. **Ineffective bargaining**

8. What role do emotional variables play in the bargaining process?
   a. They have no effect on discussions
   b. They facilitate rational decision-making
   c. **They obstruct rational decision-making**
   d. They result in speedy resolutions

9. What external factor can influence negotiation outcomes?
   a. Lack of external pressure
   b. **Economic shifts**
   c. High level of trust
   d. Effective communication

10. What might be a consequence of hidden agendas in negotiations?
    a. Increased transparency
    b. Trust-building
    c. **Erosion of trust**
    d. Quick resolution

10.6. Part B (Review Questions)

1. Discuss the common mistakes that can lead to the failure of negotiations. Provide examples and explain how each mistake contributes to the breakdown of the negotiation process.
2. Explain one example of how cultural differences can impact the negotiation process.
3. Describe the consequences of negotiators entering discussions with unrealistic expectations.
4. Discuss the role of trust in negotiations. Provide examples and explain how a lack of trust can contribute to negotiation failure.
5. Examine the impact of poor communication on the negotiation process. Include examples and discuss how effective communication can enhance the chances of successful negotiations.
6. Choose one common mistake in negotiations (e.g., inadequate preparation or emotional factors) and elaborate on how it can contribute to the failure of the negotiation process. Provide real-world examples to support your explanation.

10.7. Part C (Glossary)

Negotiation impasse: Negotiation in which one or two parties discontinue the interaction, either because one or both parties prefer no agreement, or because they could not reach an agreement despite them benefitting from doing so.
BATNA: Best Alternative to a Negotiated Agreement.
Mediation: The endeavor to resolve a conflict by the assistance of an impartial third person is known as mediation. Through the controlled process of mediation, parties can engage in active, hands-on issue negotiation.

Chapter 11

Role of Perception in Negotiation

Learning Objectives:

- Role of perception in negotiation.
- Process of perception formation in negotiation.
- Perceptual errors in negotiation.

Negotiating parties can maximize their benefits without directly competing for resources in a win−lose manner. However, instead of aspiring for mutually advantageous, or integrative agreements, negotiators frequently settle for suboptimal results. It has been identified that misperceptions among negotiating parties are a prime reason for suboptimal outcomes.[1] In negotiations, perception is very important because it affects how parties understand and react to information as well as how they approach the negotiation process in general.[2,3] Perception affects how negotiators understand the situation, create bonds with one another, and maneuver through the intricate dynamics of negotiation. Achieving virtuous negotiating outcomes requires becoming cognizant of one's own impressions as

[1]Thompson, L., & Hastie, R. (1990). Social perception in negotiation. *Organizational Behavior and Human Decision Processes*, *47*(1), 98−123.

[2]Thompson, L., Valley, K. L., & Kramer, R. M. (1995). The bittersweet feeling of success: An examination of social perception in negotiation. *Journal of Experimental Social Psychology*, *31*(6), 467−492.

[3]Ma, Z. (2006). Negotiating into China: The impact of individual perception on Chinese negotiations styles. *International Journal of Emerging Markets*, *1*(1), 64−83.

Managing and Negotiating Disagreements:
A Contemporary Approach for Conflict Resolution, 117–127
Copyright © 2024 by Bhawana Bhardwaj and Dipanker Sharma
Published under exclusive licence by Emerald Publishing Limited
doi:10.1108/978-1-83797-971-420241011

well as sensitive to those of others.[4,5] The ability to read people to identify their wants and predict their next move based on what they want to achieve is one of the most important talents of a skilled negotiator. A person's behavior, both conscious and unconscious, can reveal a lot about them.

11.1. Role of Perception in Negotiation

Understanding the true meaning concealed in spoken and nonverbal cues is a great reservoir of knowledge that can be used into a potent tool for persuasion. Thus, the outcome of negotiation largely depends on how proficiently we have mastered the skill of perception management.[6] The following are some important facets of perception's function in negotiation:

1. *Interpretation of information:* Interpretation of information plays an important role. Different people may perceive the same information differently based on their experiences, perspectives, and cultural backgrounds. Perceptions of fairness, honesty, and reliability can have a big impact on how information is received and processed during negotiations.
2. *Emotional impact:* The way that one and the other party perceive their emotions can have a significant effect on the negotiation dynamic. Emotional intelligence, or the ability to recognize and control emotions, is crucial in negotiation to understand and manage the emotionally charged aspects of the process.
3. *Building trust:* The perception of trustworthiness is a crucial element in negotiations. Trust can be impacted by past experiences, communication techniques, and reputations. Being consistent and transparent is essential to establishing trust, and people's capacity for compromise and reaching agreements can be influenced by their perceptions of one another.[7,8] In negotiations, the impression of one's credibility is vital. Reputations, communication styles, and past experiences can all affect trust. Building trust requires

---

[4]Van Kleef, G. A., & Cote, S. (2018). Emotional dynamics in conflict and negotiation: Individual, dyadic, and group processes. *Annual Review of Organizational Psychology and Organizational Behavior, 5*, 437–464.

[5]Thompson, L., Neale, M., & Sinaceur, M. (2004). The evolution of cognition and biases in negotiation research: An examination of cognition, social perception, motivation, and emotion. In M. J. Gelfand & J.-L. Brett (Eds.), *The handbook of negotiation and culture* (pp. 7–44). Standford Business Books.

[6]Jagodzinska, K. (2016). How to manage perception to win negotiations. *International Journal of Social Science Studies, 4*, 69.

[7]Butler, J. K., Jr. (1995). Behaviors, trust, and goal achievement in a win–win negotiating role play. *Group & Organization Management, 20*(4), 486–501.

[8]Boss, R. W. (1978). Trust and managerial problem solving revisited. *Group and Organizational Studies, 3*, 331–342.

being dependable and open, and people's willingness to make concessions and come to an agreement can be impacted by how they see each other.[9,10]

4. *Modes of communication*: Perceptions of communication styles, including aggressiveness, responsiveness, and listening skills, may influence the negotiation process. Misinterpreted communication might lead to misunderstandings and negotiation failures. Recognizing and adapting to the other party's chosen mode of communication is essential.[11]

5. *Cultural diversity*: It is possible for people from various cultural backgrounds to negotiate. Cultural origins and individual differences might impact perceptions of appropriate negotiation conduct, timeliness, and the value of relationships in commercial deals.[12] Furthermore, due to differences in perception and communication, inter-cultural negotiation may encounter additional difficulties. Respecting and acknowledging cultural differences are crucial for fostering fruitful communication and building rapport during negotiations.

6. *Power dynamics*: Power impressions, real or imagined, can have a significant influence on negotiation strategies and outcomes. A deep grasp of power dynamics can help negotiators better handle situations where one party may have more leverage. This understanding can also influence the strategies employed to balance or shift power.[13]

7. *Negotiation framing:* Parties' understanding of a problem's importance and potential remedies is influenced by how it is phrased.[14] Collaborating effectively and presenting negotiations favorably can promote more cooperative and fruitful problem-solving.

8. *Negotiation context*: External factors like the state of the economy, politics, or the industry may have an impact on the parties' assessments of the significance and urgency of the talks. Negotiators can anticipate problems and adjust their plans of action by having a clear understanding of the bigger picture.[15,16]

[9]Gunia, B. C., Brett, J. M., Nandkeolyar, A. K., & Kamdar, D. (2011). Paying a price: Culture, trust, and negotiation consequences. *Journal of Applied Psychology*, 96(4), 774.

[10]Ross, W., & LaCroix, J. (1996). Multiple meanings of trust in negotiation theory and research: A literature review and integrative model. *International Journal of Conflict Management*, 7(4), 314−360.

[11]Schoop, M. (2021). Negotiation communication revisited. *Central European Journal of Operations Research*, 29(1), 163−176.

[12]Brett, J. M. (2000). Culture and negotiation. *International Journal of Psychology*, 35(2), 97−104.

[13]Schaerer, M., Teo, L., Madan, N., & Swaab, R. I. (2020). Power and negotiation: Review of current evidence and future directions. *Current Opinion in Psychology*, 33, 47−51.

[14]Neale, M. A., & Bazerman, M. H. (1992). Negotiating rationally: The power and impact of the negotiator's frame. *Academy of Management Perspectives*, 6(3), 42−51.

[15]Kim, P. H., Pinkley, R. L., & Fragale, A. R. (2005). Power dynamics in negotiation. *Academy of Management Review*, 30(4), 799−822.

[16]Fülöp, M. T., Măgdaş, N., & Cordos, G. S. (2019). Theoretical background of internal and external environment of negotiation. *Annales Universitatis Apulensis: Series Oeconomica*, 21(1), 32−39.

11.2. Process of Perception in Negotiation

The perceptual process in negotiation refers to how individuals select, organize, and evaluate data from their environment to make sense of the negotiating position. Perceptual processes affect how negotiators see themselves, the other party, and the overall context of the negotiation. To successfully negotiate the complexities of inter-personal dynamics, communication, and decision-making, negotiators must understand the perceptual process. Understanding the factors that influence perception and developing self-awareness can help enhance negotiating strategies and outcomes. The following are the crucial phases of the negotiating perceptual process[17,18,19]:

1. *Sensation*: This is the stage where stimuli from the external environment are received by sensory organs. A sense organ, sensory nerve, or sensory region in the brain can be stimulated to produce the conscious or mental process of sensation. It is the physical process by which the eyes, ears, nose, tongue, and skin respond to inputs from the outside world.[20]
2. *Selection of information*: Selection occurs when negotiators decide which of the numerous stimuli in their surroundings to concentrate on. Individual objectives, expectations, and priorities all have an impact on the selection process, as does the perception of the information's applicability to the negotiation.[21] Additionally, there are multiple factors such as age, gender, education, culture, etc. to play a role in the selection of the information in the perceptual process.[22]
3. *Organization of information*: After choosing their material, negotiators arrange it in a way that makes sense to them. Information must be categorized, grouped, and organized according to patterns, similarities, and differences. Schemas, or mental frameworks, are useful for information organization. These mental models, or schemas, aid people in making sense of and interpreting new information considering prior knowledge.
4. *Interpretation*: The process of giving meaning to the ordered information is called interpretation. It involves interpreting cues and understanding the

---

[17]Alan, S., & Gary, J. (2011). Perception, attribution, and judgment of others. In *Organizational behaviour: Understanding and managing life at work* (Vol. 7). Pearson Canada Inc.

[18]Coren, S. (1980). Principles of perceptual organization and spatial distortion: The gestalt illusions. *Journal of Experimental Psychology: Human Perception and Performance*, *6*(3), 404–412.

[19]Hellriegel, D., & Slocum, J. (2011). *Organizational behavior*. Cengage Learning.

[20]Mesulam, M. M. (1998). From sensation to cognition. *Brain: A Journal of Neurology*, *121*(6), 1013–1052.

[21]Qiong, O. U. (2017). A brief introduction to perception. *Studies in Literature and Language*, *15*(4), 18–28.

[22]Brett, J. M. (2000). Culture and negotiation. *International Journal of Psychology*, *35*(2), 97–104.

implications of various cues in the context of a negotiation. Interpretations of information are influenced by individual differences. These differences encompass cultural background, values, and beliefs. For example, negotiators from more collaborative cultures may not understand aggressiveness in the same way as those from more competitive cultures.

5. *Perceptual filters*: These are distinct components that influence the selection, arrangement, and interpretation of information. These filters include things like beliefs, sentiments, experiences, and cognitive biases. Filters can affect how the opposite side intends to proceed, how important particular outcomes are to the negotiators, and how fair the process is overall.[23,24,25]

6. *Feedback/response*: The process of perception includes continuous feedback. In reaction to feedback from the other side or the negotiation environment, negotiators may alter the choice, organization, and interpretation of their material. Feedback can take the form of nonverbal cues, responses to suggestions, or adjustments to the negotiation environment.[26]

11.3. Perceptual Errors Affecting Negotiation

Perceptual errors, sometimes referred to as cognitive biases, can significantly impact the negotiation process by leading individuals to draw conclusions and render decisions that lack rationality and factual basis. Negotiators need to be aware of these perceptual errors to mitigate their effects. By actively searching out alternative perspectives, actively attempting to lessen biases, and practicing reflective thinking, negotiators can make more sane and effective judgments. Common perceptual errors that could occur during a negotiation include the following:

1. *Confirmation bias*: The search for, interpretation of, and retention of evidence in a way that is consistent with preconceived notions or expectations constitutes this prejudice. In negotiations, confirmation bias can lead to parties ignoring information that contradicts their initial positions and in favor of data that supports them.[23,27]

2. *Overconfidence bias*: One sort of cognitive bias that makes us believe that we are better than we are in some areas is called overconfidence bias. Such

[23]Berlin, L., & Hendrix, R. W. (1998). Perceptual errors and negligence. *American Journal of Roentgenology*, *170*(4), 863–867.

[24]Maule, A. J., & Hodgkinson, G. P. (2003). Re-appraising managers' perceptual errors: A behavioural decision-making perspective. *British Journal of Management*, *14*(1), 33–37.

[25]Takahashi, N., & Mashima, R. (2006). The importance of subjectivity in perceptual errors on the emergence of indirect reciprocity. *Journal of Theoretical Biology*, *243*(3), 418–436.

[26]Rassaei, E. (2013). Corrective feedback, learners' perceptions, and second language development. *System*, *41*(2), 472–483.

[27]Brett, J., & Thompson, L. (2016). Negotiation. *Organizational Behavior and Human Decision Processes*, *136*, 68–79.

people think they are better than average in terms of intelligence, honesty, or prospects and may not respect the opinions of others.[28]

3. *Anchoring bias*: This bias occurs when negotiators make decisions based too heavily on the "anchor", or initial piece of information they learn. Negotiators may not achieve their desired outcomes if they base their negotiations on an initial offer that is unfair or unjustified.[29,30]

4. *Stereotyping*: Stereotyping is the act of generalizing about someone based solely on their membership in a certain group, without considering any of their unique qualities. Stereotypes can produce biased evaluations and obstruct effective communication and teamwork in negotiations.[31] Stereotypes can act a huge barrier to reach optimum decisions in negotiation process.

5. *Fundamental attribution error*: This mistake happens when people don't consider external influences and instead attribute other people's conduct to their personalities or intentions. This might lead to misunderstandings and inaccurate evaluations of the other party's intentions and motivations during negotiations.[32]

6. *Escalation of commitment*: This bias is the tendency to continue with a course of action even when it is not working. Escalation of commitment is the propensity to "carry on" with such questionable endeavors, regardless of the likelihood of their success. Accepting loss could encourage parties to continue expending effort, resources, and concessions in an unfavorable negotiation.[33]

7. *Accessibility heuristic*: Making decisions based on easily attainable information often from recent or vivid experiences is referred to as this bias. This could lead to an overemphasis on readily available information in the context of negotiations instead of considering a greater range of relevant issues.[34]

---

[28]West, R. F., & Stanovich, K. E. (1997). The domain specificity and generality of overconfidence: Individual differences in performance estimation bias. *Psychonomic Bulletin & Review, 4*(3), 387–392.
[29]Epley, N., & Gilovich, T. (2006). The anchoring-and-adjustment heuristic: Why the adjustments are insufficient. *Psychological Science, 17*(4), 311–318.
[30]Korobkin, R., & Guthrie, C. (2003). Heuristics and biases at the bargaining table. *Marquette Law Review, 87*, 795.
[31]Blum, L. (2004). Stereotypes and stereotyping: A moral analysis. *Philosophical Papers, 33*(3), 251–289.
[32]Maruna, S., & Mann, R. E. (2006). A fundamental attribution error? Rethinking cognitive distortions. *Legal and Criminological Psychology, 11*(2), 155–177.
[33]Sleesman, D. J., Lennard, A. C., McNamara, G., & Conlon, D. E. (2018). Putting escalation of commitment in context: A multilevel review and analysis. *Academy of Management Annals, 12*(1), 178–207.
[34]Adamus-Matuszyńska, A. (2020). Heuristics and biases as sources of negotiators' errors in the pre-negotiation phase. Review of literature and empirical research. *Optimum Economic Studies, 101*(3), 79–90.

8. *Hindsight bias*: Hindsight bias is the phenomenon when people feel that they "knew it all along." People can see events as predictable or expected after they happen. This prejudice may affect subsequent discussions by creating a skewed perception of the proceedings and results.[35,36]

9. *Emotional influences*: Emotions have a significant impact on perception. Positive or negative emotions can influence how negotiators view the situation, form judgments, and communicate with the other side. Emotional intelligence, or the ability to recognize and regulate one's own feelings as well as those of others, is necessary for successful negotiation.[37,38]

11.4. Managing Perception for Effective Negotiation

Perception has a direct impact on how parties view each other, the issues at hand, and the negotiating process. Managing perception becomes an essential component of successful negotiation.[39] Through the use of these tactics, negotiators can actively control perception and foster an atmosphere that encourages candid dialogue, teamwork, and the creation of mutually agreeable solutions. The following are some strategies to manage perception for a successful negotiation:

1. *Establish trust*: Effective negotiations are built on trust. Be truthful, open, and consistent in your interactions with others and in your communication to project a trustworthy image. Keeping your word, following through on agreements, positive encounters over time are the foundation of trust.[40]

2. *Effective communication*: To guarantee that all parties understand one another, express opinions, interests, and expectations in clear and concise terms. It is important to appreciate and comprehend the viewpoint of the other person by using active listening techniques. For validating their problems that are accurately grasped, a reflective listening and paraphrasing play an important role. Additionally, it has been demonstrated that communication behavior

[35]Christensen-Szalanski, J. J., & Willham, C. F. (1991). The hindsight bias: A meta-analysis. *Organizational Behavior and Human Decision Processes*, *48*(1), 147–168.

[36]Hoffrage, U., Hertwig, R., & Gigerenzer, G. (2000). Hindsight bias: A by-product of knowledge updating? *Journal of Experimental Psychology: Learning, Memory, and Cognition*, *26*(3), 566.

[37]Zadra, J. R., & Clore, G. L. (2011). Emotion and perception: The role of affective information. *Wiley Interdisciplinary Reviews: Cognitive Science*, *2*(6), 676–685.

[38]Sjöberg, L. (2007). Emotions and risk perception. *Risk Management*, *9*(4), 223–237.

[39]Jagodzinska, K. (2016). How to manage perception to win negotiations. *International Journal of Social Science Studies*, *4*, 69.

[40]Lewicki, R. J., & Polin, B. (2013). Trust and negotiation. In M. Olekalns & W. L. Adair (Eds.), *Handbook of research on negotiation* (pp. 161–190). Edward Elgar Publishing.

causes a mirror effect, wherein the other party to the negotiation will also communicate appropriately.[41,42]

3. *Control your emotions*: Emotions influence the ability of the negotiator to accomplish negotiation goals. The likelihood of reaching the negotiation objectives increases with one's ability to manage emotions well. Effective negotiating requires emotional intelligence. Recognize your own and the other person's feelings and avoid becoming hostile or violent by controlling your emotions in a healthy way. Even in difficult circumstances, keeping a cool, collected attitude leads to successful outcomes.[43,44]

4. *Framing agenda positively*: Present topics related to negotiations in a cooperative and constructive perspective. Stressing common objectives and advantages will foster a cooperative environment. Avoid negative framing, which could elicit resistance or defensiveness. Try to come up with solutions that please everyone.[45]

5. *Be consistent*: Consistency in words and deeds fosters positivity and builds credibility. Inconsistencies can lead to misunderstandings and erode confidence. Be careful to maintain consistency in your actions and messaging throughout the negotiation process.[46]

6. *Recognize cultural difference*: Recognize how cultural quirks can affect how people perceive certain behaviors and communication approaches. Take the time to become familiar with the cultural background of the other party in order to establish rapport and prevent inadvertent misunderstandings.[47]

7. *Dealing with stereotypes and biases*: Acknowledge your own biases and misunderstandings and work to debunk them. Avoid creating assumptions about

[41]Schoop, M., Van Amelsvoort, M., Gettinger, J., Koerner, M., Koeszeig, S. T., Van der Wijst, P. (2014). The interplay of communication and decisions in electronic negotiations: Communicative decisions or decisive communication? *Group Decision Negotiation, 23*, 167–192.

[42]Schoop, M. (2021). Negotiation communication revisited. *Central European Journal of Operations Research, 29*(1), 163–176.

[43]https://www.pon.harvard.edu/daily/negotiation-skills-daily/the-limits-of-emotional-intelligence-as-a-negotiation-skill/

[44]Kelly, E. J., & Kaminskienė, N. (2016). Importance of emotional intelligence in negotiation and mediation. *International Comparative Jurisprudence, 2*(1), 55–60.

[45]Chang, L., Cheng, M., & Trotman, K. T. (2008). The effect of framing and negotiation partner's objective on judgments about negotiated transfer prices. *Accounting, Organizations and Society, 33*(7–8), 704–717.

[46]Naquin, C. E., & Kurtzberg, T. R. (2009). Team negotiation and perceptions of trustworthiness: The whole versus the sum of the parts. *Group Dynamics: Theory, Research, and Practice, 13*(2), 133.

[47]Clohisy, D. R., Yaszemski, M. J., & Lipman, J. (2017). Leadership, communication, and negotiation across a diverse workforce: An AOA critical issues symposium. *JBJS, 99*(12), e60.

other people and make an effort to understand their individuality. Encourage a friendly environment that values diversity and opposing ideas.[48]

8. *Expectation management*: Expectation management plays an important role in negotiation effectiveness. It is important to accurately convey reasonable expectations, refrain from overcommitting or making unfulfillable promises, and control the other party's expectations by giving them accurate information about the negotiating process and possible results.[49]

9. *Apply objective standards*: Base your negotiating stances on objective standards, such as industry norms, market values, or arguments backed by facts. By depersonalizing the discussion, objective criteria can facilitate the discovery of common ground and the achievement of agreement between the parties.[50,51]

10. *Respond to feedback*: It is suggested to be open to receiving input from the other side and modify your strategy as necessary. Being flexible and willing to adjust will help you gain the respect of negotiating parties by showing that you are dedicated to working together to discover win–win solutions.

11. *Look for win–win outcome*: Aim for results that both sides feel are just and advantageous. Win–win agreements increase the possibility of future cooperation and help to foster a favorable opinion of the negotiating process.

11.5. Part A (Self-assessment)

1. How does perception influence the negotiations?
   a. It has no effect on the results of negotiations
   b. **It affects how parties understand and react to the information and data**
   c. In professional negotiations, perception is irrelevant; it only matters in inter-personal connections
   d. Only those negotiators with certain cultural backgrounds should find it

2. In the context of negotiation, confirmation bias refers to———.
   a. **The propensity to look for information that supports preconceived notions**
   b. The preference for novel and contradicting data
   c. An impartial method of assessing the information
   d. Making decisions without considering one's personal values

[48]Thompson, L., Nadler, J., & Lount, R. B., Jr. (2006). Judgmental biases in conflict resolution and how to overcome them. In M. Deutsch, P. T. Coleman, & E. C. Marcus (Eds.), *The handbook of conflict resolution: Theory and practice* (pp. 243–267). John Wiley & Sons.
[49]Rubin, J. Z., Kim, S. H., & Peretz, N. M. (1990). Expectancy effects and negotiation. *Journal of Social Issues, 46*(2), 125–139.
[50]Textor, M. (2019). Perceptual objectivity and the limits of perception. *Phenomenology and the Cognitive Sciences, 18*, 879–892.
[51]Haugeland, J. (1996). Objective perception. *Perception*, (5), 268.

3. In the context of negotiation, what does emotional intelligence mean?
   a. The capacity to control feelings in order to benefit oneself.
   b. The ability to keep emotions at bay when negotiating
   c. **Being aware of and in control of one's own emotions as well as those of others**
   d. The capacity to exclude feelings from the bargaining process.

4. In negotiations, an anchoring bias is:
   a. **The propensity to place an excessive amount of weight on the initial piece of information that is obtained**
   b. The inclination for cooperative approaches to negotiating
   c. Neglecting how early offers affect the course of the negotiation
   d. Approaching the early phases of negotiations in an impartial manner

5. What is a crucial negotiating strategy for controlling perception?
   a. Ignoring the other person's communications
   b. **Establishing trust through dependable and transparent behavior**
   c. Ignoring the emotional components of the bargaining process
   d. Making use of stereotypes to comprehend the opposing side rapidly

6. How might negotiators deal with stereotypes that arise during negotiation?
   a. To make things simpler, reinforce stereotypes.
   b. Take actions that fit preconceived notions
   c. **Recognize individuality, confront electrotypes, and overcome them**
   d. Do not bargain with people who come from diverse cultural backgrounds.

7. In the perception process, what is the negotiator's dilemma?
   a. **The difficulty in accurately perceiving the motives of the other party**
   b. The challenge of presenting negotiation concerns in a favorable light
   c. The propensity to avoid emotional involvement in negotiations
   d. The difficulty in controlling confirmation bias

8. Why is it crucial for negotiators to confront biases?
   a. Biases don't affect negotiations
   b. Having biases can help people make more logical decisions
   c. **Biases can influence decisions and judgments in a way that is not rational**
   d. It is only relevant to address biases during cross-cultural negotiations.

11.6. Part B (Review Questions)

1. Describe the concept of anchoring in negotiations. In what ways might negotiators manage it?
2. How crucial it is to establish trust during the negotiating process. Give two methods for establishing and maintaining trust.
3. How can cultural differences affect perception in a negotiation? Give a concrete example to support your argument.

4. Analyze how emotional intelligence affects negotiations. Give examples and a discussion of how emotional intelligence might affect the dynamics of negotiations.
5. Discuss the difficulties in resolving biases during the negotiating process.
6. Talk about strategies that negotiators can use to get beyond prejudices and encourage impartial decision-making.
7. Analyze critically how perception affects the results of negotiations. Talk about strategies to improve perception accuracy.

11.7. Part C (Glossary)

Perception: The process by which sensory information is organized, and interpreted by an individual.
Perceptual filters: These are discrete elements that affect how information is chosen, organized, and interpreted.
Confirmation bias: This is a perceptual error which involves the search for, interpretation of, and retention of data in a manner consistent with prior assumptions or expectations of an individual.
Stereotyping: Stereotyping is the process of forming judgments about people without considering their specific characteristics based only on their affiliation with a certain group.
Escalation of commitment: Sticking with a plan of action even after it becomes obvious that it is ineffective.

11.8. Activity 11.1: Role Play "The Negotiation Game"

a. Divide the class into small groups to form a bargaining team.
b. Give each team a separate set of negotiating scenarios (such as resource distribution, business partnerships, wage negotiations, labor issues, etc.).
c. Provide each team with some hidden agenda that is important for the discussion but not clearly stated or apparent.
d. Request each group to bargain in light of the information at hand, taking into account potential perceptual inaccuracies.

Discuss and brainstorm: Conclude the role play by discussing how perception errors affected the course and the result of the negotiations.

11.9. Activity11.2: Group Project: "Negotiation and Perceptual Errors"

a. Assign each small group in the class a particular cognitive bias (such as attribution bias or cultural stereotyping) that is pertinent to cross-cultural discussions.
b. Give group instructions to research about the topic and demonstrate how their allocated bias may affect cross-cultural discussion.
c. Finish with group presentations and a class discussion about the difficulties and solutions for reducing perception errors in situations where people are not from the same culture.

Chapter 12

Team Negotiation

Learning Objectives:

- Team negotiation and its features.
- Situation conducive for team negotiation.
- Various roles in a negotiation team.
- Advantages of team negotiation.
- Challenges of team negotiation.
- Process of team negotiation.
- Effective team negotiation.

With the advancement of technology, organizations are transforming rapidly[1] and teamwork has become imperative for organizational effectiveness. Balancing innovation and optimum utilization of resources is challenging and team leadership can play a vital role in organizational success.[2] In negotiation, a facilitator may also employ an approach where groups of individuals work together to attain shared objectives or settle disputes. A type of negotiation known as "team negotiation" involves several parties working together to reach a compromise.[3]

---

[1]Sharma, D., Salehi, W., Bhardwaj, B., Chand, M., & Salihy, H. (2023). Dovetailing the human resource management with the cloud computing in the era of industry 4.0: A review. *Frontiers in Management and Business*, *4*(2), 340–351. https://doi.org/10.25082/FMB.2023.02.004

[2]Balkrishan, B., Sharma, B., Dipanker, D., & Chand, M. (2024). Exploring unexplored dimensions of organizational ambidexterity in the hotel industry: Systematic literature review, synthesis and research agenda. *International Journal of Hospitality and Tourism Systems*, *17*(1), 48–65.

[3]Halevy, N. (2008). Team negotiation: Social, epistemic, economic, and psychological consequences of subgroup conflict. *Personality and Social Psychology Bulletin*, *34*(12), 1687–1702.

Managing and Negotiating Disagreements:
A Contemporary Approach for Conflict Resolution, 129–139
Copyright © 2024 by Bhawana Bhardwaj and Dipanker Sharma
Published under exclusive licence by Emerald Publishing Limited
doi:10.1108/978-1-83797-971-420241012

The practice of bargaining between two or more groups, each represented by a team of individuals, is called a team negotiation. Large corporate transactions frequently include this kind of negotiation, which can also happen in a variety of settings like business, labor unions, international relations, legal matters, and more. Team negotiations can also occur in these situations. Each side in a team negotiation consists of two or more people, and everyone involved must decide how to settle the conflict collectively.[4] Together, the delegates from the teams discuss issues and come up with solutions that satisfy everyone. Throughout the negotiation process, a lot of discussions, exchanges, and concessions are usually made, as conflicting parties try to attain a resolution.[5]

12.1. Features of Team Negotiation

1. *Team involvement*: Team negotiation involves a group of people representing a negotiating party. These teams may comprise members from several backgrounds, specializations, and opinions.[6]
2. *Cooperation*: Cooperation among the team members and working together is underlined during the negotiating process. Team members collaborate to achieve the goals, needs, and concerns of negotiating party.[7]
3. *Communication*: Effective communication provides a formative base for effective team negotiations. To facilitate effective communication, it is important to encourage active listening, clearly state individual perspectives, keeping communication open and transparent.[8]
4. *Problem-solving*: In team negotiations, addressing complex issues and developing novel solutions are commonplace tasks. Teams' member's focus is to solve difficulties, overcome impediments, and envision a win–win outcome. Team members need to be flexible and open to exploring many options and trade-offs. Changes and adjustments are made possible by flexibility throughout the negotiation.[9]

---

[4]Thompson, L., Peterson, E., & Brodt, S. E. (1996). Team negotiation: An examination of integrative and distributive bargaining. *Journal of Personality and Social Psychology, 70*(1), 66.

[5]Gelfand, M. J., Brett, J. M., Imai, L., Tsai, H. H., & Huang, D. (2005, June). Team negotiation across cultures: When and where are two heads better than one? In *IACM 18th annual conference.*

[6]Sally, D., & O'Connor, K. (2004). Team negotiations. *Marquette Law Review, 87*(4), 26.

[7]Desivilya-Syna, H. (2011). The role of negotiation in building intra-team and inter-team cooperation. In *Negotiation excellence: Successful deal making* (pp. 361–379). World Scientific.

[8]Byers, P. (1985). Communication: Cooperation or negotiation? *Theory into Practice, 24*(1), 71–76.

[9]Polzer, J. T. (1996). Intergroup negotiations: The effects of negotiating teams. *Journal of Conflict Resolution, 40*(4), 678–698.

5. *Flexibility*: Teams must be adaptable and willing to consider different solutions and trade-offs. Adaptations and changes can be made during the negotiating process with flexibility.[10]

6. *Relationship building*: It is critical to establish and preserve a good rapport between the negotiation teams. Future cooperation and effective discussions are facilitated by mutual trust and goodwill.[11,12]

7. *Preparation*: Teams prepare thoroughly before entering discussions. This entails being aware of their own goals, evaluating the viewpoint of the other person, and foreseeing any obstacles.[13,14]

8. *Closure and implementation*: After reaching a consensus, the teams proceed to close the negotiation process by putting the terms into writing and putting the solutions that were agreed upon into action.

12.2. Application

While managing collaborative work arrangements is a challenging process, teamwork has become an essential component of modern organizational functioning. Beyond finishing the current task's objective, there are multiple dimensions of team negotiation. Team negotiation can be particularly applied in the succeeding situations[15]:

1. When there is a complex situation that calls for a wide range of skills, knowledge, or experience.

2. There is a lot of room for innovative, integrative ideas in the negotiation.

3. There are a variety of interests and constituencies presented at the negotiation table, such as in trade union talks.

4. When the negotiating party wants to strengthen its bargaining position, for example, in international settings, when teams are expected to participate.

5. You want to convey the message to the opposing side that you are serious about the discussion.

6. You regard and trust the team members.

7. You have enough time to plan and direct a team endeavor.

---

[10]Druckman, D., & Mitchell, C. (1995). Flexibility in negotiation and mediation. *The Annals of the American Academy of Political and Social Science*, *542*(1), 10–23.

[11]Naquin, C. E., & Kurtzberg, T. R. (2009). Team negotiation and perceptions of trustworthiness: The whole versus the sum of the parts. *Group Dynamics: Theory, Research, and Practice*, *13*(2), 133.

[12]Nadler, J. (2003). Rapport in negotiation and conflict resolution. *Marquette Law Review*, *87*, 875.

[13]Peleckis, K. (2014). International business negotiations: innovation, negotiation team, preparation. *Procedia-Social and Behavioral Sciences*, *110*, 64–73.

[14]Lindholst, M., Bülow, A. M., & Fells, R. (2018). The practice of preparation for complex negotiations. *Journal of Strategic Contracting and Negotiation*, *4*(1–2), 119–140.

[15]Thompson, L., Peterson, E., & Brodt, S. E. (1996). Team negotiation: An examination of integrative and distributive bargaining. *Journal of Personality and Social Psychology*, *70*(1), 66.

12.3. Various Roles in Team Negotiations

Evidently, the negotiating team comprises more than two team members. As Fig. 24 exhibits, a negotiation team consists of multiple positions. Sometimes a single person can play multiple roles.[16,17] Some common roles in negotiation teams are as follows:

- *Leader*: In a negotiation, each team often designates a leader who will render the final decision.
- *Observer*: The observer is the member of the team who pays close attention to the other party's team, observes them, and shares their findings with the leader.
- *Relater*: Relater is a team member who plays the role of fostering relationships with the other team members. His role will be ensuring coordination and congenial relationship among team members.
- *Recorder*: Team member assuming this role documents and maintains records of discussion and minutes of a negotiation.
- *Critic*: A team member playing this role critically analyzes and understands the repercussions of an agreement's concessions and the possibility of other undesirable consequences.
- *Builder*: The deal to be offered or a package for a negotiating team is prepared by a builder of the negotiation team. During negotiations, they can carry out financial tasks such as estimating the cost of an agreement.

Fig. 24.   Roles in a Team Negotiation. *Source*: Created by authors.

---

[16]https://www.pon.harvard.edu/daily/negotiation-skills-daily/negotiation-team-strategy/
[17]https://hbr.org/2009/09/how-to-manage-your-negotiating-team

12.4. Advantages of Team Negotiation[18,19]

- *Broad base of knowledge*: When well-organized, teams bring a wealth of expertise to the table and are less likely to miss crucial information. They think more cohesively and plan more effectively.
- *Quality of outcomes*: The quality of decision taken by a team is better in quality than their counterparts.[20] Negotiation is a complex cognitive task, requiring negotiation skills such as understanding the other party's preferences, interests, and substitutes. It also involves crafting counteroffers, and deciding on responses. Complex problems can be successfully handled via simultaneous data processing and augmented memory capacity of team members.[2]
- *Creativity*: Team negotiation produces better results when negotiations are difficult and call for a wide range of skills, information, or experience. Together, you can come up with more inventive solutions and assess the advantages and disadvantages of various ideas from various perspectives.
- *Better planning and effectiveness*: Involvement of team members and negotiators can develop a sense of ownership and accountability for the negotiation process and outcome. For example, a labor union negotiating with an employer can use a team approach to represent the interests and voices of its diverse members. Furthermore, they can exchange information and opinions with the employer and build legitimacy and support for the agreement among its constituents.
- *Teams set higher targets for negotiations*: Team negotiations can also create opportunities for learning, feedback, and recognition among team members, as well as for building trust and rapport with the other party.
- *Team members reinforce each other's strengths*: Team members possess complementary skills and create synergistic effect.

---

[18]Hüffmeier, J., Zerres, A., Freund, P. A., Backhaus, K., Trötschel, R., & Hertel, G. (2019). Strong or weak synergy? Revising the assumption of team-related advantages in integrative negotiations. *Journal of Management, 45*(7), 2721–2750.

[19]O'Connor, K. M. (1997). Groups and solos in context: The effects of accountability on team negotiation. *Organizational Behavior and Human Decision Processes, 72*(3), 384–407.

[20]Polzer, J. T. (1996). Intergroup negotiations: The effects of negotiating teams, *Journal of Conflict Resolution, 40*(4), 678.

12.5. Challenges of Team Negotiation[21,22]

- *Selecting your teammates*: Selecting a teammate for a team negotiation is a cumbersome job. It involves considering criteria such as negotiation proficiency, procedural expertise, and inter-personal effectiveness.
- *Communication with the team (information pooling)*: Coordination of information sharing and communication to ensure group interaction would demand a thoughtful strategy and be challenged in the case of a diverse team.
- *Team cohesion*: Team cohesion acts as a retaining force and binds members together. There can be two types of team cohesion. (a) *Common-identity groups*: In this form of groups, the members are attracted to the group for what it represents. (b) *Common-bond groups* comprise the members who are fascinated to the group due to the particular members in the group.
- *Information processing (common information bias)*: This is the propensity of group members to discuss and share the information that is common and hide the information that is unique.
- *Coordination*: Coordination is one of the biggest challenges of the negotiation because there is a need to accomplish the roles and responsibilities. Careful planning is necessary for coordination to guarantee that the team has a well-defined and adaptable division of labor and responsibility in addition to a clear and shared goal, strategy, and agenda. To make sure the team reacts to the dynamic and unpredictable negotiation environment as a cohesive team. It also involves monitoring, adjusting and communicating. For instance, to align its plans for integration, due diligence, and valuation, a merger and acquisition team negotiating with a target business must coordinate team members from several functional areas.
- *Team conflict*: Divergent personalities, competitive goals, unharmonious styles, power imbalance, and status difference or ambiguity in roles and expectations can stem conflicts within the team. On one hand, occasional conflict can stimulate critical thinking and enhance mutual understanding, respect, and cooperation. Similarly, conflict can also damage trust, communication, and decision making, as well as increase stress. For example, a government delegation negotiating with an international organization can face conflicts within its team due to conflicting agendas, priorities, and loyalties, as well as conflicts with the other party due to cultural, ideological, or procedural differences. Make sure you implement effective conflict management mechanisms to ensure your team works collaboratively toward a mutually beneficial outcome.

---

[21]Naquin, C. E., & Kurtzberg, T. R. (2009). Team negotiation and perceptions of trustworthiness: The whole versus the sum of the parts. *Group Dynamics: Theory, Research, and Practice, 13*(2), 133.
[22]https://www.pon.harvard.edu/daily/dealmaking-daily/negotiation-research-you-can-use-promoting-cooperation-between-teams-nb/

12.6. Process of Team Negotiation

The stages of team negotiation process may involve the following stages:

1. *Preparation*: This stage involves clarifying goals, objectives, and expected outcomes of the team negotiation. It also involves gathering information about the negotiating party's interests, priorities, and potential concerns. Understanding their perspective and possible points of contention is part of the preparation. Additionally, it involves coordinating with team members and delegating roles and responsibilities. This stage ensures that team members are well versed in key agendas and objectives.
2. *Opening the negotiation*: The opening of negotiation comprises the introduction and brief overview of negotiation agenda. It also involves agreeing on rules and procedures that will guide and govern the negotiation process. This stage also involves setting time limits and communication protocols.
3. *Information sharing*: This stage of team negotiation comprises information sharing by each negotiating party. In this stage, each team shares its needs, expectations, priorities, and initiation proposals. The stage can be made effective through active listening to ensure understanding and underlying interest.
4. *Problem-solving and bargaining*: This stage involves brain storming to generate creative solution. It also involves offers, counteroffers, and bargaining to reach a point of agreement.
5. *Building agreements*: Once the common ground of agreement is identified, negotiating parties prepare a draft of agreement. Such agreement may contain details regarding timelines, responsibilities, and any other conditions as agreed during negotiation.
6. *Closing the negotiation*: This stage involves ending the negotiation on a positive note, that is, signing the negotiation agreements.
7. *Implementation and control*: This stage involves putting terms of negotiation agreement into actions. It may further involve periodic review and progress of the implemented agreement.

12.7. Ensuring Effectiveness in Team Negotiation[6,15,17,24]

1. *Goal and strategy alignment*: Strategy of negotiation should be alignment with the organizational and team goals. Furthermore, it is imperative to ensure that all members of the team comprehend the benefits and objectives of the negotiation.[23]
2. *Surfacing and handling internal conflicts*: Conflict within the team can bring serious repercussions. Acknowledging divergent interests, personality differences, and a clear team vision can reduce the chances of conflict. The managers or team leader can also create a matrix of the matters that need to be handled to assess competing interests. They can further identify each issue's priorities and positions for themselves as well as for each team member.

---

[23]Brett, J. M., Friedman, R., & Behfar, K. (2009). How to manage your negotiating team. *Harvard Business Review, 87*(9), 105–109.

3. *Utilize data to support your arguments*: Conflicts of interest are frequently caused by the fact that members of a team do not have access to the same data. Negotiating team can provide better impact with the presentation of data and statistics that adequately illustrate their argument and impact of their efforts on their respective parties.

4. *Prepare together*: A negotiation's effectiveness is largely dependent on preparation. When more than one person will be negotiating, they should all prepare simultaneously. This will ensure that plans, interests, and strategies are all aligned. It will also ensure that all parties are aware of the limitations of the negotiation.

5. *Implementing a shared strategy*: Discipline breakdowns in negotiation can sabotage a team's strategy, revealing fissures that the other party exploits, often due to genuine differences in negotiation styles or lack of preparation.

6. *Ensure intra-team communication*: A team communication plan is often overlooked. Instead, they develop innovative methods, ranging from low-tech to high-tech, and from explicit to implicit. This includes using techniques like stretching and setting up chairs for sharing and passing information.

7. *Assess accountability*: Assigning roles to each team members should be accompanied by accountability to each role.

12.8. Caselet 12.1: Team Negotiation with a Diverse Team

Leading global provider of technology solutions, EPICTECH Corporation, was in the process of establishing a strategic alliance with SUN Electronics, a vital supplier. Several EPITECH's departments were involved in the negotiation including marketing, R&D, and procurement. Securing a long-term cooperation that would ensure creative product creation, mutual growth, and a solid supply chain was the main objective.

Important players of the negotiation are:

Negotiation team for EPICTECH Corporation comprised of (1) Head of Research and Development, (2) Procurement Manager, (3) Marketing Director, and (4) Legal Counsel.

The team of SUN Electronics negotiation team included (1) Chief Executive Officer, (2) Head of Sales, (3) Chief Technology Officer, and (4) Legal Advisor.

However, divergent interests of the teams made it difficult to match individual interests with the larger business objectives because each department at EPICTECH had distinct priorities and ambitions. The Head of Negotiation teams identified the following challenges with the team:

1. *Divergent interests*: It was difficult to match individual interests with the larger business objectives because each department at EPICTECH had distinct priorities and ambitions.

2. *Cultural disparities*: SUN Electronics had its headquarters in Japan, whereas EPICTECH Corporation was established in the United States. The

bargaining process became more complex due to cultural quirks and communication approaches.
3.   *Time restraints*: In order to meet market demands and seize strategic opportunities, both companies felt pressure to execute the cooperation agreement in a short amount of time.

> *Q1*. Keeping in mind the objectives of the negotiation, what strategies should be adopted to facilitate effective negotiation?

> *Q2*. How important is coordination in the above situation and how can it be ensured?

12.9. Activity 12.1: Team Negotiation and Diversity

Divide your group into two teams of employers and employees with diverse members who have come together to negotiate over the issue of workers' salary hike and bonus. Allow each member to negotiate on the issue with some assumptive facts. Conclude the session with various challenges faced by the members while negotiating as a team.

12.10. Part A (Self-assessment)

1.   What is the benefit of being well-prepared when negotiating as a team?
  a.   It gives the other team fear
  b.   It asserts authority
  c.   **It raises the possibility of success**
  d.   It speeds up negotiating

2.   What part does listening actively play in group negotiations?
  a.   It gains control of the discourse
  b.   **It shows compassion and understanding**
  c.   It scares the opposition side.
  d.   In negotiations, it is not necessary

3.   What makes flexibility crucial while negotiating as a team?
  a.   It permits one squad to rule the other
  b.   **It facilitates the investigation of substitutes and solutions**
  c.   It results in inflexible discussions
  d.   It demonstrates a lack of negotiation expertise

4.   Why is problem-solving important in team negotiations?
  a.   To give positions priority above underlying problems
  b.   **To incite additional disputes**
  c.   To deconstruct difficult issues and identify answers
  d.   To completely forego negotiation

5. What role does trust play in productive team negotiations?
   a. In negotiations, it is unimportant
   b. It asserts authority
   c. **It encourages sincere dialogue and teamwork**
   d. It gives the other team fear

6. How important is patience when negotiating as a team?
   a. It needlessly draws out the negotiation
   b. **It supports keeping focus and composure under pressure**
   c. In a negotiation, it is irrelevant
   d. It demonstrates a lack of negotiation expertise

7. In team negotiations, what constitutes a win–win solution?
   a. Solution that exclusively helps one group
   b. **A workable solution for both parties**
   c. A conflict-creating solution
   d. An approach that centers on outclassing the opposition

8. How can a team foster innovation during the bargaining process?
   a. By following strict schedules
   b. By eschewing substitute remedies
   c. By discouraging ideation meetings
   d. **By creating an atmosphere that values creative thinking**

9. How does coordination function in a negotiation team?
   a. It causes internal strife
   b. It causes the bargaining process to stall
   c. **It guarantees efficient communication and makes use of each person's unique strengths**
   d. It gives the other team fear

10. How can a negotiation process come to an end?
    a. Active listening
    b. Preparation
    c. **Closing, and agreement finalization**
    d. Solving issues

12.11. Part B (Review Questions)

1. What are the essential measures in getting ready for a group negotiation?
2. Emphasize the significance of comprehending the objectives of both your side and the other team prior to engaging in talks.
3. How can a group prepare for various negotiating scenarios and assess possible problems in an efficient manner?
4. What part does active listening play in group negotiations? How can it help to achieve positive results?

5. Which communication abilities are crucial for a team to have when negotiating? Give instances of the various applications for these skills.
6. Talk about how important teamwork is during negotiating. How can a cohesive team improve the results of negotiations?
7. Why is using a problem-solving strategy so important in group negotiations? Give an instance of a negotiation situation where innovative problem-solving was effectively used.
8. To come up with creative solutions during negotiations, how can a team foster creativity?
9. Describe the idea of win–win agreements in negotiations. Give an instance from real life where a negotiated deal was advantageous to all sides.
10. Talk about how trust functions in group negotiations. How can a team build and preserve confidence with the other team?
11. How can a team conduct itself honestly and openly when negotiating?

12.12. Part C (Glossary)

Functional conflict: Conflict that supports the goals of the individual/group or brings positive outcomes.

Team negotiation: A team negotiation involves the process of bargaining between two or more groups each represented by a team of individuals.

Group think: A psychological phenomenon known as "groupthink" occurs when members of a team/group try to reach an agreement.

Common information bias: It is sometimes referred to as shared information bias or collective information sampling bias, occurs when group members are more likely to discuss information that the entire group is already aware of the information that only some members know.

Chapter 13

Negotiation Skills: How to Stay Stronger in Negotiation

Learning Objectives:

- Key negotiation skills.
- Importance of negotiation skills.
- Application of negotiation skills.

13.1. Introduction

Negotiation plays an important role in our lives as well as in business contexts. Organizations have become considerate that the best negotiators are those who can create and assert value simultaneously. In other words, they are competitors as well as collaborators.[1] The qualities that enable us to come to agreements and settle conflicts with other parties are known as negotiation skills.[2] Negotiation is a global competence that encompasses various dimensions such as business, personal, and organizational. Effectiveness in negotiation is not only advantageous, but it also overcomes the opportunities lost due to incompetent negotiation. Negotiation skills are essential to be able to build strong personal as well as professional relationships.[3] The necessity for negotiation skills has been powered by the present interest in industrial relations.[4,5]

---

[1]https://www.pon.harvard.edu/daily/negotiation-skills-daily/top-10-negotiation-skills
[2]Roloff, M. E., Putnam, L. L., & Anastasiou, L. (2003). Negotiation skills. In J. O. Greene & B. R. Burleson (Eds.), *Handbook of communication and social interaction skills* (pp. 801–833). Routledge.
[3]Chapman, E., Miles, E. W., & Maurer, T. (2017). A proposed model for effective negotiation skill development. *Journal of Management Development, 36*(7), 940–958.
[4]Rackham, N. (1972). Developing negotiating skills. *Industrial and Commercial Training, 4*(6), 266–275.
[5]Kharbanda, O. P., & Stallworthy, E. A. (1991). Negotiation: An essential management skill. *Journal of Managerial Psychology, 6*(4), 2–52.

Managing and Negotiating Disagreements:
A Contemporary Approach for Conflict Resolution, 141–151
Copyright © 2024 by Bhawana Bhardwaj and Dipanker Sharma
Published under exclusive licence by Emerald Publishing Limited
doi:10.1108/978-1-83797-971-420241013

It has been observed that negotiations are substantially successful if we consider the psychological dynamics involved such as cognitive biases, emotional intelligence, as well as social perception.[6] A spectrum of negotiations ranging from the confrontational to the cooperative provides many options in which the outcomes can be made. Having good communication skills, including active listening skills, ability to reason, as well non-verbal communication that is paramount to understand others' perspectives and make our own interests known.[7,8] A successful negotiation also requires a well-thought-out plan to identify the Best Alternative to a Negotiated Agreement (BATNA) and conduct comprehensive research.[9]

An effective negotiation also demands strategies that help control the obstacles in negotiations such as handling difficult negotiators and managing disagreements. At the same time, ethical and green practices must be applied using standards of ethics of honesty, fairness, and integrity.[10,11] Furthermore, applying lessons in the real world or using case studies provides useful information on how to negotiate effectively. In a nutshell, growing your negotiating talents is important for handling the problems of modern life. By understanding the principles, developing communication skills, and accepting ethical issues, people can learn the art of negotiation and reach a win−win situation in both their personal and professional lives.[12,13]

13.2. Types of Negotiation Skills

A person can use a variety of skills and tactics to accomplish goals, come to agreements, and successfully settle disputes. Negotiation skills are the abilities that help to reach agreements and resolve disputes. These skills include the

[6]Ashcroft, S. (2004). Commercial negotiation skills. *Industrial and Commercial Training*, *36*(6), 229–233.

[7]Schneider, A. K. (2012). Teaching a new negotiation skills paradigm. *Washington University Journal of Law and Policy*, *39*, 13.

[8]Mircică, N. (2014). Constructive communication in effective negotiation. *Analysis and Metaphysics*, (13), 64–72.

[9]Beenen, G., & Barbuto, J. E., Jr. (2014). Let's make a deal: A dynamic exercise for practicing negotiation skills. *Journal of Education for Business*, *89*(3), 149–155.

[10]Anshima & Bhardwaj, B. (2023). Leveraging AI for the reinforcement of GHRM. In B. Bhardwaj, D. Sharma, & M. C. Dhiman (Eds.), *AI and emotional intelligence for modern business management* (pp. 64–76). IGI Global.

[11]Jangid, J., & Bhardwaj, B. (2024). Relationship between AI and green finance: Exploring the changing dynamics. In D. Sharma, B. Bhardwaj, & M. C. Dhiman (Eds.), *Leveraging AI and emotional intelligence in contemporary business organizations* (pp. 211–218). IGI Global.

[12]Make, Y. (2007). Principles and tactics of negotiation. *Journal of Oncology Practice*, *3*(2), 102–105.

[13]Downs, L. J. (2009). *Negotiation skills training*. American Society for Training and Development.

back-and-forth communication aimed at resolving conflicts between two or more persons. Any type of cooperative action, problem solving, and conflict resolution require negotiation, which can take many arrangements – verbal, nonverbal, explicit, implicit, direct, or through middlemen.[14] Some of the negotiation skills are as follows:

1. *Communication skills*: Effective communication is essential for understanding other person's point of view and effectively presenting your own. You just need to express your ideas clearly and listen to others attentively.[8] Effective communication is the key to a successful negotiation. Besides speaking effectively, negotiators should be able to listen carefully to the opinions of others and to express their ideas. A successful negotiation requires a person to have strong language skills and communication abilities.[15] The key focus of communication skills is to express ideas, proposals, and concepts in a straight and simple way:

   - *Active listening*: Paying attention to the perspectives, concerns, and intentions of others to reach areas of agreement and collaboration.
   - *Verbal convincing*: Gaining dominance over people's minds by means of persuasive language.
   - *Nonverbal communication*: Demonstrating confidence, empathy, and dependability via gestures, facial expressions, and body language.
   - *Questioning*: Use insightful questions to clarify details, make intentions known, and reveal ultimate aims and objectives.

2. *Emotional intelligence*: Emotional intelligence refers to the ability to identify, understand, and control one's own emotions as well as those of others during a negotiation. Allowing emotions to overpower rational thinking may affect the outcome. It is important to maintain emotional stability in negotiation.[16]

3. *Expectation management*: Effective negotiators put a lot of effort into making sure that both parties are happy with the agreement. Balancing your goals and the other side's expectations is important. Expectation management is the ability to coordinate and regulate expectations across all stakeholders, guaranteeing a practical comprehension of results and reducing unpleasant surprises.[17]

---

[14]https://www.pon.harvard.edu/tag/negotiation-skills/

[15]Musa, F., Mansor, A. Z., Mufti, N., Abdullah, N. A., & Kasim, F. D. (2012). Negotiation skills: Teachers' feedback as input strategy. *Procedia Social and Behavioral Sciences, 59*, 221–226. https://doi.org/10.1016/j.sbspro.2012.09.268

[16]Kim, K., Cundiff, N. L., & Choi, S. B. (2014). The influence of emotional intelligence on negotiation outcomes and the mediating effect of rapport: A structural equation modeling approach. *Negotiation Journal, 30*(1), 49–68.

[17]https://www.pon.harvard.edu/daily/conflict-resolution/managing-expectations/

4. *Problem-solving*: Successful negotiations depend on the ability of negotiators to recognize problems, come up with answers, and use your imagination to get over roadblocks. It is important to find a creative solution that benefit both sides.[18,19] The negotiation processes can help in handling a tough problem, get out of the obstacle, and get to the point of a mutual agreement. Problem-solving approach of negotiators can identify and bring forth new ideas, and analysis to tackle crucial issues. Following are essential elements of problem-solving abilities in negotiation:

   - *Analytical thinking*: Studying the issue's underlying causes, then choosing the relevant variables, and lastly assessing the possibilities in terms of feasibility and efficiency.
   - *Creativity*: Generating the ideas, preferences, and options that provide value and respect to all the stakeholders.
   - *Collaboration*: Considering the trade-offs, finding the solutions, identifying the points of agreement, and working with the modifications.
   - *Flexibility:* Maintaining a mindset and being flexible enough to explore the multiple methods and to change the plans as per the feedback and the evolving situation.

5. *Persuasion*: Persuasion is the art of getting people to embrace a specific idea, point of view, or agreement. Usually through skillful communication and reasoning, we need to convince others to value our proposal and address their concerns.[6,20,21]

6. *Rapport-building*: Rapport-building is the process of maintaining a good rapport with counterparts. Establishing trust and rapport with the other side is important for negotiation effectiveness.

7. *Active listening*: Active listening is one of the most important negotiating skills which involve giving attention to the speakers, understanding their views, and showing concern. Effective communication and teamwork are fostered through active listening, and that fosters rapport, trust, and understanding between the parties.[22,23]

---

[18]Putnam, M. E. R. L. L., & Anastasiou, L. (2003). Negotiation skills. In J. O. Greene & B. R. Burleson (Eds.), *Handbook of communication and social interaction skills* (pp. 819–852). Routledge.

[19]Menkel-Meadow, C. J., Schneider, A. K., & Love, L. P. (2020). *Negotiation: processes for problem solving*. Aspen Publishing.

[20]Sussman, L. (1999). How to frame a message: The art of persuasion and negotiation. *Business Horizons*, 42(4), 2–6.

[21]Manning, T. (2012). The art of successful persuasion: Seven skills you need to get your point across effectively. *Industrial and Commercial Training*, 44(3), 150–158.

[22]McMains, M. J. (2002). Active listening: The aspirin of negotiations. *Journal of Police Crisis Negotiations*, 2(2), 69–74.

[23]Jäckel, E., Zerres, A., & Hüffmeier, J. (2024). Active listening in integrative negotiation. *Communication Research*, 51(2), 231–254. https://doi.org/10.1177/00936502241230711.

8. *Assertiveness*: The ability to express yourself skillfully and bravely by stating your own needs, interests, and respecting the opinions and concerns of others is known as assertiveness. Assertiveness is the way that one puts forth one's interests in a very powerful way without being hostile or submissive.[24,25] Assertiveness comprises:

- *Clarity*: The characteristic of self-expression, communicating one's opinions, preferences, and priorities firmly, confidently, and in a clear and concise manner is an essential component of assertiveness.
- *Confidence*: Demonstrating confidence and steadiness, even in a challenging or aggravating environment.
- *Boundary setting*: It is important for an individual to prioritize the protection of their own self and to also express personal independence by clearly defining their own boundaries, limits, and expectations.
- *Negotiation framing*: Focus on the benefits of the cooperation, collaboration, and mutual benefit mechanisms to foster the cooperation.

9. *Adaptability*: Negotiators should be flexible and ready to adjust and articulate their strategies in a dynamic and unpredictable settings. Negotiators who are flexible can handle obstacles, react quickly to changing conditions, and use all possibilities.[26,27] Adaptability as a negotiation skill includes the following:

- *Flexibility*: Having an open mind along with a willingness to try new perspectives, facts, and ideas and being flexible to achieve negotiation goals.
- *Agility*: The flexibility to deal with a new scenario, different agendas, or newly emerging opportunities during negotiations.
- *Resourcefulness*: Applying thinking skills and resourcefulness to problem-solving and overcoming possible obstacles during negotiation.
- *Resilience*: The skill of being confident, optimistic, and persistent in achieving your objectives despite the presence of obstacles or opposition in a negotiation process.

10. *Empathy*: Empathy is defined as the ability to understand and put oneself in the position of the other person. Empathy is a feature that allows one to connect, show understanding, and gain the confidence of their counterparts

---

[24]Lee, J. I., Jang, D., Luckman, E. A., & Bottom, W. P. (2022). Wielding power in multiparty negotiations: The impact of communication medium and assertiveness. *International Journal of Conflict Management, 33*(1), 132–154.

[25]Norton, R., & Warnick, B. (1976). Assertiveness as a communication construct. *Human Communication Research, 3*(1), 62–66.

[26]Heunis, H., Pulles, N. J., Giebels, E., Kollöffel, B., & Sigurdardottir, A. G. (2024). Strategic adaptability in negotiation: A framework to distinguish strategic adaptable behaviors. *International Journal of Conflict Management, 35*(2), 245–269.

[27]Reynolds, M. (2019). *7 negotiation tactics that actually work*. Retrieved March 18, 2024, from HBS Online: https://online.hbs.edu/blog/post/negotiation-tactics-that-actually-work

which leads to better communication and collaboration.[28] The following strategies can be adopted to enhance the empathy:

- *Seeking viewpoint*: Seeking to see the situation through the other person's eyes to have a deeper understanding of their motivations, reasons, and feelings.
- *Active engagement*: Communicating sincere interest, consideration, and awareness of the other party's needs, problems, and feelings.
- *Emotional intelligence*: The skill of sensing, determining, and self-regulating one's own feelings and those of others to be used in analyzing situations with an aim to put care and sensitivity therein.
- *Relationship building*: Instances of showing respect, responsiveness, empathy, and trust throughout these actions.

Thus, negotiation skills are an array of abilities and techniques used to resolve conflicts, reach agreements, and attain goals. Negotiators can form stronger ties, promote cooperation, and come up with win−win outcomes in different scenarios through the development of these skills.

13.3. Importance of Negotiation Skills

The negotiation skills become essential to deal with and solve problems as well as effective communication in personal and professional contexts in this globally connected world. Understanding the processes via which managers pick up new skills and acquire knowledge is crucial at a time when management is more concerned with knowledge acquisition, learning, and continuous improvement.[29] Negotiation skills are essential in both personal and professional contexts due to several compelling reasons[30]:

1. *Strengthening relationships*: Negotiation skills play a substantial role in building and sustaining a strong relationship based on trust, respect, and mutual understanding. Efficient negotiators focus on conversation, trust, and cooperation, resulting in the atmosphere favorable for positive dialogue and teamwork. Through the process of listening carefully to counterpart's views and considering their interests, negotiators, thus, foster goodwill and rapport. In professional settings, the ability to make compelling relationships during negotiations is critical in the building of networks, the development

---

[28]Barkacs, L. L., & Standifird, S. (2008). Gender distinctions and empathy in negotiation. *Journal of Organizational Culture, Communications and Conflict, 12*(1), 83–92.
[29]Nadler, J., Thompson, L., Van Boven, L. (2003). *Learning negotiation skills: Four models of knowledge creation and transfer.* www.pon.harvard.edu
[30]Khan, M. A., & Baldini, G. M. (2019). Understanding the scope and importance of negotiation. In M. A. Khan & N. Ebner (Eds.), *The Palgrave handbook of cross-cultural business negotiation* (pp. 19–51). Palgrave Macmillan.

of partnerships, and the improvement of organizational performance. Similarly, in inter-personal relationships, negotiation abilities help individuals maneuver the differences, solve conflicts, and strengthen relationships with friends, family, and colleagues.[31]

2. *Goal achievement*: Negotiation skills play a very significant role in achieving personal and professional objectives. They give people the ability to represent their own interests, bargain for advantageous terms, and reach agreements. In a business realm, negotiations take place on a regular basis in various forms such as contract negotiation, sales transactions, and strategic partnerships. The skilled negotiators who use their communication skills, analytical abilities, and strategic thinking to reach deals that create value and achieve organizational objectives are referred to as effective negotiators. Likewise, these skills are very useful in our personal lives since we use them to make decisions regarding buying a house, planning a vacation or deal with conflicts within the relationships. Through the process of negotiation, an individual can articulate his/her needs, tackle the problems, and meet the goals, which is very important in achieving success.[18,32]

3. *Conflict resolution*: The fact of conflict being present in any type of human interaction is common. It may occur due to opposed views, perspectives, different interests, and various goals. The negotiation skills are of huge significance in the way conflicts are being solved through facilitating communications, understanding, and compromise. Negotiators may have different goals, conflict over those goals, but may also perceive the need to cooperate to some degree to achieve their goals.[33,34,35] Skilled negotiators possess the capacity to pay attention actively, to understand the opposite party's view, and to coproduce harmonious solutions. Through dialogue and partnership, negotiation competencies offset the tendency of conflicts to escalate, to preserve relationships, and create a cordial working environment to promote teamwork and a productive atmosphere.[34]

4. *Problem-solving and decision-making*: Negotiation skills give individuals the capability to break down complex problems and come up with solutions. Proficient negotiators go about resolving problems through interpretation of the underlying interests, identification of the common grounds and

[31]https://www.pon.harvard.edu/daily/business-negotiations/build-strong-relationships-in-business-negotiations-nb/

[32]Tasa, K., Whyte, G., & Leonardelli, G. J. (2013). Goals and negotiation. In *New developments in goal setting and task performance* (pp. 397–414). Routledge.

[33]Core, M., Traum, D., Lane, H. C., Swartout, W., Gratch, J., Van Lent, M., & Marsella, S. (2006). Teaching negotiation skills through practice and reflection with virtual humans. *Simulation, 82*(11), 685–701. https://doi.org/10.1177/0037549706075542

[34]Inayaturrahmah, R., Barkah, C. S., & Novel, N. J. A. (2022). Analysis the role of negotiation as communication skills in conflict management. *Jurnal Bisnis: Teori dan Implementasi, 13*(3), 217–227.

[35]Zartman, I. W. (2007). *Negotiation and conflict management: Essays on theory and practice*. Routledge.

creative solutions. Through risk assessment, tradeoffs analysis, and out-come examination, negotiators can optimize values and minimize negative impacts. Negotiation abilities of individuals allow them to have freedom of choice and conduct action in favor of their values, tastes, and long-term perspective.[19,36,37]

5. *Adaptability and flexibility*: Negotiation skills build on the adaptability and flexibility, allowing one to deal with the multiple situations and environmen-tal conditions successfully. Negotiators are trained to be flexible enough to adjust their strategy to the ever-changing situation, the counterpart, and the desired result, showing creativity and adaptability in the face of diffi-culty. Adaptability proves to be valuable in the current dynamic and inter-connected world where people meet all sorts of cultures, perspectives, and expectations. Competent negotiators can excel in a myriad of situations by drawing upon their inter-personal skills, cultural sensitivity, and emotional intelligence and attain the win−win agreement.[38,39]

6. *Empowerment*: Negotiating skills enable individuals to express their views and defend their rights. Effective negotiation skills such as active listen-ing, assertiveness, and problem-solving help in breaking down barriers and deliver autonomy and empowerment. Furthermore, it helps to improve self-esteem, confidence, and assertiveness. Through the acquisition of the skills and the assurance to negotiate in a constructive manner, negotiation skills build a feeling of control and belief that one can achieve his aspirations and power through challenges with self-reliance and persistence.

13.4. Situations in Which Negotiation Skills Can be Applied?

Negotiation is sometimes taught as a one-size-fits-all process, with the standard advice to be "tough on the issues and soft on the people" and to use common methods of "give and take" being applied to every negotiation, regardless of the situation or intended results.[3] However, negotiation skills are versatile and can be applied in following situations:

---

[36]Kelman, H. C. (1996). Negotiation as interactive problem solving. *International Negotiation, 1*(1), 99–123.

[37]Hopmann, P. T. (1995). Two paradigms of negotiation: Bargaining and problem solving. *The Annals of the American Academy of Political and Social Science, 542*(1), 24–47.

[38]Neville, L., Caza, B. B., & Olekalns, M. (2020). Negotiation resilience: a framework for understanding how negotiators respond to adversity. In C. Roux-Dufort Powley, E. H., Caza, B. B., & Caza, A. (Eds.), *Research handbook on organizational resilience* (pp. 70–84). Edward Elgar Publishing..

[39]Mitsea, E., Drigas, A., & Mantas, P. (2021). Soft skills & metacognition as inclusion amplifiers in the 21st century. *International Journal of Online & Biomedical Engineering, 17*(4), 121–132.

1. *Businesses negotiations:*

    - *Contract negotiations*: Negotiating over contract terms and conditions like payment terms, delivery dates, and prices.
    - *Vendor negotiations*: Bargaining for the terms, prices, and quality of goods and services with suppliers and vendors.
    - *Partnership negotiations*: Reaching mutual understanding to form business partnerships, joint ventures, or strategic alliances with potential collaborators. Commercial talks should ideally be based on mutual respect and trust.[6]
    - *Merger and acquisition negotiations*: Negotiating the clauses of mergers, acquisitions, or corporate takeovers, such as ownership structures, integration strategies, and valuation.

2. *Personal and inter-personal negotiations*:

    - *Family negotiations*: These concerns include solving disputes regarding parenting, house chores, money, and many other issues that arise in the family setting.
    - *Relationship negotiations*: These negotiations takes place in friendships, romantic relationships, or social circles, setting limits, making expectations, and finding compromises.
    - *Conflict resolution*: Coming to terms on how to deal with disagreements and conflicts with friends, neighbors, colleagues, or peers in social or personal situations.

3. *Legal negotiations:*

    - *Settlement negotiations*: The purpose of this is to end up with the less expensive and less time-consuming litigations.
    - *Contract negotiations*: These entail drafting clauses and provisions of contracts, agreements, or settlements that establish the basis of legal acts such as business partnerships or real estate transactions.
    - *Collective bargaining*: Labor unions represent the employees in the process of labor contract negotiations, agreements, and collective bargaining agreements with employers.

4. *Crisis and emergency negotiations*:

    - *Hostage negotiations*: These include talking with the hostage-holders or the offender to guarantee the release of the hostages and to find the least destructive solution.
    - *Crisis management*: It is a procedure of discussing emergency protocols, resolutions, or crisis responses during a case of terrorism, natural disaster, or another unexpected event.

5. *Employment negotiations:*

- *Salary negotiations*: Discussing compensation packages during job offers or performance reviews, including base wage, incentives, benefits, and stock options.
- *Contract negotiations*: Negotiating the terms of employment such as duties, schedules, and contract non-competition clauses.
- *Promotion negotiations*: Talking about wages, prospects for professional growth, and taking on more responsibility inside the company.

6. *Sales and customer negotiations*:

- *Price negotiations*: Bargaining with the clients or customers over the payment terms, discounts, and prices during sale transactions.
- *Service negotiations*: In service-oriented sectors, service agreements, contracts, or terms of service with clients or customers may be negotiated.
- *Customer dispute resolution*: Arranging settlements for complaints, disputes, or dissatisfaction of customers regarding goods and services.

7. *Diplomatic negotiations:*

- *International treaties*: The negotiations of such treaties, accords, or conventions take place between nations or international organizations in matters of trade, security, and environmental conservation.
- *Peace negotiations*: They include negotiations for ceasefires, peace treaties, or other means of conflict resolution between fighting groups or factions either in civil or international conflicts.
- *Diplomatic negotiations*: When diplomatic channels are used for diplomatic relations, alliances, or negotiation of international problems.

13.5. Part A (Self-assessment)

1. Negotiation is important in ——.
   a. Business relations
   b. Personal relationships
   c. Professional connection
   d. **All of the above**

2. Which of the following DOES NOT constitute negotiation skills' main function?
   a. Reaching deals that benefit both parties
   b. Handling disputes
   c. **Silencing dissenting opinions**
   d. Establishing and preserving connections

3. In conflict resolution, negotiation skills have a role in ——.
   a. Escalating confrontations
   b. Ignoring conflicts
   c. **Turning conflicts into opportunities**
   d. Avoiding conflicts completely

4. Why is active listening a vital tool for negotiators?
   a. **To hear and comprehend every concern that each party brings to the table for discussion**
   b. To listen to and consider each resolution proposal
   c. Putting on an air of interest to get the other person drop their guard.
   d. To oversee the celebration and handle future issues

5. Negotiation skills include ————.
   a. The capacity to win negotiation at all costs
   b. Manipulation strategies
   c. **Skills for coming to mutually beneficial agreements**
   d. Convincing others to accept unjust bargains

6. What is a fundamental component of effective negotiation?
   a. Avoiding any form of compromise
   b. Sticking to your guns when making demands
   c. **Actively listening and showing empathy for the other person**
   d. Taking the lead and managing the conversation

7. What are the advantages of emotional intelligence in negotiations?
   a. Dismissing emotions and concentrating only on the facts
   b. By manipulating the other person
   c. **By empathizing with them and controlling one's own**
   d. By completely avoiding emotions

13.6. Part B (Review Questions)

1. Discuss various types of negotiation skills.
2. Describe the role of negotiating skills in conflict management.
3. Explain the role that effective negotiation techniques play in organizational management.
4. Discuss the importance of good listening skills in negotiation.
5. Discuss the role of emotional intelligence in effective negotiation.

13.7. Part C (Glossary)

Salami tactics in negotiation: Negotiation by dividing demands into small manageable part and persuading the opposing side to accept each one.

Chapter 14

BATNA: Reserving Alternatives and Back Up

> **Learning Objectives:**
>
> - Understanding the concept of BATNA.
> - Benefits of BATNA in negotiation.
> - How to decide BATNA.
> - Rules for a good BATNA.
> - Importance of BATNA.

Having available options during a negotiation is a good alternative which empowers you with the confidence to either reach a mutually satisfactory agreement or walk away to a better alternative.[1]

Jane is a postgraduate student and desires to purchase a used textbook titled *Managing and Negotiating Disagreements: A Contemporary Approach for Conflict Resolution*. Used copies are available in the bookstore for $90. Although she is willing to spend up to $85 for one in good condition, her goal is to get one for $60. Joy, posted an advertisement promoting his old book *Managing and Negotiating Disagreements: A Contemporary Approach for Conflict Resolution* for $90. He will not go below that amount since he can sell it back to the bookshop for $65. When Jane arrives to look it over, she offers $65. However, they found the book in good condition and quickly agreed to $80.

[1]Sebenius, J. K. (2017). BATNA s in negotiation: Common errors and three kinds of "No". *Negotiation Journal*, *33*(2), 89–99.

Managing and Negotiating Disagreements:
A Contemporary Approach for Conflict Resolution, 153–161
Copyright © 2024 by Bhawana Bhardwaj and Dipanker Sharma
Published under exclusive licence by Emerald Publishing Limited
doi:10.1108/978-1-83797-971-420241014

Now consider the above situation again and imagine what will happen if they are unable to come to a mutually agreeable agreement, what will they do? Below are some options:

1.   Jane's alternative is to share a textbook with her roommate.
2.   Joy's option is to wait and see if a more generous buyer shows up or to sell the text to the bookstore.

The alternatives that are available to both negotiators are called the Best Alternative to a Negotiated Agreement (BATNA) and the zone which specifies the deals acceptable to both is the Zone of Possible Agreement (ZOPA).[2] Fig. 25 illustrates the BATNA and ZOPA available with Jane and Joy.

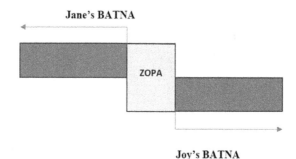

Fig. 25.   BATNA and ZOPA. *Source*: Created by authors in line with literature.

14.1. Introduction and Concept

The term BATNA was coined by Fisher et al. (1981) in their book *Getting to Yes*.[3,4,5] A well-crafted BATNA can prove to be a key driving force for a successful negotiation. Furthermore, it can help negotiating parties decide whether to accept or reject an offer.[6,7] The negotiators commonly do not accept a worse offer

[2]Yao, J., Zhang, Z. X., & Liu, L. A. (2020). When there is no ZOPA: Mental fatigue, integrative complexity, and creative agreement in negotiations. *Negotiation and Conflict Management Research*, *13*(3), 194–213. https://doi.org/10.1111/ncmr.12178
[3]Fisher, R., & Ury, W. (1981). *Getting to yes*. Houghton Mifflin.
[4]Fisher, R., Ury, W., & Patton, B. (1991). *Getting to yes: Negotiating agreement without giving in*. Penguin.
[5]https://www.pon.harvard.edu/category/daily/batna/?cid=11408
[6]Patel, B. N., & Rubin, G. D. (2016). Deal or no deal? Negotiation 101. *Journal of the American College of Radiology*, *13*(6), 756–758.
[7]Pinkley, R. L., Neale, M. A., & Bennett, R. J. (1994). The impact of alternatives to settlement in dyadic negotiation. *Organizational Behavior and Human Decision Processes*, *57*(1), 97–116.

than their BATNA.[8] Additionally, it acts as a point of leverage in negotiation and defines ZOPA. During a negotiation managers may overestimate their BATNA while investing little time in researching real options available, BATNA acts as a guiding torch for accepting or rejecting a negotiation offer. BATNA, therefore, is the next best offer you have gotten if you are negotiating pricing. Similarly, it is the finest job offer you have received while applying for a job. BATNA can be of three types listed below and displayed in Fig. 26.

1. *Walk away BATNA*: When a party decides to walk away from the negotiation if the suggested settlement is un-satisfactory. Negotiators use this tactic if there is an alternative available and the expected outcome is not attained. [9,10]
2. *Interactive BATNA*: When one or more sides in a negotiation are not cooperating with the other parties, interactive BATNAs are sought.[11]
3. *Third-party BATNA*: When two parties in a negotiation are unable to reach a consensus on their own or their disagreement is never-ending, third-party BATNAs are sought. If a negotiation impasse reached third party, BATNA can prove to be a helping hand.[12]

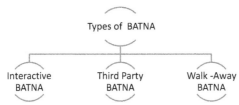

Fig. 26. Types of BATNA. *Source*: Created by authors.

14.2. Benefits of BATNA

When it comes to grounding positions on facts rather than feelings, a strong BATNA can be an important negotiation tool. Robust BATNAs also guarantee a

---

[8]Conlon, D., Pinkley, R. L., & Sawyer, J. E. (2014). Getting something out of nothing: Reaping or resisting the power of a phantom BATNA. In O. B. Ayoko, N. M. Ashkanasy, & K. A. Jehn (Eds.), *Handbook of conflict management research* (pp. 328–342). Edward Elgar.
[9]Hewlin, J. A. (2017). The most overused negotiating tactic is threatening to walk away. *Harvard Business Review*, 18.
[10]Berlin, J. W. (2008). The fundamentals of negotiation. *Canadian Association of Radiologists Journal*, *59*(1), 13.
[11]https://www.vskills.in/certification/tutorial/best-alternative-to-a-negotiated-agreement-batna/
[12]https://www.pon.harvard.edu/daily/batna/translate-your-batna-to-the-current-deal/#SnippetTab

contingency plan, ensuring that the organization won't be disrupted in the event that the negotiations fail. Some of the benefits of BATNA are as below[13]:

1. *Robust negotiation power*: BATNA enhances the negotiation power of the players. A solid ground for negotiations is established by being aware of your BATNA. Bargaining power is strong if BATNA is well-defined and strong.[14]
2. *Enhanced confidence*: Having a good BATNA helps you feel more confident when negotiating. You may make more intelligent decisions and moves with this confidence, which will improve the results. A strong BATNA gives you the confidence to withdraw from a negotiation if it does not satisfy your needs, and it can also be used as leverage to make the deal better.[15]
3. *BATNA sets the threshold*: BATNA sets the limit up to which bargaining can be stretched and protects the interest of the negotiating parties. It also helps define a ZOPA and determine the agreement's location (between each party's positions).[16]
4. *Decreased stress*: A strong BATNA reduces the urgency to come to a negotiation agreement at any cost. Consequently, one can make more rational decisions during negotiations.
5. *Better decision-making*: By understanding your BATNA, you can assess offers and proposals with greater objectivity. It assists you in determining whether the terms of the contract are preferable to what you could accomplish with your other option.[15]
6. *Planning strategies for negotiation*: A well-defined BATNA facilitates determining the acceptable/unacceptable phases which makes navigating the negotiating process simpler. Thus, strategies can be planned for the negotiation.[12]
7. *Flexibility*: A well-defined BATNA decides the flexibility to be offered during the negotiation process. If the other party declines to accommodate your expectations, you are free to explore your alternate options.[16]

[13]Kim, P. H., & Fragale, A. R. (2005). Choosing the path to bargaining power: An empirical comparison of BATNAs and contributions in negotiation. *Journal of Applied Psychology, 90*(2), 373.
[14]Lax, D. A., & Sebenius, J. K. (1985). The power of alternatives or the limits to negotiation. *Negotiation Journal, 1*(2), 163–179.
[15]Sebenius, J. K. (2001). Six habits of merely effective negotiators. *Harvard Business Review, 79*(4), 87–97.
[16]Brett, J. F., Pinkley, R. L., & Jackofsky, E. F. (1996). Alternatives to having a BATNA in dyadic negotiation: The influence of goals, self-efficacy, and alternatives on negotiated outcomes. *International Journal of Conflict Management, 7*(2), 121–138.

14.3. How to Decide a BATNA?

Negotiations can settle smoothly if we take the time to identify BATNA and consider how to make it stronger. A strong BATNA ensures better results as only those deals that are better than your BATNA will be accepted. Knowing that you are in a better position regardless of what happens will give you more confidence during the talks. If the negotiation fails or no agreement is reached, it comes down to determining what you should do to protect your interests. What is your contingency plan? A strong BATNA opens avenues for an increased number of viable options which reinforces the strength of the negotiator.

After calculating your BATNA, choose the option that will best serve your interests and be easier to achieve. Furthermore, we should remember that alternatives are not fixed and need a lot of consideration. As a result, spending some time figuring out what your BATNA is and considering how to make it stronger will help your discussions succeed. Increasing your BATNA ensures that you will get better results if you only make deals that are better than your BATNA. Thus, whatever the outcome, we will be in a better position.

While creating a BATNA, the following steps are adopted:

1. *List all the alternatives*: List as many options as you can think of that might be taken into consideration if the negotiations are unable to produce a satisfactory result.
2. *Evaluate the alternatives*: Evaluate these alternatives to decide which of the most promising options to implement as realistic steps.
3. *Identify and select the best alternative*: During the negotiation, decide which option is the best and keep it as a fallback. This is the best alternative to the current negotiation or BATNA.
4. *Identify your threshold value*: Identify the lowest valued deal acceptable for you to decide the threshold for applying BATNA.

14.4. Boosting Up Your BATNA

A strong BATNA can help you turn the tables. Following are the ways to strengthen a BATNA:

1. *Be creative*: Brainstorm to identify as many alternatives as possible. Creativity can enhance the number of available alternatives to enhance your bargaining position. Creativity also helps in planning according to the counterpart's interests and options.
2. *Expand your options*: The quantity of choices strengthens your best alternative. Another way to increase the options is to include interested third parties whose interests might align with important aspects of yours. When a third party enters the picture to undermine the strongest option on the other side, the game is played entirely different way.
3. *Involving experts:* Thirty impartial persons with the necessary experience may be able to unravel your issue and present it from a different, more appealing angle. Seek the assistance of experts in areas where your side is weak.

14.5. Rules for a Robust BATNA

1. *Do not disclose BATNA unless it is beneficial*: One should not reveal one's BATNA unless it is better than the other side thinks it is. If your BATNA is weak then revealing it will weaken your bargaining position.
2. *Separate individuals from objectives*: Getting personal during negotiation can affect the outcome. To achieve a goal, separate people from the problem during negotiations. Understand their feelings, opinions, values, and unique backgrounds to address misunderstandings and conflict directly. Imagine the situation from their perspective, and openly explore each side's perceptions. Key negotiation skills include avoiding blame.
3. *Prepare at all levels*: Being prepared is not the first step in a successful negotiation; rather, preparation is needed at every stage, from the beginning to the end of the agreement.
4. *Keep yourself free from biases*: Perceptual errors and biases may create a hurdle and optimum results may not be attained. Thinking and acting without bias and emotion can both serve to increase effectiveness.
5. *Don't bluff about your BATNA*: Avoid creating a fake or inflated BATNA to increase your negotiating leverage. If you lie, exaggerate, or misrepresent the truth, you risk losing your reputation in addition to your ethical standards.
6. *Assess the other party's BATNA*: As much as it is crucial to ascertain your BATNA, you should equally consider the options available to the other party. They could occasionally have an excessive amount of optimism about their options. Assessing the options available to other party helps in planning negotiation strategies and Framing BATNA.[17]

14.6. Why BATNA is Essential?

1. A negotiator will be in a very precarious position if they neglect to investigate their BATNA.
2. High internal pressure to reach a deal, as they will be unaware of BATNA could lead to negotiation failure.
3. The risk of reaching a deal without knowing other's options is minimized.
4. Overconfidence about proposed agreements could lead to an underestimation of the related costs.

14.7. Challenges of BATNA

Although using BATNA in negotiation processes has many benefits, there are drawbacks as well:

1. *Uncertainty*: It can be difficult to identify an accurate and trustworthy BATNA. Furthermore, it may suffer from a problem of measurement and

---

[17]Reynolds, J. W. (2014). Breaking BATNAS: Negotiation lessons from Walter White. *New Mexico Law Review, 45*, 611.

predictability.[18] The actual manifestation of an option may differ from initial assumptions, and future events and consequences are frequently unpredictable.

2. *Incomplete information*: It may be more difficult to accurately determine your BATNA if you don't have all the information regarding the interests, preferences, and available options of the other party. Inadequate information can cause errors in judgment and poor decision-making.

3. *Emotional factors*: When assessing BATNA, an emotional attachment to a specific result or solution may impair judgment. Individuals could undervalue the advantages of obtaining a negotiated agreement or exaggerate the value of their alternative.[19]

4. *Power imbalance*: The strength of a BATNA can be influenced by the power dynamics existing between the negotiation parties. The effect of BATNA may be lessened if one party is notably more powerful than the other and may be less inclined to take the other party's option into consideration.[20]

5. *Cultural and ethical considerations*: How parties view and use their BATNA may vary according to their cultural and ethical backgrounds. In one culture, anything that might be seen as a viable alternative might not be in another.

6. *Relationship impact*: Placing too much focus on BATNA may cause tension in inter-personal relationships. An agreement that is cooperative and advantageous to both parties may be undermined by an excessive focus on alternatives, which can foster a hostile and competitive environment.[21]

7. *Resources*: Calculating BATNAs can be a time-consuming, expensive, and complicated process.

14.8. Part A (Self-assessment)

1. In terms of negotiation theory, what does BATNA stand for?
   a. Fundamental Accord for Amicable Negotiation
   b. **More Sufficient Substitute for Non-Negotiation Agreement**
   c. The Greatest Substitute for a Negotiated Agreement
   d. The Advantageous Method for Negotiation Evaluation

2. Why is having a clearly defined BATNA crucial for negotiators?
   a. **To establish control over the other party**
   b. To lessen the pressure to decide all costs
   c. To do away with the necessity for negotiations
   d. To dazzle the other party with options

[18]Goovaerts, L. (2011). The challenges of BATNA. *Negociations*, *16*(2), 75–94.
[19]Van Kleef, G. A., De Dreu, C. K., Pietroni, D., & Manstead, A. S. (2006). Power and emotion in negotiation: Power moderates the interpersonal effects of anger and happiness on concession making. *European Journal of Social Psychology*, *36*(4), 557–581.
[20]Mannix, E. A., & Neale, M. A. (1993). Power imbalance and the pattern of exchange in dyadic negotiation. *Group Decision and Negotiation*, *2*, 119–133.
[21]Lempp, F. (2020). A new agent-based simulation model of bilateral negotiation. *International Journal of Conflict Management, 31*(1), 115–148.

3. Which of the following describes a weak BATNA as a possible risk?
   a. Greater ability to negotiate
   b. Overconfidence in the ability to negotiate
   c. Improved problem-solving skills
   d. **Limited flexibility and leverage**

4. What is an illustration of a BATNA among the following?
   a. **Accepting a job offer from a rival company**
   b. Bargaining with your present employer for a better wage
   c. Agreeing to terms that are unfavorable to prevent dispute
   d. Not engaging in any negotiation at all

5. What does the word "reservation value" mean in negotiations?
   a. **The negotiation's least acceptable result**
   b. Maximum achievable result
   c. Halfway point between desire and BATNA
   d. Best choice available to the opposing side

6. What part does BATNA play in the art of negotiating?
   a. It unilaterally decides the negotiation's conclusion
   b. **It establishes the framework for discussion and shapes decisions**
   c. It has no bearing on the negotiation process
   d. It only matters if the other party has a weak BATNA

14.9. Part B (Review Questions)

1. Describe the meaning of BATNA and how it affects the negotiating process.
2. Give an instance of a negotiation where having a solid BATNA would be beneficial.
3. Talk about a possible difficulty in assessing and applying BATNA during a discussion.
4. Describe in further detail the moral issues raised by utilizing BATNA in talks. Give instances to back up your claims.
5. What effects does the dynamic character of negotiations have on the assessment and efficacy of BATNA? Provide pertinent examples to support your discussion.

14.10. Part C (Glossary)

ZOPA: Zone of possible agreement is a term used in negotiations to characterize the space or range where two or more parties might work together to identify points of agreement.

Bargaining power: In business and negotiation, the term "bargaining power" describes the relative capacity of the participants in a negotiation to exercise influence and secure their desired results.

BATNA: The acronym BATNA represents Best Alternative to a Negotiated Agreement. It is a notion from negotiation theory that denotes what a side will do if talks fail to produce an agreement.

Reservation value: Least expected outcome or value from a negotiation.

14.11. Activity 14.1: BATNA in a Job Negotiation

As a job candidate, you are negotiating your pay with potential employers. An offer that pays 10% more than the existing offer on the table is your best and final offer (BATNA).

1. How specifically may you approach this pay negotiation to best utilize your BATNA?
2. Talk about the possible consequences of leaning too much on your BATNA during this negotiation.

Chapter 15

Post-negotiation Process: Evaluation and Introspection

> **Learning Objectives:**
>
> - Understanding the importance of post-negotiation process.
> - Activities to be performed after negotiation.
> - Tools for assessing the negotiation.
> - Post-negotiation evaluation questionnaire.
> - Personal excellence progress.

> The quality of a peace agreement is only equal to the quality of its implementation. While the handshake symbolizes the conclusion of a process, it simultaneously opens a new one, the need to forge a quality implementation.[1]

Negotiators typically concentrate on the deal at hand and the parties in attendance, ignoring other facets of the negotiated agreement that would affect parties outside the room and necessitate their cooperation for the agreement to be successful and implementable.[2] The execution of a negotiated agreement and its ramifications for future communication between the parties determine its success.[3] Implementing the negotiation agreement and overseeing its operation

---

[1] Jean-Paul Lederach. (2016) *After the handshake: Forging quality implementation of peace agreements*. Humanity United. Retrieved March 15, 2024, from https://www.humanityunited.org/after-the-handshake

[2] https://www.pon.harvard.edu/daily/negotiation-skills-daily/we-have-a-deal-now-what-do-we-do-three-negotiation-tips-on-implementing-your-negotiated-agreement/

[3] Mislin, A. A., Campagna, R. L., & Bottom, W. P. (2011). After the deal: Talk, trust building and the implementation of negotiated agreements. *Organizational Behavior and Human Decision Processes*, *115*(1), 55–68.

Managing and Negotiating Disagreements:
A Contemporary Approach for Conflict Resolution, 163–173
Copyright © 2024 by Bhawana Bhardwaj and Dipanker Sharma
Published under exclusive licence by Emerald Publishing Limited
doi:10.1108/978-1-83797-971-420241015

are the major tasks of the post-negotiation phase. This also involves the grievance procedures necessary in the event of a misunderstanding or contract violation. Since the relationship between labor and management is an ongoing endeavor, it is pertinent to uphold cordial relations.[4] To ensure adherence to the agreements made during the negotiation process and the positive relationship between two parties, post-negotiation actions are essential.[5] Post-negotiation typically involves the following activities:

1. *Documentation and verification*: This involves completing and examining paperwork related to the agreed-upon terms and conditions. This also involves verifying that everyone agrees with the terms and conditions. There are several ways to frame an agreement. However, it is the preference of the parties involved and the nature of the matter discussed that determine the framework of the agreement.[6] A thorough agreement that results from the conflict management negotiation process includes:
    a. Criteria for the successful implementation of an agreement.
    b. The consensus on the standards by which compliance is evaluated.
    c. The procedures and materials to carry out the agreement are spelled out clearly.
    d. The relevant stakeholders, who have given their explicit consent to participate in the implementation phase.
    e. If applicable, an organizational structure to carry out the agreement.
    f. The provision for future amendments to the existing provisions of the agreement.
    g. The role of the monitor is well defined.
    h. Procedures to manage un-intended or unforeseen difficulties in case they occur during implementation. Involvement of assistance of experts, and a temporary arrangement.
2. *Internal communication*: This involves notifying the departments and teams about the negotiation's results and terms and conditions to be followed by the company. This also involves giving instructions on how the agreement will affect different department's/company's functions.[7]

---

[4]Fisher, R., Ury, W., & Patton, B. (2011). *Getting to yes: Negotiating agreement without giving in*. Penguin Books.

[5]Burato, E., & Cristani, M. (2012). The process of reaching agreement in meaning negotiation. In *Transactions on computational collective intelligence VII* (pp. 1–42). Springer.

[6]Prietula, M. J., & Weingart, L. R. (2011). Negotiation offers and the search for agreement. *Negotiation and Conflict Management Research, 4*(2), 77–109.

[7]Mishra, K. E. (2007). *Internal communication: Building trust, commitment, and a positive reputation through relationship management with employees*. University of North Carolina at Chapel Hill.

3. *Legal review*: If legal documents are involved, ensure their accuracy and compliance with all applicable laws and regulations by conducting a complete legal assessment. Seek legal advice to resolve any doubts or possible problems.[8]
4. *Implementation*: When parties involved in the dispute bring an agreement into effect to end the discord, it is called implementation. Creating a thorough plan and detailing the implementation of the agreed-upon terms are important components of post-negotiation process. This also involves delegating and assigning tasks to groups or people to ensure efficient completion. Thus, it leads to ending the dispute and most agreement requires the reinstatement of parties previously involved in conflict. An agreement's implementation strategy and the procedure used to bring it into effect determine its success. It also depends on the parties' ability to carry out the terms of the agreement and how much they feel the sense of ownership in their agreement.[9,10] Thus, the following points summarize the success of agreement:
   a. The parties in dispute's willingness and capacity to abide by the agreement.
   b. Monitoring the protocols to ensure the effective implementation.
   c. The provision employed to manage non-compliance with the agreement through enforcement.
   d. The authority and function of the governing body or outside watchdog.
5. *Monitoring performance*: Creating measurements and tracking systems to keep an eye on how well each party is fulfilling their responsibilities. Monitoring also involves planning frequent check-ins to evaluate progress and handle any issues that may come up.

   A monitor may be assigned a responsibility to check and monitor the process. However, the role of a monitor is decided by the conflict stakeholder. The effective monitoring depends on the clarity regarding the standards to be measured and complied. The stakeholder also needs to decide the rules for winding up the negotiation agreement.[11] In this process, the roles of monitors can be:
   a. Whistle-blower who simply points out that an agreement has been broken.
   b. Enforce and oversee the implementation.
   c. Participates in upcoming negotiations over the grievances caused due to non-compliance with the negotiation agreement.

---

[8]Simmons, B. A. (1998). Compliance with international agreements. *Annual Review of Political Science*, *1*(1), 75–93.

[9]Chayes, A., & Chayes, A. H. (1993). On compliance. *International Organization*, *47*(2), 175–205.

[10]McLaughlin Mitchell, S., & Hensel, P. R. (2007). International institutions and compliance with agreements. *American Journal of Political Science*, *51*(4), 721–737.

[11]Markiewicz, A., & Patrick, I. (2015). *Developing monitoring and evaluation frameworks*. Sage Publications.

6. *Managing relationships*: By responding to issues, providing updates, and guaranteeing a cooperative execution strategy, we can cultivate a positive relationship. Keeping the lines of communication open and transparent can also help with the opposing party.[12]

7. *Feedback and evaluation*: Feedback plays an important role in ensuring the effectiveness.[13,14] It also ensures feedback on the negotiating process and results from the opposing party as well as internal stakeholders. Make use of this feedback to pinpoint areas in need of development and to strengthen your upcoming bargaining tactics.[15]

8. *Modifications and additions*: Be willing and open to modify or revise the agreement as needed in response to unforeseen difficulties or changing conditions. Remaining flexible and open to modification increases the chances of negotiation effectiveness.[16]

9. *Mechanisms for resolving disputes*: During the implementation phase, strengthen or set up procedures for settling conflicts. Make sure everyone is informed about the procedures for resolving disputes that have been agreed upon.[17]

10. *Celebrate the victory and joy*: Celebrating the success of a negotiation reinforces our happiness. Honor the completion of fruitful negotiations and the attainment of favorable accords. Express gratitude to the participating teams and promote an optimistic company culture.[18]

11. *Exchange of knowledge:* Numerous research studies have demonstrated the beneficial impact of group awareness support on cooperative learning. To improve organizational knowledge, compile and disseminate lessons learnt from the negotiating process.[19,20]

---

[12]Mnookin, R. H., Peppet, S. R., & Tulumello, A. S. (2000). *Beyond winning: Negotiating to create value in deals and disputes*. Harvard University Press.

[13]Maslovat, D., & Franks, I. M. (2019). The importance of feedback to performance. In M. Hughes, I. M. Franks, & H. Dancs (Eds.), *Essentials of performance analysis in sport* (pp. 3–10). Routledge.

[14]Chur-Hansen, A., & McLean, S. (2006). On being a supervisor: The importance of feedback and how to give it. *Australasian Psychiatry, 14*(1), 67–71.

[15]Park, C., Wilding, M., & Chung, C. (2014). The importance of feedback: Policy transfer, translation and the role of communication. *Policy Studies, 35*(4), 397–412.

[16]Hart, E., & Schweitzer, M. E. (2020). Getting to less: When negotiating harms post-agreement performance. *Organizational Behavior and Human Decision Processes, 156*, 155–175.

[17]https://www.mckinsey.com/capabilities/operations/our-insights/managing-conflict-effectively-in-negotiations

[18]https://hbr.org/2022/01/celebrate-to-win

[19]Fisch, D., Kalkowski, E., & Sick, B. (2011). Collaborative learning by knowledge exchange. In C. Müller-Schloer, H. Schmeck, & T. Ungerer (Eds.), *Organic computing—A paradigm shift for complex systems* (pp. 267–280). Springer Science & Business Media.

[20]Erkens, M., & Bodemer, D. (2019). Improving collaborative learning: Guiding knowledge exchange through the provision of information about learning partners and learning contents. *Computers & Education, 128*, 452–472.

12. *Reconvening sessions*: Arrange follow-up meetings with the other side to talk about the situation, resolve any issues, and improve the collaboration.
13. *Record-keeping and archiving*: For future reference, keep an extensive file of all papers and correspondence pertaining to the negotiation.

15.1. Assessing the Effectiveness of Negotiation Process

Developing a more reflective style of negotiation is one of the finest methods to get better at it. Post-negotiation appraisal is most beneficial in complex team situations. The evaluation can help the negotiation teams by highlighting areas in which further training is needed and by offering a helpful log of the negotiating process.[21],[22] The evaluation process consists of three steps: the first is to analyze the results and consider what you could have done differently, the second is to revisit the goal statements and assess whether you truly completed the task at hand, and the final step is to assess how the negotiation will impact your short and long-term objectives.

The following tools can be used for assessing the effectiveness of negotiation process.

15.2. Post-negotiation Evaluation Questionnaire

A post-negotiation evaluation questionnaire is a tool used to assess and gather feedback on the negotiation process after it has concluded. It is designed to capture insights from the participants involved in the negotiation, helping to identify strengths, weaknesses, and areas for improvement. The purpose of such a questionnaire is to enhance future negotiation strategies, refine communication practices, and ensure that lessons learned are incorporated into future negotiations. This technique has been used by various organizations to understand the effectiveness and success of negotiation.[23],[24],[25]

Components of post-negotiation evaluation questionnaire: A post-negotiation evaluation questionnaire can typically involve the following components:

---

[21]Scanzoni, J., & Godwin, D. D. (1990). Negotiation effectiveness and acceptable outcomes. *Social Psychology Quarterly*, 239–251.

[22]Fells, R., & Sheer, N. (2019). *Effective negotiation: From research to results*. Cambridge University Press.

[23]Coleman, P. T., & Lim, Y. Y. J. (2001). A systematic approach to evaluating the effects of collaborative negotiation training on individuals and groups. *Negotiation Journal*, *17*(4), 363–392.

[24]Delaney, M. M., Foroughi, A., & Perkins, W. C. (1997). An empirical study of the efficacy of a computerized negotiation support system (NSS). *Decision Support Systems*, *20*(3), 185–197.

[25]Mumpower, J. L., Sheffield, J., Darling, T. A., & Milter, R. G. (2004). The accuracy of post-negotiation estimates of the other negotiator's payoff. *Group Decision and Negotiation*, *13*, 259–290.

a. *Preparation and planning*: This component focuses on the effectiveness of preparation and planning involved in the negotiation process. The focus of this component is to receive feedback for understanding the preparation and clarity regarding the goals of the negotiation. The response can be collected on a rating scale. Sample questions are as follows:
    1. Did you feel adequately prepared for the negotiation?
    2. Were the negotiation objectives clear and well defined?

b. *Communication and relationship building*: This component assesses the communication effectiveness process adopted during negotiation and the role of negotiation approach in relationship building among conflicting parties. Some of the representation questions assessing this component may be as given below:
    1. How effective was communication between your team and the other party?
    2. Were relationship-building strategies successful?

c. *Flexibility and adaptability*: This component assesses the adaptability of negotiation parties as per the changing circumstances during negotiation process. Examples of questions to be asked for assessing flexibility and adaptability are as follows:
    1. Did your team demonstrate flexibility in response to changing circumstances?
    2. Were adaptations to the negotiation strategy made when necessary?

d. *Agreement and outcome*: The extent to which the objectives of negotiation are met and parties are satisfied with the outcome can be measured through this component. Examples of questions are as follows:
    1. Did the final agreement meet your team's objectives?
    2. Were both parties satisfied with the negotiated outcome?

e. *Implementation and follow-up*: This component intends to measure the effectiveness of implementation negotiation agreement. This component seeks to answer the following questions:
    1. Were implementation plans clearly outlined in the agreement?
    2. Is the follow-up process well defined and understood?

f. *Overall satisfaction*: It involves measuring the overall satisfaction of negotiation parties for the negotiation process. The example question is as follows:
    1. How satisfied are you with the process of the negotiation conducted?

Apart from the above scale-based responses, open ended questions are also asked to understand other dimensions of negotiations. For example:

1. What aspects of the negotiation process worked well?
2. What challenges or issues did you encounter during the negotiation?
3. Are there any suggestions for improvement in future negotiations?

The questionnaire can be distributed among team members and other stake-holders involved in the negotiation process. The responses can provide valuable insights into the effectiveness of the negotiation strategy, communication prac-tices, and overall satisfaction with the outcome. The feedback collected can then be analyzed to inform future negotiations and improve the organization's overall negotiation capabilities.

15.3. PEP (Personal Excellence Progress)

Personal excellence programs strive to achieve the goal of personal growth and development we need to understand our own strengths and weaknesses. A per-sonal excellence program can be a valuable tool in the context of negotiations, helping individuals enhance their negotiation skills, build effective strategies, and achieve successful outcomes. Here's how a personal excellence plan can be applied to negotiation:

1. *Define negotiation goals*: Clearly articulate your negotiation goals within the framework of your personal excellence plan. Identify both short and long-term objectives related to the negotiation process.
2. *Develop communication skills*: Include communication skills enhancement in your plan. Effective negotiation requires strong communication, active lis-tening, and the ability to convey ideas persuasively. Consider specific actions to improve these skills.
3. *Identify core values in negotiation*: Understand and incorporate your per-sonal values into the negotiation process. Define the ethical principles and boundaries that will guide your decision-making during negotiations.
4. *Set SMART objectives for negotiations*: Apply the SMART criteria (Specific, Measurable, Achievable, Relevant, Time-bound) to your negotiation goals. Break down larger negotiation objectives into smaller, manageable tasks with clear timelines.
5. *Plan negotiation strategies*: Develop comprehensive strategies for different negotiation scenarios. Consider factors such as BATNA (best alternative to a negotiated agreement), concessions, and collaborative problem-solving approaches.
6. *Continuous learning and skill development*: Regularly update your plan with opportunities for learning and skill development related to negotiation. This could involve reading negotiation literature, attending workshops, or seeking mentorship from experienced negotiators.
7. *Build relationships and networks*: Include relationship-building strategies in your plan. Successful negotiation often relies on strong interpersonal connec-tions. Identify key stakeholders and cultivate relationships that can enhance your negotiation effectiveness.
8. *Assess and manage risks*: Develop a risk assessment strategy within your plan. Anticipate potential challenges and devise contingency plans to address unexpected issues that may arise during negotiations.

9. *Evaluate and learn from past negotiations*: Incorporate a reflection and feedback loop in your plan. Evaluate the outcomes of past negotiations, identifying strengths and areas for improvement. Adjust your strategies based on lessons learned.
10. *Self-care and well-being*: Recognize the importance of personal well-being during negotiations. Ensure that your plan includes provisions for stress management, maintaining a healthy work–life balance, and addressing any personal factors that may affect your negotiation performance.
11. *Cultural awareness and sensitivity*: If you are engaging in cross-cultural negotiations, incorporate cultural awareness and sensitivity training into your plan. Understand the cultural nuances that may impact negotiation dynamics.
12. *Regular plan review and adaptation*: Periodically review and update your personal excellence plan to align with evolving negotiation goals, changing circumstances, and new learnings.

By integrating negotiation-specific components into a personal excellence plan, individuals can systematically enhance their negotiation skills, adapt to different situations, and ultimately improve their overall effectiveness in the negotiation process.

15.4. Part A (Self-assessment)

1. What is the post-negotiation process's main goal?
    a. First agreement
    b. **Relationship management and implementation**
    c. Court records
    d. Planning before negotiations

2. Which of the following is essential for preserving a good relationship during the post-negotiation phase?
    a. Disengagement
    b. Documentation
    c. Feedback and assessment
    d. **Internal communication**

3. What does "performance monitoring" mean in the context of negotiations?
    a. Pre-negotiating assessments
    b. Competitor monitoring
    c. **Tracking progress toward fulfilling negotiated requirements**
    d. Assessing negotiation tactics

4. Why is post-negotiation process ongoing improvement important?
    a. Enhancing legal compliance
    b. **Fostering pleasant relationships**
    c. Refining negotiating methods for future success
    d. Expediting the negotiation process is just one of the benefits

5. Which action is related to modifying an agreement's terms in light of evolving circumstances?
   a. Relationship management
   b. Evaluation and feedback
   c. **Modifications and amendments**
   d. Dispute resolution

15.5. Part B (Review Questions)

1. Describe the role that legal review plays in the post-negotiation process. Give an illustration.
2. Describe the essential components of a successful post-negotiation implementation plan.
3. In what ways can organizations cultivate a constructive rapport in the aftermath of the negotiating process? Give a minimum of three tactics.
4. Talk about the importance of evaluation and feedback in the post-negotiation phase. How can businesses use input to make ongoing improvements?
5. Analyze the difficulties involved in putting negotiated agreements into practice and provide solutions.
6. Select an actual instance of a fruitful post-negotiation procedure. Examine the elements that made it successful and the lessons that can be drawn from it.

15.6. Part C (Glossary)

Personal excellence plan: Conflict that supports the goals of the individual/group or brings positive outcomes.

Whistle blowing[26,27]: Whistleblowing is characterized as a dissenting act of public accusation against an organization.

Post-negotiation evaluation questionnaire: A post-negotiation evaluation questionnaire is a tool used to assess and gather feedback on the negotiation process after it has concluded.

Divide your group into two sub-groups. Assign your instructor the role of facilitator. Conduct a negotiation session over duties to be performed in an upcoming event in your organization. Assess the effectiveness of negotiation through post-negotiation effectiveness questionnaire given in Table 4.

---

[26]Near, J. P., & Miceli, M. P. (1996). Whistle-blowing: Myth and reality. *Journal of Management*, 22(3), 507–526.

[27]Jubb, P. B. (1999). Whistleblowing: A restrictive definition and interpretation. *Journal of Business Ethics*, 21, 77–94.

Table 4.   Activity.

Statement	Not at All	No	May Be	To Some Extent	To a Great Extent
	1	2	3	4	5
1. Did a deal come to an end during the negotiation?					
2. Did you make a mistake by failing to adjust to new knowledge or come up with innovative solutions?					
3. Is there something you might be doing better for yourself than what you agreed upon or the option that was accessible to you when the negotiations ended?					
4. Did a genuine disagreement for which you were unable to reach a mutually acceptable solution cause the negotiations to end?					
5. If negotiations resulted in a resolution, did you get the issue somewhat closer to your goal?					
6. Did you feel sufficiently prepared for the engagement from your pre-negotiation preparation?					
7. Were the needs, advantages, and disadvantages of the opposing side sufficiently and accurately anticipated?					
8. If negotiations resulted in a resolution, did you get the issue somewhat closer to your goal?					
9. Did you feel sufficiently prepared for the engagement from your pre-negotiation preparation?					

Table 4. (*Continued*)

Statement	Not at All	No	May Be	To Some Extent	To a Great Extent
	1	2	3	4	5
10. How well did you evaluate your own requirements, advantages, and disadvantages?					
11. Did you get the issue somewhat closer to your goal?					
12. Did you establish a sufficiently ambitious goal?					
13. Did your realistic setting and solid support enable you to meet your goal?					
14. Did you learn anything that surprised you?					
15. Did you extend the initial proposal? Was that really necessary?					
16. Did your habit of compromise work? Did the increments get too big? Did you give in too much too often?					
17. Did your habit of compromise work?					
18. Was the overall amount of concessions you made about the same as or less than the overall amount made by the other side? If not, what justification exists?					
19. Did the opposing side endorse the stance you took from them?					
20. How successfully did you manage your responses to the strategies used by the opposition?					

Chapter 16

Third-party Interventions: When Negotiation Doesn't Work

Learning Objectives:

- Third-party peace making.
- Forms of third-party intervention.
- Understanding mediation.
- Understanding conciliation.
- Understanding adjudication.

In the context of conflict resolution, third-party interventions refer to the involvement of an independent, impartial party to assist in the resolution of disagreements or conflicts. Third-party interventions are used to facilitate communication, negotiation, and settling disagreements in a mutually accepted form.[1] Third parties typically do not hold a strong partisan stance on the issue at hand; instead, they try to assist parties in reaching a settlement. Invited or uninvited, formal, or informal, acting alone or on behalf of a group or constituency, more or less "neutral," advising or directing, and favoring the content (result) and/or process (method) of their intervention are all possible outcomes for third parties.[2] Tactics employed by third parties to aid in conflict resolution include open dialogues, fostering understanding, and identifying mutually acceptable solutions rather than formal and confrontational processes like litigation. However, the success of the approach is contingent on the willingness of stakeholders to participate and look

---

[1]Rubin, J. Z. (1980). Experimental research on third-party intervention in conflict: Toward some generalizations. *Psychological Bulletin*, *87*(2), 379.
[2]Lewicki, R. J., Weiss, S. E., & Lewin, D. (1992). Models of conflict, negotiation and third party intervention: A review and synthesis. *Journal of Organizational Behavior*, *13*(3), 209–252.

Managing and Negotiating Disagreements:
A Contemporary Approach for Conflict Resolution, 175–184
Copyright © 2024 by Bhawana Bhardwaj and Dipanker Sharma
Published under exclusive licence by Emerald Publishing Limited
doi:10.1108/978-1-83797-971-420241016

forward to the areas of agreement. Involving a third party can help prevent conflict escalation, save time and resources, and lead to more amicable and long-term outcomes. The method of intervention chosen is determined by the nature of the conflict and the preferences of the parties involved.

16.1. Forms of Third-party Intervention in Conflict Management

Commonly used forms of third-party interventions are as follows:

16.1.1. Mediation

Mediation entails a neutral third party, known as a mediator, who assists disputing parties in communicating, identifying concerns, and working together to find solutions. The mediator does not make decisions for the parties, but rather helps them toward a mutually acceptable agreement. Mediation is frequently utilized in family disagreements, industrial problems, and legal disputes.[3,4,5,6]

Mediator: A mediator is a neutral party that assists disputants in communicating and understanding each other's viewpoints.[7] The mediator facilitates a structured dialogue, helps identify underlying issues, and supports the development of mutually agreeable solutions. Mediation is often less formal than legal proceedings and allows for more flexibility in finding creative solutions.[8]

Mediation approaches: Fig. 27 describes the types of mediation approaches[9,10,11]:

---

[3]Bercovitch, J. (2009). Mediation and conflict resolution. In J. Bercovitch, I. W. Zartman, & V. Kremenyuk (Eds.), *The SAGE handbook of conflict resolution* (pp. 340–357). SAGE.

[4]Ott, M. C. (1972). Mediation as a method of conflict resolution: Two cases. *International Organization, 26*(4), 595–618.

[5]Winslade, J., & Monk, G. D. (2000). *Narrative mediation: A new approach to conflict resolution*. John Wiley & Sons.

[6]Jeong, H. W. (2009). *Conflict management and resolution: An introduction*. Routledge.

[7]Silbey, S. S., & Merry, S. E. (2018). Mediator settlement strategies. In C. Menkel-Meadow (Ed.), *Mediation* (pp. 183–208). Routledge.

[8]Shapiro, D., Drieghe, R., & Brett, J. (1985). Mediator behavior and the outcome of mediation. *Journal of Social Issues, 41*(2), 101–114.

[9]Benedikt, A., Susło, R., Paplicki, M., & Drobnik, J. (2020). Mediation as an alternative method of conflict resolution: A practical approach. *Family Medicine & Primary Care Review, 22*(3), 235–239.

[10]Alfini, J. J. (1996). Evaluative versus facilitative mediation: A discussion. *Florida State University Law Review, 24*, 919.

[11]Roberts, K. M. (2007). Mediating the evaluative-facilitative debate: Why both parties are wrong and a proposal for settlement. *Loyola University Chicago Law Journal, 39*, 187.

1. *Facilitative mediation*: In this, a mediator plays the role of a facilitator by structuring the process to support the parties in the attainment of a mutually agreeable decision. The only role of the mediator is asking questions, validating the information, and normalizing the parties. The mediators do not recommend or advice the conflicting parties. The mediator is responsible for the process while the parties are responsible for the outcome.
2. *Evaluative mediation*: In this process, mediator may point out weaknesses of the parties and may make formal and informal recommendations. Thus, the mediator takes the responsibility of structuring the process as well as directly or indirectly influencing the decisions. Conflicting parties are mostly present in the mediation. However, the mediator may also meet with the parties in isolation as well.
3. *Transformative mediation*: This approach particularly attempts to transform the relationship between conflicting parties by empowering each party and recognizing the needs, interests, and values of other parties involved. Like facilitative mediation, the process allows and supports the parties in mediation to determine the direction of their own process.

Merits of mediation:

1. *Less expensive*: Mediation is a relatively less expensive method than the court trial or arbitration.
2. *Quick method*: This is a quick method of conflict resolution.
3. *Relatively simpler method*: As mediation does not include cumbersome procedures and just relies on a general rule of fairness, hence it is considered a simple approach to conflict settlement.
4. *Flexibility*: Mediation permits the conflicting parties to modify and readjust the issues of conflict taken up for discussion. The flexibility allows negotiators to act as problem solvers rather than problem creators.
5. *Acceptable solution*: As the agreement of mediation is in consent with the parties involved, the acceptability of the solution is high. Thus, the agreements are more likely to be fulfilled.

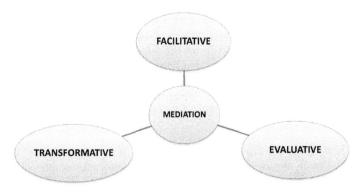

Fig. 27.   Types of Mediation.

Demerits of mediation:

1. *Mediation does not guarantee a settlement*: As mediation is intended to bring the conflicting parties together, it is not necessary that the parties agree on a particular outcome.
2. *Lacks procedures*: Mediation process lacks structured procedures and thus may not bring out desired outcomes and sometimes inequitable settlement.
3. The legal instance cannot be set in mediation. The methods cannot be used to settle legal matters.
4. No formal investigation processes. The mediators have to rely on the information presented by the conflicting parties and no formal investigation of facts and data can be conducted.

16.1.2. Conciliation

This is a third-party intervention where a conciliator helps parties to examine their interests and try to come to a consensus. The conciliator may offer recommendations and fill in communication gaps to promote resolution. It is a voluntary procedure because the parties to a dispute consent voluntarily to have their disagreement settled through conciliation. Furthermore, it is a flexible process where the parties can decide the time and place for conciliation, structure, content, and terms of negotiations.[12,13]

Conciliation is a process where a reliable third party acts as a go-between for the adversaries to identify problems, reduce hostilities, and promote direct communication – typically through negotiation. While conciliation and mediation share the goal of fostering a constructive working relationship between the disputing parties, conciliation differs from mediation. The "conciliator" is an unbiased third party who helps the parties reach a mutually agreeable resolution by facilitating their talks. Even though it sounds a lot like mediation, these two approaches to conflict resolution are very different from one another. Through settlement proposals, the conciliator offers the parties involved an advice on potential solutions and participates in a relatively direct role in the actual resolution of the conflict. The conciliator helps in communication and problem-solving but does not impose a decision. The neutral party in conciliation is typically viewed as an authoritative entity tasked with determining what is best for the parties. The terms of settlement are frequently developed and proposed by the conciliator, not the parties. The parties decide on the suggestions offered by conciliators after approaching the conciliator for advice. In this sense, a conciliator's role and a mediator's role are different. The mediator always upholds objectivity and neutrality. A mediator neither limits their attention to conventional concepts of culpability nor takes full responsibility for coming up with solutions.[14]

---

[12]Chalmers, W. E. (1948). The conciliation process. *ILR Review*, *1*(3), 337–350.
[13]Reif, L. C. (2007). The use of conciliation or mediation for the resolution of international commercial disputes. *Canadian Business Law Journal*, *45*, 20.
[14]Wenying, W. (2005). The role of conciliation in resolving disputes: A PRC perspective. *Ohio State Journal on Dispute Resolutions*, *20*, 421.

Rather, a mediator acts as a partner with the parties, helping them to discover the best course of action to accomplish their goals. The main responsibility of a mediator is to support the parties' own dialogue, representation of their own interests, and search for a good, reasonable, and sustainable solution together. In mediation, the parties take an active part by expressing their interests, outlining potential solutions, and deciding how to respond to one other's suggestions. The parties visit the mediator to work out the best solution on their own.

Characteristics of conciliation[15,16,17]:

a. *Voluntary procedure*: It is a voluntary procedure because the parties to a dispute consent voluntarily to have their disagreement settled through conciliation.
b. *Flexible*: Parties can decide the time and place for conciliation, structure, content, and terms of negotiations.
c. *Non-binding*: The decision suggested is not binding on the disputing parties.

16.1.3. Arbitration

Arbitration is a form of alternative dispute resolution (ADR) in which an impartial arbitrator evaluates the arguments and evidence presented by both parties and renders a decision. An arbitrator is a neutral third person who mediates disputes between parties in a dispute without taking a case to court. Due to its general speed and flexibility compared to traditional litigation, arbitration is a preferred method of dispute resolution. It is often employed as a formal alternative to litigation in labor negotiations and corporate disputes.[18,19]

Features of arbitration[20]:

1. *Voluntary agreement*: Generally, parties choose to arbitrate disputes willingly, either by mutual agreement after a disagreement occurs or by a pre-existing agreement (like a contract with an arbitration clause).
2. *Neutral third party*: The matter is heard by an arbitrator or panel of arbitrators. These people are typically unbiased, unbiased specialists in the pertinent topic.

---

[15]Watson, V. (1966). Possibilities and limitations of conciliation procedures. *Journal of Industrial Relations*, *8*(1), 25–35.
[16]Loquin, E. (2019). Notions of conciliation, mediation and arbitration. *International Business Law Journal*, *6*, 549–566.
[17]Terry, S. (1987). Conciliation: Responses to the emotional content of disputes. *Mediation Quarterly*, *16*, 45–52.
[18]Paulsson, J. (2013). *The idea of arbitration*. OUP Oxford.
[19]Elkouri, F., Elkouri, E. A., Ruben, A. M., American Bar Association, & Employment Law. (1973). *How arbitration works* (p. 2). Bureau of National Affairs.
[20]Stipanowich, T. J. (2010). Arbitration: The new litigation. *University of Illinois Law Review*, *2010*, 1.

3. *Decision is binding*: In most cases, the arbitrator's ruling is legally enforceable in court. Non-binding arbitration is a situation in which the parties may agree to a ruling that is advisory only and not enforceable absent consent from both parties.
4. *Confidentiality*: The specifics of the disagreement are not made public during arbitration hearings, which are frequently private.
5. *Limited rights of appeal*: An arbitrator's judgment can often only be appealed under limited circumstances, which helps to provide a more definitive and final outcome.
6. *Costs and efficiency*: Considering the probable time and money involved in court procedures, arbitration is sometimes viewed as a more cost-effective option than litigation, even though there may be costs involved.

16.1.4. Adjudication

In the process of adjudication, a judge or other comparable authority considers the evidence and contentions made by the parties to a dispute before rendering a decision. This procedure is frequently employed in court systems to settle disputes and carry out justice, and it is usually connected to formal legal processes. Adjudication is extensively used in many different legal circumstances, including administrative law, civil litigation, and ADR procedures like building and contract disputes.[21,22]

A wide range of situations calls for adjudication, such as administrative hearings, civil court trials, labor disputes, and contract disputes. It offers a substitute for expensive and time-consuming court cases. Many times, adjudication is thought to be a quicker and less expensive option than traditional litigation. It assists parties in avoiding legal actions and speeds up the resolution of conflicts. There can be choices for appealing the adjudicator's decision to a higher authority, depending on the jurisdiction and circumstances of the dispute. In the legal system, adjudication is crucial because it offers a quick and convenient way to settle disagreements, particularly in situations where a formal court ruling is needed. It is a crucial part of justice and conflict resolution, with the goal of bringing clarity and closure to contentious subjects.

The following are some of the key components of adjudication:

1. In adjudication, the facts are examined, the law or pertinent contract provisions are interpreted, and a judgment or decision is rendered by an impartial and neutral decision-maker.[23]
2. It is a formal, systematic process and may involve the parties to the dispute submitting their arguments, supporting documentation, and legal reasoning.[23]

---

[21]Sarat, A., & Grossman, J. B. (1975). Courts and conflict resolution: Problems in the mobilization of adjudication. *American Political Science Review, 69*(4), 1200–1217.
[22]Gent, S. E., & Shannon, M. (2010). The effectiveness of international arbitration and adjudication: Getting into a bind. *The Journal of Politics, 72*(2), 366–380.
[23]Matheson, I. (1983). Adjudication and dispute settlement. *Victoria University of Wellington Law Review, 13*, 151.

3. Statutes, regulations, and legal precedents serve as the foundation for adjudication. These legal precepts are applied by the adjudicator to the facts and contentions made throughout the hearings.[23]
4. Since adjudication procedures are typically held in public, the legal system is transparent. Public access is granted to courtrooms, and decisions are frequently made available to the public.
5. Parties have the option to appeal an adjudication judgment in several legal systems. Higher courts could examine the legal logic and soundness of the initial ruling through appeals.
6. Adjudication can be used in a range of legal situations, such as criminal cases, administrative law cases, civil disputes, and regulatory difficulties.[22]
7. A judge, magistrate, administrative tribunal, or another person with the authority to make legal decisions provides a verdict for adjudication.[24]
8. Parties submit evidence, make legal arguments, and present their cases in formal legal proceedings known as adjudication. When compared to certain other forms of ADR, such as mediation, this procedure is frequently more formal and regimented.

    Generally, the parties concerned are bound by the decision or judgment made during adjudication. This implies that they must abide by the ruling, and frequently, there are procedures in place to make sure the ruling is carried out.[25]
9. The adjudication decision is legally binding on the parties in many cases. This implies that they must abide by the ruling, which may need to be legally enforced.[26]

16.2. Part A (Self-assessment)

1. What is a third party's main function in resolving disputes?
    a. Making decisions
    b. Advising
    c. Advocacy
    d. **Neutral facilitator**

2. The role of the third party under the facilitative model of third-party conflict resolution is mainly to ——.
    a. Make a binding decision
    b. Assess the case's merits
    c. **Assist the parties in coming to their own accord**
    d. Represent one of the disputing parties.

---

[24]https://www.oxfordlearnersdictionaries.com/definition/english/adjudication
[25]Fuller, L. L. (1978). The forms and limits of adjudication. *Harvard Law Review*, *92*, 353.
[26]Peters, C. J. (2002). Participation, representation, and principled adjudication. *Legal Theory*, *8*(2), 185–219.

3. Which of the following describes a type of third-party intervention in which an impartial third party assists parties in dispute to come to a voluntary agreement?
   a. Litigation
   b. Arbitration
   c. **Mediation**
   d. Negotiation

4. What is the main benefit of resolving conflicts through the mediation of a neutral third party?
   a. Quick decision-making
   b. **Impartiality**
   c. Speed
   d. Formal legal processes

5. Which phrase describes a decision rendered by a third party that the disputing parties must abide by legally?
   a. Mediation
   b. **Arbitration**
   c. Mediation
   d. Assistance

6. When it comes to resolving conflicts, which ethical value ought a third party to put first?
   a. Partiality
   b. **Neutrality**
   c. Advocacy
   d. Favoritism

7. Which third-party conflict resolution model emphasizes transforming the relationships between the parties involved in the conflict?
   a. Facilitative
   b. Evaluative
   c. **Transformative**
   d. Directive

8. A third party mediating a conflict at work is more likely to——.
   a. Render a decision
   b. Offer legal counsel
   c. **Encourage dialogue and compromise**
   d. Advocate on behalf of the employer.

9. What possible drawbacks would there be to employing technology to resolve disputes between third parties?
   a. Enhanced communication
   b. Increased accessibility
   c. Improved communication
   d. **Limited confidentiality**

16.3. Part B (Review Questions)

1. Explain mediation process and discuss about its role in resolving disputes. Give instances that show how successful mediation can be in various situations.
2. Examine and contrast mediation with other forms of conflict resolution, including litigation and arbitration. Draw attention to the benefits and drawbacks of each strategy.
3. Examine the fundamental ideas and methods of mediation. In what ways can a mediator help parties in disagreement communicate and work together?
4. Discuss about the moral issues surrounding the mediation profession. What moral principles should a mediator adhere to guarantee an unbiased and equitable process?
5. Examine a case study about the use of mediation to resolve disputes. Give clear examples of the difficulties the mediator is facing and suggest solutions.
6. Analyze how cultural variations affect the mediation process and how a mediator should handle cultural differences?
7. Explain conciliation's main tenets and define it in relation to dispute resolution. Give instances to show how conciliation is different from other approaches like arbitration and mediation.
8. Examine and contrast conciliation with ADR procedures, emphasizing the benefits and drawbacks of selecting conciliation in particular circumstances.
9. Consider the function of a conciliator in resolving disputes between people. In what ways does the conciliator help parties in conflict to communicate and work together?
10. Discuss the relevance of establishing confidence during the conciliation process. Give examples of techniques a conciliator can use to build and preserve trust between parties in conflict.
11. Examine the moral issues surrounding conciliation. What moral standards ought a conciliator to uphold in order to guarantee an impartial and equitable resolution process?
12. Examine a case study where conciliation was used to successfully settle a conflict at work. Determine the conciliator's main actions and assess the result.
13. Analyze how cultural diversity affects the conciliation procedure. In what ways may a conciliator improve conflict resolution by skillfully navigating cultural differences?
14. Analyze the impact of power dynamics in disputes and talk about the ways in which a conciliator might resolve power disparities to promote a more just outcome.
15. Talk about the drawbacks and advantages of conciliation in international disputes. In what ways might conciliation help settle conflicts across different countries or cultures?
16. Explain third-party conflict management and the function of a third party in dispute resolution. In this case, compare the functions of conciliators, arbitrators, and mediators.
17. Talk about the benefits and drawbacks of utilizing third parties to mediate disputes. Give instances that show when involving a third party could be very advantageous.

18. Examine the essential abilities and characteristics of a third-party dispute resolution professional. What role do these abilities have in successful dispute resolution?
19. Examine the many methods of third-party conflict resolution, including transformative, evaluative, and facilitative models. Give instances of the circumstances in which each model might work well.
20. Talk about the moral issues surrounding third-party conflict resolution. What moral standards should a third party adhere to guarantee an impartial and equitable outcome?

16.4. Part C (Glossary)

Conciliators: The third party involved in conducting conciliation.

Alternate dispute resolution: Alternate dispute resolution (ADR) encompasses a variety of procedures and methods used to settle disagreements outside of the conventional courtroom litigation process. ADR procedures are intended to be less confrontational, more flexible, and more efficient than traditional court cases. Example – mediation, conciliation, arbitration, etc.

Mediators: A mediator is a neutral party that assists disputants in communicating and understanding each other's viewpoints.

Arbitrator: An arbitrator is a neutral third person who mediates disputes between parties in a dispute without taking a case to court.

16.5. Role Play: Resolving Conflict Through Mediation

The mid-sized technology corporation Rainbow Corporation was facing a growing conflict between its product development and sales teams. A misunderstanding over project timeframes caused the conflict, which resulted in delays and costs for both departments. Team morale and production had started to suffer as a result of the strained relationships between the members. Three players are:

Sara – Sales Manager.
Devi – Product Development Manager.
Mike – Mediator.

Instructions: Ask three volunteers from the group to assume the above-mentioned roles and discuss the outcomes.

Chapter 17

Changing Dimensions of Conflict Management: Digital Technology and Artificial Intelligence

Learning Objectives:

- Understanding the role of digital technology and AI in conflict resolution.
- Online dispute resolution (ODR).
- Online negotiation and negotiation support system.
- Models of ODR.

The proliferation of the digital technology and the amplified use of social networking sites have changed workplace dynamics in recent years. Ensuring a balance between innovation and performance has become vital for organizational success. Technology and artificial intelligence (AI) have become an important part of business functions.[1] Employees are engaged in virtual social relations and build virtual lives.[2] These social and virtual relationships are used for various activities such as enhancing social capital, information sharing, managing social

---

[1]Bhardwaj, B., Sharma, D., & Dhiman, M. C. (2023). Artificial intelligence vs emotional intelligence: Unraveling the companionship and paradoxes. In B. Bhardwaj, D. Sharma, & M. Dhiman (Eds.), *AI and emotional intelligence for modern business management* (pp. 1–13). IGI Global. https://doi.org/10.4018/979-8-3693-0418-1.ch001
[2]Sindermann, C., Yang, H., Yang, S., Elhai, J. D., & Montag, C. (2022). Willingness to accept (WTA), willingness to pay (WTP), and the WTA/WTP disparity in Chinese social media platforms: Descriptive statistics and associations with personality and social media use. *Acta Psychologica, 223*, 103462.

Managing and Negotiating Disagreements:
A Contemporary Approach for Conflict Resolution, 185–198
Copyright © 2024 by Bhawana Bhardwaj and Dipanker Sharma
Published under exclusive licence by Emerald Publishing Limited
doi:10.1108/978-1-83797-971-420241017

relationships, etc.[3,4] Use of smartphones has made it possible to access social media sites anywhere and anytime. However, in the late 1980s and early 1990s, case-based reasoning and machine learning were utilized to construct negotiation support systems (NSSs) and ODR tools. Game theory has also been shown to aid in the process of negotiation and dispute resolution.[5]

17.1. Role of Digital Technology and AI in Conflict Resolution

Conflict resolution in the digital age and AI-driven companies presents new difficulties and opportunities. Integrating AI with different aspects of personal and professional life has revolutionized how people communicate, engage, and even resolve disputes.[6,7] There are several ways in which digital improvements and AI can help in conflict resolution. However, it has been discovered that computers cannot totally replace human roles, but can augment them to improve their efficacy and efficiency.[8] Digital era and AI have influenced the conflict resolution trends also.[9] The role of technology in dispute resolution is explained below.

17.1.1. Online Dispute Resolution (ODR)

The use of digital technology, particularly the internet, to expedite the resolution of disagreements between parties is referred to as ODR. Individuals, businesses, and organizations can use ODR platforms to resolve disputes without resorting

---

[3]Tandon, A., Dhir, A., Islam, N., Talwar, S., & Mäntymäki, M. (2021). Psychological and behavioral outcomes of social media-induced fear of missing out at the workplace. *Journal of Business Research*, *136*, 186–197.

[4]Luqman, A., Talwar, S., Masood, A., & Dhir, A. (2021). Does enterprise social media use promote employee creativity and well-being? *Journal of Business Research*, *131*, 40–54.

[5]Zeleznikow, J. (2021). Using artificial intelligence to provide intelligent dispute resolution support. *Group Decision and Negotiation*, *30*(4), 789–812.

[6]Bhardwaj, B., Sharma, D., & Dhiman, M. C. (Eds.). (2023). *AI and emotional intelligence for modern business management*. IGI Global. https://doi.org/10.4018/979-8-3693-0418-1

[7]Chaisse, J., & Kirkwood, J. (2022). Smart courts, smart contracts, and the future of online dispute resolution. *Stanford Journal of Blockchain Law & Policy*, *4*(1), 62–14.

[8]Bhardwaj, B., Sharma, D., & Dhiman, M. C. (2023). Artificial intelligence vs emotional intelligence: Unraveling the companionship and paradoxes. In B. Bhardwaj, D. Sharma, & M. Dhiman (Eds.), *AI and emotional intelligence for modern business management* (pp. 1–13). IGI Global. https://doi.org/10.4018/979-8-3693-0418-1.ch001

[9]Sharma, D., Bhardwaj, B., Dhiman, M. C. (2024). *Leveraging AI and emotional intelligence in contemporary business organizations*. IGI Global. https://doi.org/10.4018/979-8-3693-1902-4

to traditional legal proceedings, which can be time-consuming and costly.[10,11] Information and communication technology (ICT) can be used to augment dispute resolution techniques. ODR is the process of resolving conflicts via the use of digital technology and alternative dispute resolution methods like mediation, conciliation, and arbitration.[12]

ODR is sometimes taken too literally to indicate e-ADR or ADR made possible by technology. Thus, it may refer to techniques that predominantly use ADR techniques with significant ICT assistance. This could involve the first filing, the impartial appointment, the processes for gathering evidence, and oral hearings, conversations, and even the making of legally enforceable judgments. ODR is merely an alternative dispute resolution process that upholds due process standards all the way through.[13] The combination of ADR with ICT led to the development of ODR as a mechanism for resolving online issues for which the more established channels of dispute resolution were either unreliable or ineffective.[11]

The advent of COVID-19 as a pandemic in early 2020 has emphasized the significance of developing ODR systems.[14] Adieu, Amica, IMMEDIATION, MODRON, and Our Family Wizard are some examples of the ODR systems.[5,15,16] These systems are intended to enable dispute settlement through digital means, giving users a simple and effective approach to address problems. These platforms are examples of how technology can be leveraged to provide accessible and user-friendly solutions for dispute resolution. Some of the examples of ODR are:

   a. *IMMEDIATION*: IMMEDIATION is an ODR platform designed to facilitate negotiation, mediation, and arbitration for a wide range of disputes. It leverages technology to support both parties and professional mediators in reaching mutually beneficial solutions.[17]

---

[10]Katsh, M. E., & Rabinovich-Einy, O. (2017). *Digital justice: Technology and the internet of disputes*. Oxford University Press.

[11]Cortés, P. (2010). *Online dispute resolution for consumers in the European Union* (p. 266). Taylor & Francis.

[12]Utama, G. S. (2017). Online dispute resolution: A revolution in modern law practice. *Business Law Review, 3*(3), 1–6. https://law.uii.ac.id/wp-content/uploads/2017/04/V-01-No-03-online-dispute-resolution-a-revolution-in-modern-law-practice-gagah-satria-utama.pdf

[13]Mania, K. (2015). Online dispute resolution: The future of justice. *International Comparative Jurisprudence, 1*(1), 76–86.

[14]Sourdin, T., & Zeleznikow, J. (2020). Courts, mediation and COVID-19. *Australian Business Law Review, 48*(2), 138–158.

[15]Schmitz, A. J., & Zeleznikow, J. (2022). Intelligent legal tech to empower self-represented litigants. *Ohio State Legal Studies Research Paper*, (688), 23.

[16]Rajendra, J. B., & Thuraisingam, A. S. (2022). The deployment of artificial intelligence in alternative dispute resolution: The AI augmented arbitrator. *Information & Communications Technology Law, 31*(2), 176–193.

[17]https://www.immediation.com/

b. *MODRON*: MODRON is an ODR platform that focuses on resolving disputes related to e-commerce transactions, consumer rights, and digital services. It aims to provide an efficient way for consumers and businesses to address issues that arise in the online marketplace.[5]

c. *Our Family Wizard*: Our Family Wizard is designed to assist separated or divorced parents in co-parenting effectively. It provides tools for communication, scheduling, sharing important information, and managing expenses related to children's needs.[18]

d. *Adieu*: It offers tools and resources to assist users in making important decisions and resolving conflicts in these sensitive areas. Adieu is a platform that focuses on helping individuals navigate through difficult life situations, such as divorce, separation, and end-of-life planning.[5]

e. *Amica*: Amica is an online platform that specializes in divorce and separation cases. It provides tools for creating legally binding agreements, managing financial aspects, and addressing child custody arrangements. The platform aims to simplify and streamline the divorce process.[19]

Additionally, TEAMS and ZOOM offer video conferencing platform ensuring communication of people sitting at distant places. Some technological platforms have recently enabled apps to offer sophisticated chat robots.

It has also been observed that professional advice is also provided to disputing parties regarding alternatives available to them, that is, their BATNA.[20] The access to tools such as MODRIA[21] has played an important role in ODR by offering various features. There are developing countries like India which has also reoutlined their dispute resolution system with the introduction of various ICT enabled ODR initiatives such as e-Courts Mission Mode Project and e-Lok Adalats.[22]

Features of ODR: Online conflict resolution has shown advantages in several ways. Some of the features of ODR are as follows:

a. *Case management*: This form of ODR plays a role in filing and managing cases and disputes in a diverse way. Conflicting parties are permitted to input data, request pertinent information from users, and give them templates to start a disagreement settlement. Traditionally, these activities

---

[18]Zeleznikow, J. (2021). Online support for the resolution of disputes. *Academia Letters*, 2.

[19]https://agami.in/odr/

[20]Stranieri, A., Zeleznikow, J., Gawler, M., & Lewis, B. (1999). A hybrid rule–neural approach for the automation of legal reasoning in the discretionary domain of family law in Australia. *Artificial Intelligence Law*, 7(2–3), 153–183.

[21]Modria and the Future of Dispute Resolution. https://www.odreurope.com/news/articles/online-dispute-resolution/1172-modria-and-the-future-of-dispute-resolution

[22]Designing the Future of Dispute Resolution THE ODR POLICY PLAN FOR INDIA. Retrieved February 21, 2024, from https://www.niti.gov.in/sites/default/files/2023-03/Designing-The-Future-of-Dispute-Resolution-The-ODR-Policy-Plan-for-India.pdf

were supported manually making it expensive, time-consuming, and error-prone process.[11,23]

b. *Triaging system of ODR*: Triaging systems support in beginning and advancing high-risk cases. They provide advice that is timely and pertinent to provide bail petitions. Intelligent ODR systems are capable of triaging and incorporating agreement-producing document writing tools.[5,17]

c. *Advisory ODRs*: These ODR systems help with reality testing and advice by providing copies of legislation, case studies, and films of desirable and undesirable behavior. BATNA advising systems, for example, provide information on the most likely outcome of a disagreement. Such platforms provide advice to disputants on their BATNAs. They also facilitate bargaining, and assist litigants in concentrating on solutions that are interest based not person based. For example, GETAID system used in Australia is an example of Advisory ODR.[24,25]

d. *Communication tools*: ODR system supports online process such as mediation, negotiation, conciliation, and facilitation. These systems can also facilitate face-to-face communication.[26]

e. *Drafting or agreement technologies*: These ODRs aid in drafting settlement agreements. They facilitate preparing agreements or plans that are satisfactory to all parties. They can be used to construct appropriate agreements when a negotiated settlement is reached.[13]

f. *Decision support tools*: Software that makes use of AI or game theory can be used to help negotiate trade-offs if the parties involved are unable to come to an agreement. These services are offered by Smartsettle and Family Winner. Experts in the field (such as attorneys and mediators) might offer insightful guidance on trade-offs. Appropriate decision support tools are essential in their absence.[13]

g. *Data analysis for insight*: AI can analyze massive volumes of data to provide insights into patterns, trends, and viable remedies in complex situations. AI tools can swiftly analyze and categorize documents, emails, and communication to uncover relevant information.

h. *Predictive analytics*: Using past data and trends, AI algorithms can forecast probable outcomes and provide recommendations. This assists parties in understanding the potential ramifications of their decisions and making more informed judgments during the negotiation process.

---

[23]Shang, C. S., & Guo, W. (2020). The rise of online dispute resolution-led justice in China: An initial look. *ANU Journal of Law and Technology, 1*(2), 25–42.

[24]Lodder, A. (2001). *DiaLaw on legal justification and dialogical models of argumentation* (Vol. 42). Springer and Business Media.

[25]Schoop, M. (2010). *Support of complex electronic negotiations. Handbook of group decision and negotiation* (pp. 409–423). Springer.

[26]Beal, B. L. (1999). Online mediation: has its time come. *Ohio State Journal on Dispute Resolution, 15*, 735.

i. *Natural language processing* (NLP): NLP enables AI systems to interpret and analyze human language. Chatbots and virtual assistants employ this technology to help parties through conflict resolution processes, answer queries, and provide pertinent information.

j. *Facilitating communication*: Technology and AI can help parties in conflict communicate more effectively. Video conferencing, messaging platforms, and collaboration tools enable parties to participate in talks from a distance, bypassing geographical obstacles and allowing for more effective communication.

k. *Reducing bias*: By focusing on objective data and patterns rather than personal biases, AI has the potential to eliminate bias in conflict resolution. This can result in more fair and equitable outcomes.

l. *Improved mediation*: Mediators can utilize AI tools to analyze communication and negotiation trends in order to discover potential areas of agreement and impediments. This can assist mediators in guiding parties toward resolutions that are agreeable to all parties.

m. *Efficiency and speed*: AI-powered platforms may automate administrative activities such as document management and scheduling, allowing conflict resolution procedures to move more swiftly and efficiently.

17.1.2. *Online Negotiation and Negotiation Support Syspetms(NSS)*[7,27]

Online negotiation makes use of electronic media and internet networks. It is a simpler approach than traditional negotiation. Online negotiation does not include face-to-face interaction and proves less complicated, easier, and cost effective.[28] There are various dispute resolution and negotiation tools available today to assist parties in managing disagreements, reaching agreements, and streamlining the negotiating process.[29] NSSs are intended to assist and counsel negotiators. They are employed to organize and examine the issue, extract preferences, and apply them to the creation of a utility function, identify workable and effective substitutes, illustrate various facets of the issue and the process, and promote dialogue. Several NSSs have recently been put online and utilized for conducting commercial negotiations, research, and education. These systems provide important intelligent advice and support. The use of digital technology to support negotiation started decades back. However, contemporary organizations

[27]Chaisse, J., & Kirkwood, J. (2022). Smart courts, smart contracts, and the future of online dispute resolution. *Stanford Journal of Blockchain Law & Policy*, 4(1), 62–14.
[28]Sagala, L. M., & Marpaung, D. S. H. (2021). Penegakkan Hukum serta Upaya Penyelesaian Sengketa Online Marketplace melalui Mekanisme Online Dispute Resolution. *Widya Yuridika*, 4(2), 421–434. https://doi.org/10.31328/wy.v4i2.2414
[29]Kersten, G. E., & Lo, G. (2003). Aspire: an integrated negotiation support system and software agents for e-business negotiation. *International Journal of Internet and Enterprise Management*, 1(3), 293–315.

also use AI to facilitate negotiation processes. Traditional AI has included major components of rule-based reasoning, case-based reasoning, and machine learning. These processes were distinguished from other less cognitive but more numerically based techniques such as operations research and statistics:

a. *DEUS*: This form of NSS is used for exhibiting the level of disagreement, with respect to each item. These are based on rule-based reasoning, case-based reasoning, and machine learning.[30]
b. *INSPIRE*: It is a template-based NSS based on utility functions.[31] It helps in tracking offers made by the disputing parties. This system displays both previous and present offers and uses utility functions to evaluate proposals. The current version of this NSS enables preference specification and offers evaluation, communication management, graphical display of the negotiation process, post-agreement analysis, and other services. The system can be used as a demonstration decision support system, a demonstration negotiation assistance system, a game, and a negotiation simulator, and it can also be utilized for research and teaching.[31,32]
c. *Negoisst*: This system offers communication support, conflict management, contract management, and decision support. It makes it possible for human negotiators to carry out intricate electronic negotiations.[33]
d. *Aspire*: This system is a hybrid of INSPIRE and Atin. This is a rule-based negotiation software that oversees the process and gives the user suggestions.[34]
e. *NEGOPLAN*[35]: A prototype expert system shell for strategic decision support and negotiation assistance is called negoplan. The problem is represented and modified using rule-based formalism, and the user has strong control over the solution process.

---

[30]Lodder, A. R., & Zeleznikow, J. (2010). *Enhanced dispute resolution through the use of information technology.* Cambridge University Press.

[31]Kersten, G. E., & Noronha, S. J. (1998). Negotiation support systems and negotiating agents. In *Modèles et Systèmes Multi-Agents pour la Gestion de l'Environement et des Territoires* (pp. 307–316).

[32]Kersten, G. E., & Noronha, S. J. (1998). Negotiation support systems and negotiating agents. In *Modèles et Systèmes Multi-Agents pour la Gestion de l'Environement et des Territoires* (pp. 307–316).

[33]Schoop, M., Jertila, A., & List, T. (2003). Negoisst: A negotiation support system for electronic business-to-business negotiations in e-commerce. *Data & Knowledge Engineering, 47*(3), 371–401.

[34]Kersten, G. E., & Lo, G. (2003). Aspire: An integrated negotiation support system and software agents for e-business negotiation. *International Journal of Internet and Enterprise Management, 1*(3), 293–315.

[35]Noronha, S., & Szpakowicz, S. (1996). Negoplan: A system for logic-based decision modelling. In *Advances in artificial intelligence: 11th biennial conference of the Canadian Society for Computational Studies of Intelligence, AI'96 Toronto, Ontario, Canada, May 21–24, 1996 Proceedings 11* (pp. 417–428). Springer.

f.   *Smartsettle*: Smartsettle is an online platform that helps parties discuss and settle disputes by utilizing algorithms and AI. It aids in the discovery of mutually beneficial solutions through a fair and efficient procedure. This is a neutral NSS that generates possible agreements based on party preferences while eliciting and managing preferences for any number of parties with opposing agendas on any number of problems.[36]

g.   *Modria*: Modria offers an **ODR** platform that may be utilized for various problems, from e-commerce disputes to legal conflicts. It provides a structured discussion process that assists parties in reaching agreements without the need for traditional legal actions.[37,38]

h.   *Cybersettle*: This platform helps in settling claims and disputes. This platform can be used for proposing bids and settlement offers to reach a point of agreement. This platform simplifies financial settlement and negotiation. Two parties can effectively negotiate and settle financial transactions through this private, secure, and GenAI-enhanced environment.[39]

i.   *Immediation*: This platform combines mediation and technology. Through this app, remote mediation sessions to support negotiations and settlement discussions can be provided.[16]

j.   *Rechtwijzer*: This online platform has been used by the Dutch Legal Aid Board that helps individuals to navigate legal matters and dispute resolution. It provides guidance and information for mediation and negotiation.[40,41]

k.   *Virtual courthouse*: Virtual courthouse is a platform for online conflict resolution that courts, mediators, and arbitrators utilize to manage and settle disputes outside of traditional courtrooms. It provides virtual hearing rooms as well as document exchange and communication options.[42]

l.   *Relativity trace*: Relativity trace, while not entirely a dispute resolution tool, is an AI-powered platform used for compliance and e-discovery. By analyzing communication and data, it can help in identifying possible conflicts and settling disputes.

m.   *JAMSConnect*: JAMSConnect is a well-known **ADR** provider's online platform. It enables parties to participate in virtual ADR procedures and

---

[36]https://www.smartsettle.com/

[37]Clift, H. (2015). Online resolution: Is this the future for disputes? *Proctor, 35*(5), 34–35.
[38]Exon, S. N. (2017). Ethics and online dispute resolution: From evolution to revolution. *Ohio State Journal on Dispute Resolution, 32*, 609.

[39]https://www.cybersettle.com/

[40]van Veenen, J. (2008, December). Online integrative negotiation tools for the Dutch Council for Legal Aid. In *Proceedings of the 5th international workshop on online dispute resolution (ODR workshop'08). (JURIX 2008), Firenze, Italy*. (CEUR Workshop Proceedings, Vol. 430, pp. 23–31). https://www.ceur-ws.org

[41]Zeleznikow, J. (2021). Using artificial intelligence to provide intelligent dispute resolution support. *Group Decision and Negotiation, 30*(4), 789–812.

[42]https://www.pon.harvard.edu/daily/mediation/dispute-resolution-using-online-mediation/

provides communication, document exchange, and settlement discussion capabilities.[43]

n. *Digital arbitrator*: Digital arbitrator is a platform powered by AI that offers conflict resolution services such as technology-assisted negotiation, mediation, and arbitration. It tries to improve efficiency by streamlining the resolution process.

17.2. Models of ODR

The ODR can be adopted in three different ways:

17.2.1. Tiered Dispute Resolution Models

These models provide an end-to-end dispute resolution solution by filtering the disagreements through several ODR processes. For example, The Zhejiang, China-based Online Dispute Diversification Resolution Platform (ODDRP) offers a five-tiered complete methodology for resolving disputes. The platform includes online consultation, online evaluation, online and offline mediation, online arbitration, and online litigation. Thus, the selection of model will possible depend depend on the kinds of conflicts that are being settled.[44]

17.2.2. Hybrid Models of Dispute Resolution

A hybrid dispute resolution model improves on the established offline dispute resolution procedures while also creating ODR options for more accessibility and efficiency. The concurrent integration of ICT with traditional conflict resolution procedures boosts their effectiveness and steadily increases public confidence in the use of technological instruments in the process.[39]

17.2.3. AI-Based ODR

With the advent of AI in organization, the functioning of the organizations has transformed completely. AI-based ODR platforms such as Smartsettle and Cybersettle have transitioned to novel mechanisms like algorithmic resolutions or blind-bidding, signifying that ODR has ample potential for growth and expansion because of technology advancements in this domain.[37,45]

---

[43]https://www.jamsadr.com

[44]Designing the Future of Dispute Resolution THE ODR POLICY PLAN FOR INDIA. Retrieved February 21, 2024, from https://www.niti.gov.in/sites/default/files/2023-03/Designing-The-Future-of-Dispute-Resolution-The-ODR-Policy-Plan-for-India.pdf

[45]Zeleznikow, J. (2021). Using artificial intelligence to provide intelligent dispute resolution support. *Group Decision and Negotiation*, *30*(4), 789–812.

17.3. Merits of ODR

1. *Time saving*: ODR can expedite the process since it gives parties greater flexibility than asynchronous communication methods. This is so that parties can work whenever it is convenient for them thanks to ODR.[13]
2. *Convenient*: The procedure of ODR is more convenient because, through the use of asynchronous communications, all parties are able to respond with preparedness and without succumbing to intimidation or bullying.[46] Additionally, some academics believe that asynchronous interactions that enable parties must deliberate more carefully before communicating than while conversing verbally.[47] Additionally, it enables channels of communication that are not available in more traditional offline judicial processes. Additionally, ODR frequently employs private procedures that motivate parties to be more forthcoming in a setting of trust that promotes settlement.[48] ODR enables the parties to get to work on resolving their conflicts right away. Additionally, it permits impartial third parties to support the involved parties even after crucial communications.[49]
3. *Cost effectiveness*: Because there is no travel or lodging costs — which, in cases of international consumer disputes, are usually greater than the dispute's value — ODR is less expensive than offline procedures. Self-representation and quick settlements are made possible by the informal methods of ODR, which save money and time to be incurred for legal procedures.[50,51]
4. *Advantages over litigation*: The fact that the parties have more control over the decision-making and the processes is the main benefit. As an example, in In consensual ODR, the parties draft their own agreement rather than having a third party impose it. There might not always be clear-cut victors and losers as a result.[52] The parties may also decide on the neutral third party and procedure that works best for them. Experts in the specific field of dispute,

---

[46]Rule, C. (2002). Online dispute resolution for businesses. In *B2B, E-commerce, consumer, employment, insurance, and other commercial conflicts (San Francisco: Jossey Bass)*. John Wiley & Sons.

[47]Kaufmann-Kohler, G., & Schultz, T. (2004). *Online dispute resolution: Challenges for contemporary justice*. Kluwer Law International BV.

[48]Ponte, L. M., & Cavenagh, T. D. (2005). *Cyberjustice, online dispute resolution for E-commerce*. Parson Prentice Hall.

[49]Carneiro, D., Novais, P., Andrade, F., Zeleznikow, J., & Neves, J. (2014). Online dispute resolution: an artificial intelligence perspective. *Artificial Intelligence Review, 41*, 211–240.

[50]Gramatikov, M. (Ed.). (2012). *Costs and quality of online dispute resolution: A handbook for measuring the costs and quality of ODR*. Maklu.

[51]Bakhramova, M. (2022). The origins of the ODR system and its advantages over other ADR methods. *BARQARORLIK VA YETAKCHI TADQIQOTLAR ONLAYN ILMIY JURNALI, 2*(1), 527–530.

[52]Wissler, R. L. (1995). Mediation and adjudication in the small claims court: The effects of processes and case characteristics. *Law and Society Review, 29*(2), 323.

neutral third parties, can serve as a substitute for attorneys and expert witnesses in certain cases. Judges, on the other hand, are required to adhere to established protocols and precedents. The rules of evidence do not hold when using consensual ODR procedures. In addition, judicial enforcement is costly, time-consuming, and complex, especially when it comes to enforcing cross-border decisions.[53,54]

5. *Control over the outcome*: Consensual ODR increases choices for resolving disputes, and offers the parties greater control over the results. Agreements can be reached by parties without being constrained by legal restrictions. Furthermore, when a decision is made willingly by the parties, there is a greater likelihood of voluntary compliance.

6. *Personalised solutions*: AI can assist in the generation of personalized solutions based on the individual demands and goals of the parties concerned. This personalization can lead to more satisfying results.[55]

7. *User feedback and learning*: AI may collect user feedback to continuously enhance the conflict resolution process. AI systems can change and develop their tactics over time by analyzing user interactions and outcomes. AI can support in giving the feedback regarding conflict management styles and behavior during ODR.[56]

17.4. Challenges of ODR[47,57]

1. *Lack of face-to-face interaction*: Facial expressions, tone of voice, and body language are crucial components of communication. Ineffective non-verbal cues can encourage identity fraud[58] and result in misunderstandings. Other online technologies, like video conferencing, could make up for the ODR but cannot fully replace it. Technology and impartial third parties are crucial for

---

[53]Aziz, T. N. R. A., & Hamid, N. A. A. (2020). The settlement of disputes through online dispute resolution (ODR): A literature review. *Asian Journal of Research in Business and Management, 2*(4), 90–98.

[54]Cashman, P., & Ginnivan, E. (2019). Digital justice: Online resolution of minor civil disputes and the use of digital technology in complex litigation and class actions. *Macquarie Law Journal, 19*, 39.

[55]Westin, C., Borst, C., Kampen, E. J., Nunes, T. M., Boonsong, S., Hilburn, B., Cocchioni, M., & Bonelli, S. (2022). Personalized and transparent AI support for ATC conflict detection and resolution: An empirical study. In *Proceedings of the 12th SESAR Innovation Days, Budapest, Hungary* (pp. 5–8).

[56]Carneiro, D., Gomes, M., Novais, P., & Neves, J. (2011). Developing dynamic conflict resolution models based on the interpretation of personal conflict styles. In *Progress in artificial intelligence: 15th Portuguese conference on artificial intelligence, EPIA 2011, Lisbon, Portugal, October 10–13, 2011. Proceedings 15* (pp. 44–58). Springer.

[57]Kaufmann-Kohler, G., & Schultz, T. (2004). *Online dispute resolution: Challenges for contemporary justice*. Kluwer Law International BV.

[58]Conley Tyler, M. H., & McPherson, M. W. (2006). Online dispute resolution and family disputes. *Journal of Family Studies, 12*(2), 165–183.

producing communications that are relevant and fostering a sense of confidence. Neutral third parties must receive distinct training considering this. Though it differs from physical conversations, written messages can also be interpreted. Face-to-face interactions have been said to favor people who are more articulate and physically appealing, and they may also give rise to bias on physical characteristics such as nationality, sex, religion, or sexism.[59,60]

2. *Technical difficulties*: As more and more individuals use computers on a regular basis, the claim that ODR favors those who are computer literate is becoming less and less persuasive. Parties can possess varying degrees of expertise. Furthermore, there are disparities in technological advancements across nations, meaning that there are no uniform standards.[47]

3. *Proliferation of online platforms*: Online platforms and social media have a wider reach. Conflicts can quickly escalate on social media platforms and other online spaces, reaching a wider audience and intensifying emotions. The rapid spread of information can create rumors and opinions can amplify conflicts before they can be effectively managed.[61]

4. *Anonymity and trolling*: The anonymity provided by the digital realm can lead to toxic behavior and trolling, making conflict resolution more challenging. People might be more inclined to engage in aggressive behavior when they can hide behind a screen name.[62]

5. *Algorithmic amplification*: AI algorithms can unintentionally amplify conflicts by showing users content that aligns with their existing views, creating echo chambers, and reinforcing divisive opinions.

6. *Trust building*: In offline ADR processes, trust establishment and restoration are often crucial. However, trust-related issues can provide even greater obstacles to resolution for disputants who have only ever interacted virtually. Maintaining relationships, be they personal or professional, helps guarantee that transaction parties will act appropriately and cooperatively. Online disputants frequently express their reluctance to come to a resolution because they lack confidence that the other side would honor the terms of the mediated agreement or follow the arbitrator's ruling. Even when it is obvious that both parties would benefit from working through ODR to reach a settlement, this lack of confidence might prevent resolution from happening.[56,63]

---

[59]Raines, S. S. (2006). Mediating in your pajamas: The benefits and challenges for ODR practitioners. *Conflict Resolution Quarterly, 23*(3), 359–369.

[60]Orji, U. J. (2012). Technology mediated dispute resolution: Challenges and opportunities for dispute resolution. *CTLR, 18*(5), 124–134.

[61]Reuter, C., Stieglitz, S., & Imran, M. (2020). Social media in conflicts and crises. *Behaviour & Information Technology, 39*(3), 241–251.

[62]Kim, M., Ellithorpe, M., & Burt, S. A. (2023). Anonymity and its role in digital aggression: A systematic review. *Aggression and Violent Behavior*, 101856.

[63]Lewicki, R. J., & Wiethoff, C. (2000). Trust, trust development, and trust repair. In M. Deutsch P. Coleman, & E. C. Marcus (Eds.), *Handbook of conflict resolution: Theory and practice*. Jossey-Bass.

7. *Legal difficulties*: Many challenges develop when there are unclear legal require-
    ments for ODR, especially when public enforcement becomes necessary.

17.5. Part A (Self-assessment)

1. What is the full form meaning of ODR?
    a. Online database retrieval
    b. Open dispute resolution
    c. Offline dispute resolution
    d. **Online dispute resolution**

2. Which of the following describes ODR's main benefit?
    a. Inaccessible
    b. Protracted procedure
    c. **Economical**
    d. Insufficient adaptability.

3. What technology is frequently applied to ODR procedures?
    a. Morse code
    b. Telepathy
    c. **Blockchain**
    d. AI

4. In ODR, what function does an impartial third party serve?
    a. The aggressor
    b. The decision-maker
    c. **the arbitrator or mediator**
    d. The witness

5. Which element supports ODR's effectiveness?
    a. In-person communication
    b. Complexity
    c. **Distance in geography**
    d. Language obstacles

6. Which internet-based dispute resolution tool is most frequently utilized in
    consumer disputes?
    a. Platforms for social networking
    b. Video streaming
    c. **Dedicated ODR platforms**
    d. Internet-based gaming platforms

7. What is the main objective of ODR's?
    a. Increasing the amount of paperwork
    b. Promoting litigation
    c. **Facilitating ODR**
    d. Prolonging disputes

8. In what ways does ODR facilitate access to justice?
    a. By increasing the complexity of the legal procedure
    b. By restricting the choices available for resolving disputes
    c. **By offering an affordable and easily accessible method of resolution**
    d. By eliminating specific categories of problems

17.6. Part B (Review Questions)

1. Describe three benefits of ODR over traditional dispute resolution techniques.
2. Explain how technology can improve the effectiveness of ODR procedures.
3. Identify two ODR platforms that would work well for settling this disagreement.
4. Describe the possible courses of action for the conflicting parties in the ODR procedure.
5. Describe a potential problem that could occur during online mediation and offer a solution.
6. Explain how, in an online environment, the mediation process's secrecy is preserved.
7. Discuss the merits and demerits of ODR.

17.7. Part C (Glossary)

Online dispute resolution (ODR): The use of digital technology, particularly the internet, to expedite the resolution of disagreements between parties is referred to as online dispute resolution.

Negotiation support system (NSS): NSSs are a form of group decision support systems that focus on computerized assistance for such situations where group members have a strong disagreement over a decision.[64]

Virtual courthouse: Virtual courthouse is a platform for online conflict resolution that courts, mediators, and arbitrators utilize to manage and settle disputes outside of traditional courtrooms.

---

[64]Jelassi, M. T., & Foroughi, A. (1989). Negotiation support systems: An overview of design issues and existing software. *Decision Support Systems*, 5(2), 167–181.